The Highly Sensitive Person

Books by
Elaine N. Aron, Ph.D.

The Highly Sensitive Person

The Highly Sensitive Parent

The Highly Sensitive Person Workbook

The Highly Sensitive Person in Love

The Highly Sensitive Child

Psychotherapy and the Highly Sensitive Person

The Undervalued Self

The Highly Sensitive Person

How to Thrive When the World Overwhelms You

25TH ANNIVERSARY EDITION

Elaine N. Aron, Ph.D.

CITADEL PRESS
Kensington Publishing Corp.
www.kensingtonbooks.com

CITADEL PRESS BOOKS are published by

Kensington Publishing Corp.
119 West 40th Street
New York, NY 10018

First published in hardcover by Birch Lane Press, a division of Carol Publishing Group.

All Kensington titles, imprints, and distributed lines are available at special quantity discounts for bulk purchases for sales promotions, premiums, fund-raising, educational, or institutional use. Special book excerpts or customized printings can also be created to fit specific needs. For details, write or phone the office of the Kensington sales manager: Kensington Publishing Corp., 119 West 40th Street, New York, NY 10018, attn: Sales Department; phone 1-800-221-2647.

ISBN-13: 978-08065-4057-3
ISBN-10: 0-8065-4057-5

First Citadel Press hardcover printing: June 2020

10 9 8 7 6 5 4 3 2

Printed in the United States of America

Library of Congress Control Number: 2019951449

Electronic edition:

ISBN-13: 978-0-8065-3670-5 (e-book)
ISBN-10: 0-8065-3670-5 (e-book)

To Irene Bernadicou Pettit, Ph.D.—being both poet and peasant,
she knew how to plant this seed and tend it until it blossomed.

To Art, who especially loves the flowers—one more love we share.

Acknowledgments

I especially want to acknowledge all the highly sensitive people I interviewed. You were the first to come forward and talk about what you had known very privately about yourself for a long time, changing yourselves from isolated individuals to a group to be respected. My thanks also to those who have come to my courses or seen me for a consultation or in psychotherapy. Every word of this book reflects what you all have taught me.

My many student research assistants—too many to name—also earn a big thanks, as do Barbara Kouts, my agent, and Bruce Shostak, my editor at Carol, for their effort to see that this book reached all of you. Barbara found a publisher with vision; Bruce brought the manuscript into good shape, reining me in at all the right places but otherwise letting me run with it as I saw it.

It's harder to find words for my husband, Art. But here are some: Friend, colleague, supporter, beloved—thanks, with all my love.

I believe in aristocracy, though—if that is the right word, and if a democrat may use it. Not an aristocracy of power . . . but . . . of the sensitive, the considerate. . . . Its members are to be found in all nations and classes, and all through the ages, and there is a secret understanding between them when they meet. They represent the true human tradition, the one permanent victory of our queer race over cruelty and chaos. Thousands of them perish in obscurity, a few are great names. They are sensitive for others as well as themselves, they are considerate without being fussy, their pluck is not swankiness but the power to endure . . .

—E. M. Forster, "What I Believe,"
in *Two Cheers for Democracy*

Contents

Author's Note, 2020

for the 25th Anniversary Edition

This twenty-fifth anniversary gives us a so many reasons to celebrate. A huge reason is the exponentially growing scientific research on the trait. That is why this note is so long, because I have tried to review the best of it for you, while keeping it easy to read. It is my conviction that knowing about the accumulating research will enhance your understanding of yourself. Perhaps you will want to share it with others as well.

Even in 1998, three years after this book was first published, I could write a new preface titled "A Celebration." It was an invitation for all of us to feel good about how many people had discovered they were highly sensitive (HSPs) and found the book useful, and that the idea was catching on in the scientific world. Now we can celebrate about fifty times more of the same. *The Highly Sensitive Person* has been translated into at least thirty-one languages (I lose count). There have been articles about high sensitivity in numerous media outlets and on websites throughout the world. There is the documentary *Sensitive: The Untold Story* and the feature film, *Sensitive and in Love*. There have been twice-a-year HSP Gathering Retreats, frequent international research conferences, and numerous seminars and webinars for the public on the subject in the U.S. and Europe, plus YouTube videos, books, magazines, newsletters, and websites, and all sorts of services exclusively for highly sensitive persons—most good and some, well, not as good.

About sixty thousand subscribe to my free e-mail newsletter at hsperson.com, where there are now hundreds of articles and blog posts I have written over the years, all archived so that you can search and find something on almost every aspect of being highly sensitive. This is all because you have discovered that you are highly sensitive. I know that for many of you it has changed your life, so we have reason to celebrate this growth over twenty-five years.

A Surprise Party—Some History

Let me start with some history. First, I did not intend to write a self-help book. I explain this because some have imagined that I was just looking for a new angle to write a flashy book that would catch the public's attention. Far from it. I began with some personal curiosity about the term after it had been applied to me by a psychotherapist. I read what I could find—almost nothing—about "sensitivity," even though the term was often used in case descriptions. It was as though this lack was saying, "Of course we all know what sensitive means."

Next, I did some interviews, with about forty people who thought they might be sensitive. Then my husband and I designed a self-report measure of it and began to study a little more deeply. The local newspaper got wind of it and published an article titled "Born to Be Mild" in the Sunday Lifestyle section, with a big photo of us. The response was huge. People were writing and calling me (pre-Internet), wanting to know more. So I finally agreed to do a lecture at the local library. It was standing room only, and many people were turned away. What was happening here?

To be obliging, I held a few courses in my living room, mostly listening to people giving good advice to each other, with me taking notes. Being an introvert, I did not want to do these courses anymore, so someone suggested I write a book. It was not easy finding a publisher. All the big ones either said, "Everyone's sensitive—no news here," or "Not enough are highly sensitive—the market's too small for us." But the book did find a home, and meanwhile, our research on the subject progressed—not for the book, but for the sake of understanding this big thing I had by the tail.

Psychologists have asked me (and I'm sure more only thought but didn't ask), "How could you have discovered an entirely new trait?" The answer is that sensitivity is not new at all but just difficult to observe by watching how people behave, which is usually how psychology proceeds. Hence, psychologists and people in general were coming up with names for it that were close but not quite on it, such as *shyness, inhibitedness,* or *introversion.* It is especially hard for others to observe our trait because it really means observing our not "behaving," at least at first. Hence, assumptions were often made that we are anxious generally, or simply afraid of people, or don't like them. Hardly. As I say in the book, 30 percent of HSPs are extraverts!

Further, we are so responsive to our environments that we can be somewhat like chameleons when around others, doing whatever it takes to fit in. All I "discovered" was a better term for the trait, and that meant a better understanding of it, because I happened to be in the position of being both a curious scientist and a highly sensitive person who could know this experience from the inside. (It also helped that my husband, not an HSP, is a consummate researcher.)

So in a sense this is a surprise party: A surprise to me how this has all turned out and a surprise to every HSP who has discovered they have a trait they had no name for. Shall we continue? I know that for a party, it will be a lot of science, but that's key to the celebration.

What's New, What's Not

Before I go into the recent research, I should say what's not new in this book. This is not a total revision. Given that it was written so long ago, at the very beginning of a minor revolution, I have sometimes thought I should revise it. But when I look it over, there's not much I would change. It does the job well, with three exceptions.

First, I needed to bring you up to date on greatly expanded scientific research. There are probably three times as many studies as I discussed in the previous Author's Note.

Second, there is now a simple, comprehensive description of the trait, "DOES," that expresses its facets nicely. **D** is for depth of processing. Our fundamental characteristic is that we observe and reflect before we act. We process everything more than others do, whether we are conscious of it or not. **O** is for being easily overstimulated; if you are going to pay more attention to everything, you are bound to tire sooner. **E** is for giving emphasis to our emotional reactions and having strong empathy, which among other things motivates us to notice and learn. **S** is for being sensitive to all the subtleties around us. I will say more about these four aspects of sensitivity when I discuss the research.

Third, I have mostly rewritten Chapter 9 on "Medics, Medications, and HSPs." Due to continuing medical research, this is the one part of the book that felt out of date. In particular, I no longer discuss at length the medications for treating anxiety and depression, common issues for HSPs. These medications have proliferated since 1996, and so has the research, pro and con, about them. Further, new discoveries are being made yearly about how to treat these two problems, given how widespread they are. Mostly, I will stick with the research where I am an expert.

The Research That Makes It All Real

Since the research began on high sensitivity, under the scientific term of Sensory Processing Sensitivity (SPS which is *unrelated* to *Sensory Processing Disorder*), about a hundred papers on it have appeared in scientific journals, most no longer with me as one of the authors. Many are excellent experimental studies, and I will focus on those standouts in this review, updated since the 2012 Author's Note. I doubt that I will update this summary of the research again—it will become too long. But unless there are dramatic changes, this should be a good representation of what is to come. For the future, we will continue to update a list of a few of the best studies at www.hsperson.com.

I have tried to keep what follows both brief and interesting to show you why it matters to you while retaining enough detail to satisfy curiosity. Those of you with a greater scientific background or deeper interest can find the full methodology and results by reading the articles themselves. The references are in the Notes. Links to many of the complete articles are also on hsperson.com. Further, I and my collaborators published a good scientific summary of the theory and research in 2012, and another that I was involved in was published in 2019.

I should add that concepts very much like sensitivity are being studied by other researchers. If you are interested in this work, you can look up terms such as *biological sensitivity to context* (authors will be Thomas Boyce, Bruce Ellis, and others) and *orienting sensitivity* (the main authors will be David Evans and Mary Rothbart).

Measuring Your Sensitivity

The first published studies my husband and I did generated the self-test you have in this book and a slightly different version especially for research, called the Highly Sensitive Person (HSP) Scale. This research was also intended to demonstrate that high sensitivity is not the same as introversion or "neuroticism" (professional jargon for a tendency to be depressed or excessively anxious). We were right (remember, 30 percent of HSPs are extraverts). The trait was moderately associated with neuroticism, partly because the questions in measures of neuroticism can apply to most HSPs to some degree (I worry; sometimes I am sad; etc.). The association is also due simply to the majority of the items in the present scale being negatively worded, so we will probably revise it in the not-too-distant future.

Measures for Children

Meanwhile, the present scale functions very well, and there is now one for children and adolescents. And perhaps most exciting, there is a behavioral measure by Francesca Leonetti and others that professionals can use for identifying high sensitivity in children too young to talk. Again, when you can only watch behaviors, sensitivity is not easy to separate from shyness, fearfulness, or in young children, just plain being difficult. But we knew what to look for and it worked.

If you have read *The Highly Sensitive Child*, you saw a test for parents to help them identify sensitivity in their child. That test was well done (interviews, a large number of items narrowed down to the most effective), but it had not been further validated or published until 2018.

What does all of this mean for you? You can count on the HSP Scale being valid and reliable.

As Other Researchers Use the Scale

Of course, others began using the scale. In fact, one study looked at twenty-nine uses of it in research, and it was clear that it works well. Some researchers have found within the main scale three major factors. (I am not going into detail because it can be confusing: If you read the studies, you will see that they tried to use these factors as *separate* measures—but of what? To be an HSP, you would be fairly high on all three.) Fortunately things got clearer when the authors of the study looking at all twenty-nine uses—plus another study designed to look specifically for one factor versus three—concluded that yes, there are three factors within the measure, but there is an overarching basic trait measured by the overall scale. With such varied items—from sensitivity to pain, to caffeine, and to hunger to a rich inner life and conscientiousness, there were bound to be factors that clumped similar items together. But that is simply the nature of your trait! It affects everything about you. It is your "style."

Further, although the measure suggests that the trait has some similarities and associations with introversion or neuroticism, after considering these and a number of other personality variables, the results of many studies lead to the conclusion that these other measures of personality explain no more than one third of the "variance" on the HSP Scale. How you score on it is not very affected by how you might score on other personality tests. That is, knowing about your sensitivity makes a unique contribution to knowing about *you*.

Differential Susceptibility

Still, there was that high association of sensitivity with neuroticism, and I had a hunch about why. Another series of studies, published in 2005, verified it: HSPs with a troubled childhood are more at risk of becoming depressed, anxious, and shy than those with a similar childhood who are not highly sensitive. But HSPs with good-enough childhoods were no more at risk than others. Another study the same year by Miriam Liss and others found the same result, mainly for depression.

These findings about HSPs with poor childhoods being more depressed than those with similar childhoods without the trait seem to indicate vulnerability. The exciting news, however, is that *vulnerability* is not the right term. These are differences in *susceptibility*, to both positive and negative environments. This is now called "differential susceptibility," first thoroughly studied by Jay Belsky and Michael Pluess. That is, it refers to those high in what Michael Pluess calls environmental sensitivity (ES; being high in ES is the same as being an HSP, as it is studied with the same HSP Scale). On many measures (happiness, sensitivity to positive images, social skills, number of illnesses or injuries, etc.), HSPs with good-enough childhoods can be doing even better than those without the trait. If you are sensitive to your environment, it is reasonable that you would pick up on the positive more than others would. For example, in the study mentioned above, that described a measure of high sensitivity in children too young to read and answer a questionnaire, there was also a measure of the quality of the parenting the children were receiving. We will come across this measure again. It is generally thought that the best parenting is "authoritative," somewhere between being "authoritarian" (too strict) and "permissive" (too—well, permissive). In this study of small children, the quality of parenting affected highly sensitive children more.

Differential susceptibility is not only to childhood events, but to interventions meant to help them when they are older. One study found that among preteen girls in a program designed to prevent their becoming depressed as teenagers, only those who were highly sensitive had benefited from it one year later. Another study of boys in an intervention to prevent bullying found that only the highly sensitive boys benefited.

What does differential susceptibility mean for you? If you tend to be depressed or anxious, it may mean that you were more affected by a difficult childhood (troubles at home or at school) than other adults with similar childhood experiences. (Or that you are simply under too much stress, or something else is making you depressed or anxious.) While someone might tell you that you are making too much of your childhood problems, this research says you are probably not. You really were more affected and would benefit or have already benefited from help if you sought it, even if others would not feel the need. More important, and a special reason for hope—you may well gain more from help than others would. On the other hand, this research also means that if you had a reasonably good childhood, people who do not know you well may hardly notice your sensitivity. They will be too busy admiring its parts—your creativity, conscientiousness, kindness, and foresight. You have probably learned to take downtime when you need it, which is more often than others do, and avoid overstimulating environments, but only people close to you see this side of you.

Learning from the Past to Prepare for the Future

One of the most fascinating studies of differential susceptibility took place in a refugee camp in Syria. The researchers measured by self-report the level of war trauma in 579 children, the level of their sensitivity, and the level of functioning of their family before the war. Surprisingly, HSCs (highly sensitive children) with bad childhoods were *less* traumatized by their experiences in war zones than those who were not HSCs, and amazingly, HSCs with poor childhoods were also less distressed than HSCs with *good* childhoods.

It seems that differential susceptibility might be about learning better from our prior experiences, as suggested by computer simulations about how the trait evolved (more on that later), not simply about needing to have a good childhood in order to succeed. When HSPs have had a good childhood, they are prepared to live and work in a good-enough world, among the majority of people, who are either not much affected by their childhoods or had good-enough childhoods. Perhaps with a very negative childhood, an HSP is prepared to live in a very negative world, among other people who are stressed by it.

A study of kindergarten-age children's reactions to positive and negative changes in how they are being parented found that HSCs were more affected, "for better and for worse," by their parents changing at all than whether their parenting strategy was the best—better with no change, worse with change. The same measure of parenting was used in this study as was used in the study developing the observational measure with younger children. In the younger HSCs, we saw that parenting style itself affected them more than others, not changes in parenting style. Maybe getting older means getting more used to the ways of one's parents' parenting style, and this is why change is the bigger problem for HSCs at this age. This suggests that high sensitivity really might involve a strategy of using the past to better predict the future. Hence, changes that made a parent's future behavior less predictable seemed to be more of a problem than poor parenting. (However, there was little or no really bad parenting in these studies. "Authoritarian" parenting is not the same as abuse, nor is "permissive" parenting the same as neglect.) Bottom line: a good childhood may be less important than a somewhat predictable one.

However, not every study has found differential susceptibility. For example, one would expect that with a good childhood, life satisfaction would be higher for HSPs than for those who were not HSPs and had a similar good childhood. But unexpectedly, a study found that having a good childhood was not associated with greater life satisfaction for HSPs than those without the trait, at least on the measures used. That is, HSPs in this study did not appear to show special susceptibility to a good childhood. But research is like that—our understanding is often two steps forward and one back.

There are also studies indicating "vantage sensitivity" for HSPs, a new concept created by Michael Pluess and Jay Belsky to highlight the specific potential for sensitive people to benefit from positive circumstances and interventions—as in the study mentoned above, in which highly sensitive girls benefited from an intervention but were not worse off than those without the trait if not given the intervention. That is, in some studies of some situations, high sensitivity yields only advantages and no disadvantages.

Quite a few clinical studies have been done of the relationship between being highly sensitive and, for example, struggling more with negative emotions, more physical symptoms when stressed, stress at work, Type I diabetes, and anxiety. Alas, these studies did not take into account the role of childhood experiences, making it seem that all HSPs have these problems, when differential susceptibility would definitely predict that that would be mostly true of those with poor childhoods. Further, one wonders if these same problems would have occurred if the subjects in the studies had known about their trait and been able to adjust their personal and work lives accordingly. We also hope that future studies will include interventions to treat or prevent these problems, as we may see again that HSPs gain more from these interventions than others do.

The Genetics of This Trait

There is considerable research giving us confidence that this is largely a genetically determined trait—I use the word "largely" only because scientists never say "always," "never," or "proven." (Be suspicious of those who do.) True scientists know their theories and measurements are always improving. For example, it seemed fairly certain from research done in Denmark by Cecilie Licht and others that high sensitivity is related to a certain variation in the genetics that determine how much serotonin is available in the brain. Low serotonin is another case of differential susceptibility, in that it is associated with depression but also bestows advantages. However, since the Licht study, another unpublished study did not find this association. I still suspect they are related, but time will tell.

Chunhui Chen and his associates, working in China, took a different approach. Rather than looking at a specific gene with known properties, they looked at all of the gene variations affecting the amount of dopamine available in our brain (ninety-eight in all); dopamine is another chemical necessary for the transmission of information in certain areas of the brain. They found the HSP Scale is associated with ten variations on seven different dopamine-controlling genes.

So which genes are involved? Probably those affecting serotonin and dopamine, and more. There is a movement now away from what are called single candidate gene studies towards genome-wide studies. These will give us a better picture of the variety of genes involved in the trait and what they cause to happen in the brain. In you!

However, more support for this trait being genetically determined, whatever the genes, comes from studies of differential susceptibility. Robert Keers and Michael Pluess looked at the quality of childhood implied by various "material" measures such as the families' social class, financial distress, parents' employment status, type of housing, and so forth. Poor material conditions are known to be associated on average with poorer parenting and poorer mental health in adulthood. Keers and Pluess looked at nine genes thought to lead to high environmental sensitivity (in this study it was not possible to use the HSP Scale) and found that those with more of those genes who had a poor material environment in childhood had more problems in adulthood when under stress, but that having those genes and a good material environment in childhood made for greater resilience in adulthood when under stress.

Finally, Marinus van Ijzendoom and Marian Bakemans-

Kranenburg conducted a "meta-analysis" of twenty-two experiments involving 3,257 participants, with various problems being measured, several genetic variations associated with differential susceptibility being compared to others that were not, and with several interventions. They found that there was a very significant difference in the outcome of the interventions depending on the genetic variations being studied—with genes for sensitivity, the interventions were more effective. Thus, we know the genes governing high sensitivity are real.

What does all of this mean for you? This trait is an intrinsic part of you, and even if you or others wished you were less sensitive, you cannot eliminate it. You can improve very much how you live with it, however, and take better advantage of it by knowing its nature. Indeed, I hope by now you are seeing it is a true advantage.

What Is the Nature of This Difference?

Understanding why we evolved as we did tells us much more about ourselves than I knew when I wrote this book. At that time, I thought our sensitivity had evolved because the trait served the larger group, as sensitive individuals can sense a danger or opportunity that the others miss, while these others serve by doing something about it once they are alerted. This may still be partly true, but that may only be a side effect of the trait.

Many species—it's over one hundred so far, including fruit flies and some fish species—have a minority that are highly sensitive. Although the trait leads to different behaviors, obviously depending on whether you are a fruit fly, fish, bird, dog, deer, monkey, or human, a general description of it would be that the minority that has inherited it has adopted a survival strategy of pausing to check, observe, and reflect on or process what has been noticed before choosing an action. The others pay less attention and are less sensitive to their environments.

Depth of Processing Is the Key—but Difficult to Observe

Slowness to act, however, is not the hallmark of the trait. When sensitive individuals see right away that their situation is like a past one, thanks to having learned so thoroughly from thinking over that last time, they can react to a danger or opportunity faster than others. For this reason, the most basic aspect of the trait—the depth of processing—has been difficult to observe. Without knowing about it, when someone paused before acting, others could only guess what was happening inside that person. Again, often HSPs were thought to be inhibited, shy, fearful, or introverted. Some HSPs accepted those labels, having no other explanation for their hesitancy. Indeed, feeling different and flawed, some of us found the label "shy" or "fearful of social judgment" self-fulfilling, as I describe in chapter 5. Others knew they were different but hid it and adapted, acting in most ways like the less sensitive majority. This is probably especially true of highly sensitive men.

Finding Us Through a Computer Simulation

The current best explanation for your high sensitivity comes from a computer model done by biologists in the Netherlands. Max Wolf and his colleagues were curious about how high sensitivity might evolve as a trait, so they set up a situation using a computer program in order to keep all other factors out of the picture. Then they varied just a few things at a time and watched what happened when they ran out the various possible situations and strategies to see if being highly responsive could be a successful enough trait to remain in a population (traits that make us unsuccessful at life don't last long).

The sensitive strategy was tested by setting up a scenario in which they varied how much an individual who learned from Situation A—depending on how sensitive the individual is to everything that happened there—was more successful at Situation B because of that information. (They also had to vary the amount of benefit that came with being successful in Situation B). The alternative scenario was that variations in sensitivity made no difference. Learning from Situation A provided no help in Situation B, because events in A and B had nothing to do with each other. The question was: Under what conditions will you see the evolution of two types of individuals, one using the strategy of learning from experience and one not?

It turned out that there only had to be a small benefit for the two strategies to emerge. Why didn't every individual develop a strategy of sensitivity? Partly because in real life remembering Situation A when in Situation B does not always help and involves extra effort, but mainly because being sensitive is only an advantage when those who are sensitive are a minority. Why a minority? If everyone were sensitive it would be no advantage, as when everyone knows a shortcut and uses it. So many would be making use of the information that it would benefit no one (as often happens now because GPS tells everyone the short cuts).

Paying Attention Has Its Cost

In short, high sensitivity, or *responsivity*, as these biologists also called it, involves paying more attention to details than others do, then using that knowledge to make better predictions in the future. Sometimes you are better off doing so; other times it is a waste of energy or worse. What if events now have nothing to do with your past experiences? Suppose you are at the horse races and the first two races are won by horses with jockeys wearing red silks. Of course you are one of the few to notice. Would you bet on red silks in the third race or, if that fails, do it in the fourth? Your subtle red-silk strategy could be a costly mistake.

Further, when a past experience was very bad, an HSP can overgeneralize and avoid or feel anxious in too many situations, just because the new ones resemble in some small way the past bad one.

The biggest cost to us of being highly sensitive, however, is that our nervous systems can only take in so much. Everyone has a limit as to how much information or stimulation can be absorbed before one becomes overloaded, overstimulated, overaroused, overwhelmed, and just over! We simply reach that point sooner than others. Fortunately, as soon as we get some downtime we recover nicely.

Are We a Distinct Category of People?

Although I said in this book that usually you are either highly sensitive or not, I had no direct evidence for that point. I assumed it because Jerome Kagan of Harvard found it true for the trait of inhibitedness in children, and that seemed to be an understandable misnomer for sensitivity, given that it was based on observing children who do not rush into a room full of complicated, strange toys, but pause to look at it first. But many scientists thought sensitivity must be more like height, with most people in the middle, not a distinct category, like apples and oranges. For a doctoral thesis at the University of Bielefeld in Germany, Franziska Borries did a particular kind of statistical analysis that allows one to distinguish between categories and dimensions. In a study of over nine hundred people who took the HSP Scale, she found that being highly sensitive is indeed a category, not a dimension. Mostly, you either are or you are not.

Research continues on the question, however. Another study did not find two groups. (Ah, science!) Two other studies of this question, using a different method, found three groups that are somewhat distinct—those who are highly sensitive, very roughly 20–35 percent; a group with medium sensitivity, maybe 40–47 percent; and one with low sensitivity, 25–35 percent. But it's difficult to know the exact percentage of HSPs in any given population, as there will always be reasons why there might be more or less in the particular sample studied. For example, many studies use psychology majors as subjects, but more of these may be highly sensitive. Plus, a test is not the trait but a rough measure of it. Some people will score in the middle for reasons unrelated to their actual sensitivity level. For example, some people just rate everything lower or higher than others, and some may be distracted when tested, and so on. Also, men tend to score slightly lower on the HSP Scale, even though there is reason to think that there are just as many males born with the trait. Somehow taking the test seems to affect men differently, probably depending on the culture they are in.

The bottom line is that you are part of a special minority—hardly alone, but not like most of those around you. Moreover, it is an invisible difference, and it affects you in many ways when you are interacting with others who are not very sensitive at all. Don't forget those advantages: You notice things they do not!

DOES Describes It

When I wrote *Psychotherapy and the Highly Sensitive Person* in 2011 (to help therapists understand us better, including that our trait is not an illness or flaw), I created the acronym DOES in order to help therapists assess for this trait. I've come to like it as a way of describing both us and the research about us.

D Is for Depth of Processing

At the foundation of the trait of high sensitivity, as I just explained, is the tendency to process information more deeply. When people are given a phone number and have no way to record it at the moment, they will probably try to process it in some way in order to remember it, by repeating it many times, thinking of patterns or meanings in the digits, or noticing the numbers' similarity to something else. If you don't process it in some way, you know you will forget it. HSPs simply tend to process everything more, relating and comparing what we notice to our past experience with other similar things. We do it whether we are aware of it or not. When we decide without knowing how we came to that decision, we call this intuition, and HSPs have good (but not infallible!) intuition. When you make a decision consciously, you may notice that you are slower than others because you think over all the options so carefully. That's depth of processing too.

Studies supporting the depth-of-processing aspect of the trait have compared the brain activation of sensitive and nonsensitive people doing various perceptual tasks. Research by Jadzia Jagiellowicz and her colleagues found that the highly sensitive use more of those parts of the brain associated with "deeper" processing of information, especially on tasks that involve noticing subtleties. In another study, by ourselves and others, those with and without the trait were given perceptual tasks whose difficulty—meaning they require more brain activation or effort—is known to depend on the culture a person is from. The less sensitive persons' brains showed the usual effort being made, according to the culture they were from, but the effort made by the highly sensitive subjects' brains apparently did not change, regardless of their culture. It was as if they found it natural to look beyond their cultural expectations to how things "really are."

Research by Bianca Acevedo and her associates verified the findings of Jagiellowicz, that the brains of the highly sensitive do tend to elaborate sensory input more thoroughly. Acevedo's research has also shown more brain activation in HSPs than in others in an area called the insula, a part of the brain that integrates moment-to-moment knowledge of inner states and emotions, bodily position, and outer events. Some have called it the seat of consciousness. If we are more aware of what is going on both inside and outside, this greater activation of the insula would be exactly the result one would expect. All of these findings suggest deeper processing in the brains of the highly sensitive.

O Is for Overstimulation

If you are going to notice every little thing in a situation, and if the situation is complicated (many things to remember), intense (noisy, cluttered, etc.), or goes on too long (a two-hour commute), it seems obvious that you will also have to wear out sooner from having to process so much so thoroughly. Others, not noticing much or any of what you have, will not tire as quickly. They may even think it quite strange that you find it too much to sightsee all day and go to a nightclub that night. They might talk blithely on when you need them to be quiet a moment so that you can have some time just to think, or they might enjoy an "energetic" restaurant or a party when you can hardly bear the noise. Indeed this is often the behavior we and others have noticed most—that HSPs are easily stressed by overstimulation (including social stimulation), or having learned their lesson, that they avoid intense situations more than others do.

A study by Friederike Gerstenberg in Germany compared highly sensitive and not as highly sensitive people on the task of deciding whether or not a T turned in various ways was hidden among a great many Ls turned various ways on a computer screen. HSPs were faster and more accurate, but also more stressed than others after doing the task. Was it the perceptual effort or the emotional effect of being in the experiment? Whatever the reason, they were feeling stressed. Just as we say a piece of metal shows stress when it is overloaded, so do we.

A study of highly sensitive parents found that they were more affected by the level of chaos in their homes than those lacking their degree of sensitivity. Interestingly, the ratings of observers who came to each home agreed with the sensitive parents, while the less sensitive parents were apparently not experiencing the chaos as much. Maybe they were fortunate, but they were also not as able to see objectively the nature of their environment.

High sensitivity, however, is not mainly about being distressed by high levels of stimuli, as some have suggested, although that naturally happens when too much comes at us. Be careful not to mix up being an HSP with some problem condition: sensory discomfort can by itself be a sign of a disorder due to problems with sensory processing rather than having unusually good sensory processing. For example, sometimes persons with autistic spectrum disorders complain of sensory overload, but at other times they underreact. Their problem seems to be a difficulty recognizing where to focus attention and what to ignore. When speaking with someone, they may find the person's face no more important to look at than the pattern on the floor or the type of lightbulb above them. Naturally they can complain intensely about being overwhelmed by stimulation. They may even be more aware of subtleties, but in social situations especially they are more often noticing something irrelevant, whereas HSPs would be paying more attention to subtle facial expressions, at least when not overaroused. Those with high-functioning autism can train themselves to pay attention to social cues, but apparently they must make a great effort, while HSPs notice subtle social cues easily and usually enjoy it, even if they tire after a while by doing so much of it so well. The understanding of the autism spectrum is constantly changing, however, so there may be changes in how it is viewed. Yet we know that the brain functions differently in HSPs and those with autism spectrum disorders. Being highly sensitive and being on the spectrum are different things. Of course anyone with a disorder or other brain situation such as ADHD, schizophrenia, posttraumatic stress disorder, or even Down syndrome will also have temperament traits, possibly including high sensitivity. But high sensitivity is not a variation of any of these.

What does all of this about overstimulation mean for you? Being easily overstimulated is the only negative part of DOES, and it is easily solved by getting more downtime than others so that you can process all that you have taken in and avoiding as much as you can situations that involve high levels of stimulation. This book will help with that.

E Is for Emotional Reactivity

Data from surveys and experiments had already found some evidence that HSPs react more to both positive and negative experiences, but a series of studies done by Jadzia Jagiellowicz and colleagues found that HSPs particularly react more than those without the trait to pictures with a "positive valence." This was even more true if they had had a good childhood. In her studies of the brain done with Bianca Acevedo, this reaction to positive pictures was not only in the areas associated with the initial experience of strong emotions, but also in "higher" areas of thinking and perceiving, some of the same areas as those found in the depth-of-processing brain studies. That this stronger reaction to positive pictures is enhanced by a good childhood fits with the research on differential susceptibility, and explains why HSPs in good environments are gaining more from those environments than others— they notice and respond more to moments like a smile or a nod from a parent or teacher (or as adults, from an employer or friend).

E is also for empathy. In the study by Bianca Acevedo and her associates that I mentioned earlier, HSPs and those not so sensitive looked at photos of both strangers and loved ones expressing happiness, sadness, or a neutral feeling. In all situations, when there was emotion in the photo, HSPs showed increased activation in the insula, but also more activity in their mirror neuron system, especially when looking at the happy faces of loved ones.

The brain's "mirror neurons" were only discovered in the last twenty years or so, initially in monkeys. When we humans are watching someone else do something or feel something, this clump of neurons fires in the same way as some of the neurons in the person we are observing. As an example, the same neurons fire, to varying degrees, whether we are kicking a soccer ball, see someone else kicking a soccer ball, hear the sound of someone kicking a soccer ball, or hear or say the word *kick*. Not only do these amazing neurons help us learn through imitation, but in conjunction with the other areas of the brain associated with empathy that were also shown in this study to be especially active for HSPs, the mirror neuron area helps us know others' intentions and how they feel. Hence they are thought to be partly responsible for the universal human capacity for empathy.

In other words, sometimes HSPs do not just know how someone else feels but actually feel that way themselves to some extent. This is very familiar to sensitive people. *Anyone's* sad face tended to generate more activity in these mirror neuron areas in HSPs than in others. When seeing photos of their loved ones being unhappy, HSPs also showed more activation in areas suggesting they wanted to do something, to act, even more than in areas involving empathy (perhaps we learn to cool down our intense empathy in order to help). Overall, brain activation indicating empathy was stronger in HSPs than those without the trait when looking at photos of *anyone's* face showing strong emotion of *any* type (and even more so for people close to them than strangers) and more for happy than unhappy expressions.

There is a common misunderstanding that emotions cause us to think illogically. But the actual research, reviewed by psychologist Roy Baumeister and his colleagues, has placed emotion at the center of wisdom. One reason is that most emotion is felt after an event, which apparently serves to help us remember what happened and learn from it. The more upset we are by a mistake, the more we think about it and will be able to avoid it the next time. The more delighted we are by a success, the more we think and talk about it, going over how we did it, causing us to be more likely to be able to repeat it.

Other studies discussed by Baumeister that explore the contribution of emotion to clear thinking find that unless people have some emotional reason to learn something, they do not learn it very well or at all. This is why tests are given—to motivate learners to have that thrill of a good score or distress of a poor one, and we have found that HSPs are far more affected by test scores. This is one reason why it is easier to learn a foreign language in the country where it is spoken—we are highly motivated to find our way, converse when spoken to, and generally not seem foolish.

From this point of view about emotions, it would seem almost impossible for an HSP to process things deeply without having stronger emotional reactions to motivate them. And remember, when HSPs react more, it is as much or more to positive emotions, such as curiosity, anticipation of success (using that shortcut others don't know about), a pleasant desire for something, satisfaction, joy, and contentedness. Perhaps everyone reacts strongly to negative situations, but maybe HSPs have evolved so that we especially relish a good outcome and figure out more than others how to make it happen. I imagine that we can plan an especially good birthday celebration, anticipating the happiness it will bring. Think a moment about the ways your relatively stronger emotions help you. I know one way: Reacting before others do in a way appropriate to a situation, such as tears at a memorial service, makes you an "emotional leader."

S Is for Sensing the Subtle

Most of the studies already cited required perceiving subtleties. This is often what we are most aware of personally—the little things we notice that others miss. Given that, and because I called the trait "high sensitivity," many have thought the *senses* are the heart of the trait. (To correct this confusion and emphasize the role of processing, we used "sensory *processing* sensitivity" as its more formal, scientific designation.) However, this trait is not so much about extraordinary senses—there are, after all, sensitive people who have poor eyesight or hearing. And while it is true that some sensitive people report that one or more senses are very acute, even in these cases it could be that they process the sensory information more carefully rather than having something unusual about their eyes, nose, skin, taste buds, or ears. Again, the brain areas that are more active when sensitive people perceive are those that do the more complex processing of sensory information—not so much the areas that recognize alphabet letters by their shape or even the areas that read words, but the areas that catch the subtle meaning of words.

Our awareness of subtleties is useful in an infinite number of ways, from simple pleasure in life to strategizing a response based on our awareness of others' nonverbal cues (that they may have no idea they are giving off) about their mood or trustworthiness. Of course, when we are worn out we may be the least aware of anything, subtle or gross, except our own need for a break.

New Research on a Variety of Topics Important for You

Creativity, Awe, Regulating Your Strong Emotions

You may be interested to know that a study has finally demonstrated that we are more creative, by at least some measures, than those without our trait. There is also evidence that creativity (like depth of processing) is driven by emotions, strong and subtle, and negative emotions as well as positive. In addition, there is a strong relationship between being an HSP and feelings of awe, a very intense emotion that can add to the pleasure and meaning in life, but can also be overwhelming.

This brings us to emotional regulation—having the right emotion at the right time and in the right amount. (This does not mean learning to be bland. Intense awe, joy, or creative energy at the right time and place can *be* the right amount.) Many studies show HSPs having trouble with emotions—anxiety, in particular—especially, as I said, if they had difficult childhoods. However, the negative emotions are greatly decreased by personality qualities or skills labeled together as part of the trait of mindfulness: nonreactivity, nonjudging, acceptance, ability to describe feelings, and acting with awareness. Anxiety is lower in HSPs with this trait, particularly when we have the quality of acceptance.

The subject of acceptance of what you feel in the moment brings us to another study about emotional regulation and HSPs. (Two of the four authors were the authors of the mindfulness-trait study above.) Again, the study found we had more depression, anxiety, and so forth, but how we regulated these emotions was the key. We have some important skills, such as knowing what we feel, but need to improve on others. As with the mindfulness trait, at the top of the list was acceptance of your feelings. Other traits on the list included not feeling ashamed of them; believing you can cope with them as well as others do; trusting that your feelings will not, as we sometimes can feel, last forever; and assuming there's hope.

There is an emotion many HSPs seem to have that cannot be regulated away by the better attitudes discussed above. That is the depression that occurs when there is less sun, in winter or areas prone to clouds or rain. I found in an early survey, and now other researchers have found it too, that many HSPs have Seasonal

Affective Disorder. This does not mean every HSP; it is just a bit more common in us. But if you do have it, it is nothing to worry about. There are treatments, usually a light therapy lamp, but you have to have the right kind for the right amount of time and be consistent with it. You can learn more about this from a knowledgeable professional.

Research on HSPs in Relationships

I have written extensively on our relationships in this book and in *The Highly Sensitive Person in Love*, but I wish there was more research on this subject. Still, there is some. The first study begins with the idea that you process information more deeply and therefore might prefer to do so in your conversations with those with whom you are close. In 2010, my husband and I, and others, explored whether HS partners in a relationship would indeed be more bored when they "wish the conversation were more deep or personally meaningful." This was especially true when they answered yes to liking "to spend time reflecting or thinking about the meaning of your experience." The results were stronger for HS women but significant for both genders. Interestingly, they did not report themselves to be less satisfied with their relationship than those without this trait (and without this problem), even if they said they were bored in this way. Also interesting was that in general, people are happier when they have more meaningful conversations. So go ahead and push for what you want. What's good for HSPs is often what's good for everyone.

I conducted the second study when writing *The Highly Sensitive Person in Love*. It was an anonymous survey of "Temperament and Sexuality," using a newsletter mailing list of about six hundred HSPs. They were asked to complete the survey and return it in the envelope provided, and also to ask someone else they thought was not highly sensitive to do the survey and return it separately. We received back 308 from women and 135 from men. You can read all of the results in that book, but here is a taste: HSPs were more likely to see sex as having a quality of mystery or power; to have difficulty returning abruptly to ordinary activities after sex; and be less aroused than others by strong, explicit sexual cues. The following two items were true for all HSPs, but especially for men: "Liking to have things be the same each time you have sex" and not particularly enjoying variety in sexual activities.

On the other hand, HSPs were no different in the number of sexual partners lived with; duration of most recent sexual event; sex being one of the most satisfying parts of life; preferring being active and deciding what the pair will do; or frequency of orgasm and masturbation. HSPs' sexuality was not affected more than others' by physical or emotional problems or medications. HSPs did not report more sexual dysfunction or being sexually abused more often than others, and if abused, having these experiences affect their sexual life more than others.

Compared to other women, highly sensitive women were less likely to associate sex with feeling sad, scared, or afraid and more likely to associate it with feeling loved. They also considered more the impact of a sexual relationship on the other person; were more cautious about sexually transmitted diseases or pregnancy; needed to feel loving towards a partner in order to enjoy sex; and were less able to take sex lightly. To me the first sentence is explained by the second and our choosing to pause-to-check before proceeding—in sexuality as well as in other areas of life.

HSPs appeared to enjoy sexuality more but engage in it less, perhaps because sexuality, being a source of general stimulation, is potentially a source of overarousal when life is already full of stimulation.

I hope this information is helpful to some of you. Maybe understanding your style in this area will help you express your wishes to someone who is not highly sensitive without feeling you are "weird"!

A third study relevant to relationships specifically is the research I already described that found HSPs show more activation in areas of the brain associated with greater empathy.

Parenting

My husband and I were interested in how HSPs experience being parents, so in an online survey, we asked over a thousand of them a number of questions covering three areas. The first was about their relationship with their "co-parent" (e.g., "my partner thinks I am a good parent," "my partner is a good parent," "having a child has made difficulties in our relationship.") The good news here is that HS parents reported no more relationship difficulties than those without the trait.

The second topic was how difficult they found parenting to be (e.g., "each day is full of hassles," "I don't get enough time to myself," "I regret having become a parent"). The third topic was how attuned they felt to their child. ("I know what my child needs even before he lets me know," "I stay calm with my child no matter what," "one of my strengths is the creativity I bring to parenting"). HS mothers reported more parenting difficulties and more attunement to their children, whereas HS fathers scored significantly higher only on attunement to their child, perhaps because they spent less time with their children. (These results were not affected by parents' level of stress outside the home, their education, marital status, age, or their children's ages.)

It seems obvious that for HS parents to use the advantages of their trait, such as attunement, they must control the overstimulating part of parenting, and my book *The Highly Sensitive Parent* aims to help with that as much as possible. In particular, that book recommends HS parents not try to "go it alone," as they see some parents doing. They must have help in some way, especially while children are young, in order to be the best possible parents.

Evidence for HS parents needing help is going to accumulate as the research increases on parent burnout in general and HS parents are found to be particularly susceptible. One study, already mentioned, found HS parents are more affected by chaos in their homes. Even more telling is a study of the self-reported parenting styles of HSPs, which found that of the three styles measured—authoritarian, permissive, and authoritative—they were more likely to display the first two, which are considered less desirable than the firm but gentle authoritative style. The authors conclude that HS parents were probably trying to control the stimulation caused by their children's behavior (probably especially uncontrolled behavior, such as tantrums or chaotic noise, but also probably constant talking or arguing) by either using an authoritative or strict style, or else simply letting the children go unguided, using a permissive style. An interview study of four highly sensitive mothers seemed to verify that pattern.

Finally, in a study of those raising children with autism spectrum disorders, HS parents did not have more difficulties than others unless they were finding the decisions they had to make too difficult. This is interesting because difficulty making decisions is a result of depth of processing, and parents in the survey study reported that the large number of decisions involved in parenting was definitely one of the difficulties they experienced.

HSPs and Work

The subject of work and career is discussed in the book, but here is the research published on the subject since the book was written. A study done by Bhavini Shrivastava of HSPs in an information technology firm in India found that they felt more stressed than others by their work environment, but were actually seen as more productive than others by their managers. Maike Andresen and her collaborators in the department of Human Resource Management at the University of Bamburg, Germany, studied how being an HSP affected the "turnover intentions" (either to resign or a company's intention to "let them go") of employees working abroad. They found that HSPs were more often sent overseas on important assignments but were higher on turnover-intention measures, with stress being the reason. Since organizations sent unusually high numbers of HSPs to these positions, they apparently thought HSPs were especially suited for these jobs (with their empathy, conscientiousness, etc.). Hence, the conclusion was that more preparation and support to help them deal with the stress would allow them to be retained in these roles.

Research on those with the intention and sense of having the ability to start one's own business (entrepreneurial intention) has tended to identify a "heroic," extraverted, not-very-sensitive type. However, HSPs have also been found to have a strong entrepreneurial intention, being skilled at recognizing opportunities (depth of processing, aware of subtle stimuli, creativity, etc.) and motivated to be self-employed and manage their own energy and resources—something I discuss in the chapter on work.

Finally, John Hughes, an interim CIO and an author on best practices for CEOs, has written on the reasons HSPs make exceptional leaders. First, they notice what others miss, having a greater sense of what is happening for their team. Second, they prefer to process more than simply to take action, often standing back to let others on their team receive credit. Third, and most important, they exhibit what is called "resonant leadership," obtaining a "feel" for what is going on, often nonverbal, so that they lead with understanding and empathy. Such leaders tend to "say and do the right things at just the right time. This isn't luck or magic, it's their innate ability to feel deeply, process richly, and patiently consider the right words and actions for the moment."

Every Highly Sensitive Person Is Different, and Different at Different Times

DOES is a wonderful general guideline for understanding high sensitivity, as is the research on what the average HSP is like on various measures or in different situations, or even how their brain functions. But you are unique, not identical to a general description or like any statistically average—actually nonexistent—person. (Ever seen a family with 2.12 children?) You know you also differ moment to moment. For example, depending on how you are feeling, you may not reflect before acting or notice subtleties even as much as those around you who do not have the trait. HSPs also differ enormously from each other. We have other traits, different histories, and are just different. In our enthusiasm to identify ourselves as a group—even as a misunderstood minority (I hope not too much of that)—we do not want to forget that we are not identical by any means. In particular, we are not all, or all the time, aware, conscientious, wonderful people!

Take the O facet (easily overstimulated). Two types of sensitive people may behave quite differently when being bothered by loud noise or rude, upsetting people. One type may rarely complain or be visibly bothered by such things because such people avoid these situations or quietly exit them. They will simply not, for example, stay in a job if there are constant annoyances but would escape to another workplace, become self-employed, or quietly tolerate the annoyances while strategizing to have them corrected. Another type of HSP, usually those with a more stressful past, will feel more victimized and upset, and at the same time be less able to place themselves in the right environments and avoid the wrong ones. Maybe people like that feel you have to please others or prove something. In the workplace, they may not quit a job until a crisis occurs so that everyone working there knows about their "oversensitivity." Such HSPs are often the ones others notice, never imagining that the quiet, creative, empathic types are also HSPs.

Final Thoughts

Studying high sensitivity has been an amazing journey for me. As I said at the start of this note, I began only with an interest in the subject for myself. Then, having a scientific background in psychology, I did some interviews, still curious about it. Then, as I like to put it, I found I was walking down a street and a parade began to form behind me, a parade of people who were highly sensitive and had never heard the term before. We are still not only a minority but an invisible one. Some of us answer true to every question on the self-test in this book. But others answer false to all of them. They are also invisible and we live among them.

Of course we are not entirely invisible. To others our most obvious "problem" is that we "overreact" compared to others—the O of being overstimulated and the E of stronger emotional reactions. But since we are a minority, of course we are not reacting as most people do. It's the more noticeable O and E that have made it seem to us and others that we have a flaw. Further, as we have learned from differential susceptibility, those HSPs with a troubled past have less control over their reactions, hence the trait becomes associated with people having difficulties, or even seems to be a disorder, in these cases.

The few observable things we do that would indicate D and S, depth of processing and awareness of subtleties, can be easily overlooked or misunderstood. For example, if we are seen taking our time before entering a situation or making a decision, that can seem, again, to be different, a potential problem, and therefore a flaw. It is easy to overlook how good those decisions can be when finally made. Further, this sort of slowness can be caused by many things besides sensitivity, such as fear or even low intelligence. It's what's going on inside, out of sight, that most clearly sorts the highly sensitive minority from others. Thank goodness for the brain research that shows these differences and for the studies finding the advantages of high sensitivity. Thank you, all of you, who have stepped forward and said, "Yes, that's what goes on inside of me, too. Even if others can't see it."

Now after twenty-five years, those without the trait understand it better. Let's help them know even more and that we do not want to be seen as better than others, but certainly not worse. We can do it. We have been doing it. Let's celebrate! Maybe with a parade!

Preface

"Cry baby!"
"Scaredy-cat!"
"Don't be a spoilsport!"

Echoes from the past? And how about this well-meaning warning: "You're just too sensitive for your own good."

If you were like me, you heard a lot of that, and it made you feel there must be something very different about you. I was convinced that I had a fatal flaw that I had to hide and that doomed me to a second-rate life. I thought there was something wrong with me.

In fact, there is something very right with you and me. If you answered true to twelve or more of the questions on the self-test at the beginning of this book, or if the detailed description in chapter 1 seems to fit you (really the best test), then you are a very special type of human being, a highly sensitive person—which hereafter we'll call an HSP. And this book is just for you.

Having a sensitive nervous system is normal, a basically neutral trait. You probably inherited it. It occurs in about 15–20 percent of the population. It means you are aware of subtleties in your surroundings, a great advantage in many situations. It also means you are more easily overwhelmed when you have been out in a highly stimulating environment for too long, bombarded by sights and sounds until you are exhausted in a nervous-system sort of way. Thus, being sensitive has both advantages and disadvantages.

In our culture, however, possessing this trait is not considered ideal and that fact probably has had a major impact on you. Well-meaning parents and teachers probably tried to help you "overcome" it, as if it were a defect. Other children were not always as nice about it. As an adult, it has probably been harder to find the right career and relationships and generally to feel self-worth and self-confidence.

What This Book Offers You

This book provides basic, detailed information you need about your trait, data that exist nowhere else. It is the product of five years of research, in-depth interviews, clinical experience, courses and individual consultations with hundreds of HSPs, and careful reading between the lines of what psychology has already learned about the trait but does not realize it knows. In the first three chapters you will learn all the basic facts about your trait and how to handle overstimulation and overarousal of your nervous system.

Next, this book considers the impact of your sensitivity on your personal history, career, relationships, and inner life. It focuses on the advantages you may not have thought of, plus it gives advice about typical problems some HSPs face, such as shyness or difficulty finding the right sort of work.

It is quite a journey we'll take. Most of the HSPs I've helped with the information that is in this book have told me that it has dramatically changed their lives—and they've told me to tell you that.

A Word to the Sensitive-But-Less-So

First, if you have picked up this book because you're the parent, spouse, or friend of an HSP, then you're especially welcome here. Your relationship with your HSP will be greatly improved.

Second, a telephone survey of three hundred randomly selected individuals of all ages found that while 20 percent were extremely or quite sensitive, another 22 percent were moderately sensitive. Those of you who fall into this moderately sensitive category will also benefit from this book.

By the way, 42 percent said they were not sensitive at all—which suggests why the highly sensitive can feel so completely out of step with a large part of the world. And naturally, it's that segment of the population that's always turning up the radio or honking their horns.

Further, it is safe to say that everyone can become highly sensitive at times—for example, after a month alone in a mountain cabin. And everyone becomes more sensitive as they age. Indeed, most people, whether they admit it or not, probably have a highly sensitive facet that comes to the fore in certain situations.

And Some Things to Say to Non-HSPs

Sometimes non-HSPs feel excluded and hurt by the idea that we are different from them and maybe sound like we think we are somehow better. They say, "Do you mean I'm not sensitive?" One problem is that "sensitive" also means being understanding and aware. Both HSPs and non-HSPs can have these qualities, which are optimized when we are feeling good and alert to the subtle. When very calm, HSPs may even enjoy the advantage of picking up more delicate nuances. When overaroused, however, a frequent state for HSPs, we are anything but understanding or sensitive. Instead, we are overwhelmed, frazzled, and need to be alone. By contrast, your non-HSP friends are actually more understanding of others in highly chaotic situations.

I thought long and hard about what to call this trait. I knew I didn't want to repeat the mistake of confusing it with introversion, shyness, inhibitedness, and a host of other misnomers laid on us by other psychologists. None of them captures the neutral, much less the positive, aspects of the trait. "Sensitivity" does express the neutral fact of greater receptivity to stimulation. So it seemed to be time to make up for the bias against HSPs by using a term that might be taken in our favor.

On the other hand, being "highly sensitive" is anything but positive to some. While sitting in my quiet house writing this, at a time when no one is talking about the trait, I'll go on record: This book will generate more than its share of hurtful jokes and comments about HSPs. There is tremendous collective psychological energy around the idea of being sensitive—almost as much as around gender issues, with which sensitivity is often confused. (There are as many male as female babies born sensitive; but men are not supposed to possess the trait and women are. Both genders pay a high price for that confusion.) So just be prepared for that energy. Protect both your sensitivity and your newly budding understanding of it by not talking about it at all when that seems most prudent.

Mostly, enjoy knowing that there are also many like-minded people out there. We have not been in touch before. But we are now, and both we and our society will be the better for it. In chapters 1, 6, and 10, I will comment at some length on the HSP's important social function.

What You Need

I have found that HSPs benefit from a fourfold approach, which the chapters in this book will follow.

1. *Self-knowledge.* You have to understand what it means to be an HSP. Thoroughly. And how it fits with your other traits and how your society's negative attitude has affected you. Then you need to know your sensitive body very well. No more ignoring your body because it seems too uncooperative or weak.

2. *Reframing.* You must actively reframe much of your past in the light of knowing you came into the world highly sensitive. So many of your "failures" were inevitable because neither you nor your parents and teachers, friends and colleagues, understood you. Reframing how you experienced your past can lead to solid self-esteem, and self-esteem is especially important for HSPs, for it decreases our overarousal in new (and therefore highly stimulating) situations.

Reframing is not automatic, however. That is why I include "activities" at the end of each chapter that often involve it.

3. *Healing.* If you have not yet done so, you must begin to heal the deeper wounds. You were very sensitive as a child; family and school problems, childhood illnesses, and the like all affected you more than others. Furthermore, you were different from other kids and almost surely suffered for that.

HSPs especially, sensing the intense feelings that must arise, may hold back from the inner work necessary to heal the wounds from the past. Caution and slowness are justified. But you will cheat yourself if you delay.

4. *Help With Feeling Okay When Out in the World and Learning When to Be Less Out.* You can be, should be, and need to be involved in the world. It truly needs you. But you have

to be skilled at avoiding overdoing or underdoing it. This book, free of the confusing messages from a less sensitive culture, is about discovering that way.

I will also teach you about your trait's effect on your close relationships. And I'll discuss psychotherapy and HSPs—which HSPs should be in therapy and why, what kind, with whom, and especially how therapy differs for HSPs. Then I'll consider HSPs and medical care, including plenty of information on medications like Prozac, often taken by HSPs. At the end of this book we will savor our rich inner life.

About Myself

I am a research psychologist, university professor, psychotherapist, and published novelist. What matters most, however, is that I am an HSP like you. I am definitely not writing from on high, aiming down to help you, poor soul, overcome your "syndrome." I know personally about *our* trait, its assets and its challenges.

As a child, at home, I hid from the chaos in my family. At school I avoided sports, games, and kids in general. What a mixture of relief and humiliation when my strategy succeeded and I was totally ignored.

In junior high school an extrovert took me under her wing. In high school that relationship continued, plus I studied most of the time. In college my life became far more difficult. After many stops and starts, including a four-year marriage undertaken too young, I finally graduated Phi Beta Kappa from the University of California at Berkeley. But I spent my share of time crying in rest rooms, thinking I was going crazy. (My research has found that retreating like this, often to cry, is typical of HSPs.)

In my first try at graduate school I was provided with an office, to which I also retreated and cried, trying to regain some calm. Because of such reactions, I stopped my studies with a master's degree, even though I was highly encouraged to continue for a doctorate. It took twenty-five years for me to gain the information about my trait that made it possible to understand my reactions and so complete that doctorate.

When I was twenty-three, I met my current husband and settled down into a very protected life of writing and rearing a son. I was simultaneously delighted and ashamed of not being "out there." I was vaguely aware of my lost opportunities to learn, to enjoy more public recognition of my abilities, to be more connected with all kinds of people. But from bitter experience I thought I had no choice.

Some arousing events, however, cannot be avoided. I had to undergo a medical procedure from which I assumed I would recover in a few weeks. Instead, for months my body seemed to resound with physical and emotional reactions. I was being forced to face once again that mysterious "fatal flaw" of mine that made me so different. So I tried some psychotherapy. And got lucky. After listening to me for a few sessions, my therapist said, "But of course you were upset; you are a very highly sensitive person."

What is this, I thought, some excuse? She said she had never thought much about it, but from her experience it seemed that there were real differences in people's tolerance for stimulation and also their openness to the deeper significance of an experience, good and bad. To her, such sensitivity was hardly a sign of a mental flaw or disorder. At least she hoped not, for she was highly sensitive herself. I recall her grin. "As are most of the people who strike me as really worth knowing."

I spent several years in therapy, none of it wasted, working through various issues from my childhood. But the central theme became the impact of this trait. There was my sense of being flawed. There was the willingness of others to protect me in return for enjoying my imagination, empathy, creativity, and insight, which I myself hardly appreciated. And there was my resulting isolation from the world. But as I gained insight, I was able to reenter the world. I take great pleasure now in being part of things, a professional, and sharing the special gifts of my sensitivity.

The Research Behind This Book

As knowledge about my trait changed my life, I decided to read more about it, but there was almost nothing available. I thought the closest topic might be introversion. The psychiatrist Carl Jung wrote very wisely on the subject, calling it a tendency to turn inward. The work of Jung, himself an HSP, has been a major help to me, but the more scientific work on introversion was focused on introverts not being sociable, and it was that idea which made me wonder if introversion and sensitivity were being wrongly equated.

With so little information to go on, I decided to put a notice in a newsletter that went to the staff of the university where I was teaching at the time. I asked to interview anyone who felt they were highly sensitive to stimulation, introverted, or quick to react emotionally. Soon I had more volunteers than I needed.

Next, the local paper did a story on the research. Even though there was nothing said in the article about how to reach me, over a hundred people phoned and wrote me, thanking me, wanting help, or just wanting to say, "Me, too." Two years later, people were still contacting me. (HSPs sometimes think things over for a while before making their move!)

Based on the interviews (forty for two to three hours each), I designed a questionnaire that I have distributed to thousands all over North America. And I directed a random-dialing telephone survey of three hundred people as well. The point that matters for you is that everything in this book is based on solid research, my own or that of others. Or I am speaking from my repeated observations of HSPs, from my courses, conversations, individual consultations, and psychotherapy with them. These opportunities to explore the personal lives of HSPs have numbered in the thousands. Even so, I will say "probably" and "maybe" more than you are used to in books for the general reader, but I think HSPs appreciate that.

Deciding to do all of this research, writing, and teaching has made me a kind of pioneer. But that, too, is part of being an HSP. We are often the first ones to see what needs to be done. As our confidence in our virtues grows, perhaps more and more of us will speak up—in our sensitive way.

Instructions to the Reader

1. Again, I address the reader as an HSP, but this book is written equally for someone seeking to understand HSPs, whether as a friend, relative, advisor, employer, educator, or health professional.

2. This book involves seeing yourself as having a trait common to many. That is, it labels you. The advantages are that you

can feel normal and benefit from the experience and research of others. But any label misses your uniqueness. HSPs are each utterly different, even with their common trait. Please remind yourself of that as you proceed.

3. While you are reading this book, you will probably see everything in your life in light of being highly sensitive. That is to be expected. In fact, it is exactly the idea. Total immersion helps with learning any new language, including a new way of talking about yourself. If others feel a little concerned, left out, or annoyed, ask for their patience. There will come a day when the concept will settle in and you'll be talking about it less.

4. This book includes some activities which I have found useful for HSPs. But I'm not going to say that you *must* do them if you want to gain anything from this book. Trust your HSP intuition and do what feels right.

5. Any of the activities could bring up strong feelings. If that happens, I do urge you to seek professional help. If you are now in therapy, this book should fit well with your work there. The ideas here might even shorten the time you will need therapy as you envision a new ideal self—not the culture's ideal but your own, someone you can be and maybe already are. But remember that this book does not substitute for a good therapist when things get intense or confusing.

This is an exciting moment for me as I imagine you turning the page and entering into this new world of mine, of yours, of *ours*. After thinking for so long that you might be the only one, it is nice to have company, isn't it?

Are You Highly Sensitive?

A SELF-TEST

Answer each question according to the way you feel. Answer true if it is at least somewhat true for you. Answer false if it is not very true or not at all true for you.

I seem to be aware of subtleties in my environment.	**T**	**F**
Other people's moods affect me.	**T**	**F**
I tend to be very sensitive to pain.	**T**	**F**
I find myself needing to withdraw during busy days, into bed or into a darkened room or any place where I can have some privacy and relief from stimulation.	**T**	**F**
I am particularly sensitive to the effects of caffeine.	**T**	**F**
I am easily overwhelmed by things like bright lights, strong smells, coarse fabrics, or sirens close by.	**T**	**F**
I have a rich, complex inner life.	**T**	**F**
I am made uncomfortable by loud noises.	**T**	**F**
I am deeply moved by the arts or music.	**T**	**F**
I am conscientious.	**T**	**F**
I startle easily.	**T**	**F**
I get rattled when I have a lot to do in a short amount of time.	**T**	**F**
When people are uncomfortable in a physical environment I tend to know what needs to be done to make it more comfortable (like changing the lighting or the seating).	**T**	**F**
I am annoyed when people try to get me to do too many things at once.	**T**	**F**
I try hard to avoid making mistakes or forgetting things.	**T**	**F**
I make it a point to avoid violent movies and TV shows.	**T**	**F**

I become unpleasantly aroused when a lot is going on around me.   **T F**

Being very hungry creates a strong reaction in me, disrupting my concentration or mood.   **T F**

Changes in my life shake me up.   **T F**

I notice and enjoy delicate or fine scents, tastes, sounds, works of art.   **T F**

I make it a high priority to arrange my life to avoid upsetting or overwhelming situations.   **T F**

When I must compete or be observed while performing a task, I become so nervous or shaky that I do much worse than I would otherwise.   **T F**

When I was a child, my parents or teachers seemed to see me as sensitive or shy.   **T F**

SCORING YOURSELF

If you answered true to twelve or more of the questions, you're probably highly sensitive.

But frankly, no psychological test is so accurate that you should base your life on it. If only one or two questions are true of you but they are *extremely* true, you might also be justified in calling yourself highly sensitive.

Read on, and if you recognize yourself in the in-depth description of a highly sensitive person in chapter 1, consider yourself one. The rest of this book will help you understand yourself better and learn to thrive in today's not-so-sensitive world.

The Highly
Sensitive Person

1

The Facts About Being Highly Sensitive

A (Wrong) Sense of Being Flawed

In this chapter you will learn the basic facts about your trait and how it makes you different from others. You will also discover the rest of your inherited personality and have your eyes opened about your culture's view of you. But first you should meet Kristen.

She Thought She Was Crazy

Kristen was the twenty-third interview of my research on HSPs. She was an intelligent, clear-eyed college student. But soon into our interview her voice began to tremble.

"I'm sorry," she whispered. "But I really signed up to see you because you're a psychologist and I had to talk to someone who could tell me—" Her voice broke. "Am I *crazy*?" I studied her with sympathy. She was obviously feeling desperate, but nothing she had said so far had given me any sense of mental illness. But then, I was already listening differently to people like Kristen.

She tried again, as if afraid to give me time to answer. "I feel so different. I always did. I don't mean—I mean, my family was great. My childhood was almost idyllic until I had to go to school. Although Mom says I was always a grumpy baby."

She took a breath. I said something reassuring, and she plunged on. "But in nursery school I was afraid of everything. Even music time. When they would pass out the pots and pans to pound, I would put my hands over my ears and cry."

She looked away, her eyes glistening with tears now, too. "In elementary school I was always the teacher's pet. Yet they'd say I was 'spacey.' "

Her "spaciness" prompted a distressing series of medical and psychological tests. First for mental retardation. As a result, she was enrolled in a program for the *gifted*, which did not surprise me.

Still the message was "Something is wrong with this child." Her hearing was tested. Normal. In fourth grade she had a brain scan on the theory that her inwardness was due to petit mal seizures. Her brain was normal.

The final diagnosis? She had "trouble screening out stimuli." But the result was a child who believed she was defective.

Special But Deeply Misunderstood

The diagnosis was right as far as it went. HSPs do take in a lot—all the subtleties others miss. But what seems ordinary to others, like loud music or crowds, can be highly stimulating and thus stressful for HSPs.

Most people ignore sirens, glaring lights, strange odors, clutter and chaos. HSPs are disturbed by them.

Most people's feet may be tired at the end of a day in a mall or a museum, but they're ready for more when you suggest an evening party. HSPs need solitude after such a day. They feel jangled, overaroused.

Most people walk into a room and perhaps notice the furniture, the people—that's about it. HSPs can be instantly aware, whether they wish to be or not, of the mood, the friendships and enmities, the freshness or staleness of the air, the personality of the one who arranged the flowers.

If you are an HSP, however, it is hard to grasp that you have some remarkable ability. How do you compare inner experiences? Not easily. Mostly you notice that you seem unable to tolerate as much as other people. You forget that you belong to a group that has often demonstrated great creativity, insight, passion, and caring—all highly valued by society.

We are a package deal, however. Our trait of sensitivity means we will also be cautious, inward, needing extra time alone. Because people without the trait (the majority) do not understand that, they see us as timid, shy, weak, or that greatest sin of all, unsociable. Fearing these labels, we try to be like others. But that leads to our becoming overaroused and distressed. Then *that* gets us labeled neurotic or crazy, first by others and then by ourselves.

Kristen's Dangerous Year

Sooner or later everyone encounters stressful life experiences, but HSPs react more to such stimulation. If you see this reaction as part of some basic flaw, you intensify the stress already present in any life crisis. Next come feelings of hopelessness and worthlessness.

Kristen, for example, had such a crisis the year she started college. She had attended a low-key private high school and had never been away from home. Suddenly she was living among strangers, fighting in crowds for courses and books, and always overstimulated. Next she fell in love, fast and hard (as HSPs can do). Shortly after, she went to Japan to meet her boyfriend's family, an event she already had good reason to fear. It was while she was in Japan that, in her words, she "flipped out."

Kristen had never thought of herself as an anxious person, but suddenly, in Japan, she was overcome by fears and could not sleep. Then she became depressed. Frightened by her own emotions, her self-confidence plummeted. Her young boyfriend could not cope with her "craziness" and wanted to end the relationship. By then she had returned to school, but feared she was going to fail at that, too. Kristen was on the edge.

She looked up at me after sobbing out the last of her story.

"Then I heard about this research, about being sensitive, and I thought, Could that be me? But it isn't, I know. Is it?"

I told her that of course I could not be sure from such a brief conversation, but I believed that, yes, her sensitivity in combination with all these stresses might well explain her state of mind. And so I had the privilege of explaining Kristen to herself—an explanation obviously long overdue.

Defining High Sensitivity—Two Facts to Remember

FACT 1: Everyone, HSP or not, feels best when neither too bored nor too aroused.

An individual will perform best on any kind of task, whether engaging in a conversation or playing in the Super Bowl, if his or her nervous system is moderately alert and aroused. Too little arousal and one is dull, ineffective. To change that under-aroused physical state, we drink some coffee, turn on the radio, call a friend, strike up a conversation with a total stranger, change careers—anything!

At the other extreme, too much arousal of the nervous system and anyone will become distressed, clumsy, and confused. We cannot think; the body is not coordinated; we feel out of control. Again, we have many ways to correct the situation. Sometimes we rest. Or mentally shut down. Some of us drink alcohol or take a Valium.

The best amount of arousal falls somewhere in the middle. That there is a need and desire for an "optimal level of arousal" is, in fact, one of the most solid findings of psychology. It is true for everyone, even infants. They hate to feel bored or overwhelmed.

FACT 2: People differ considerably in how much their nervous system is aroused in the same situation, under the same stimulation.

The difference is largely inherited, and is very real and normal. In fact, it can be observed in all higher animals—mice, cats, dogs, horses, monkeys, humans. Within a species, the percentage that is very sensitive to stimulation is usually about the same, around 15–20 percent. Just as some within a species are a little bigger in size than others, some are a little more sensitive. In fact, through careful breeding of animals, mating the sensitive ones to each other can create a sensitive strain in just a few generations. In short, among inborn traits of temperament, this one creates the most dramatic, observable differences.

The Good News and the Not-So-Good

What this difference in arousability means is that you notice levels of stimulation that go unobserved by others. This is true whether we are talking about subtle sounds, sights, or physical sensations like pain. It is not that your hearing, vision, or other senses are more acute (plenty of HSPs wear glasses). The difference seems to lie somewhere on the way to the brain or in the brain, in a more careful processing of information. We reflect more on everything. And we sort things into finer distinctions. Like those machines that grade fruit by size—we sort into ten sizes while others sort into two or three.

This greater awareness of the subtle tends to make you more intuitive, which simply means picking up and working through information in a semiconscious or unconscious way. The result is that you often "just know" without realizing how. Furthermore, this deeper processing of subtle details causes you to consider the past or future more. You "just know" how things got to be the way they are or how they are going to turn out. This is that "sixth sense" people talk about. It can be wrong, of course, just as your eyes and ears can be wrong, but your intuition is right often enough that HSPs tend to be visionaries, highly intuitive artists, or inventors, as well as more conscientious, cautious, and wise people.

The downside of the trait shows up at more intense levels of stimulation. What is *moderately* arousing for most people is highly arousing for HSPs. What is *highly* arousing for most people causes an HSP to become very frazzled indeed, until they reach a shutdown point called "transmarginal inhibition." Transmarginal inhibition was first discussed around the turn of the century by the Russian physiologist Ivan Pavlov, who was convinced that the most basic inherited difference among people was how soon they reach this shutdown point and that the quick-to-shut-down have a fundamentally different type of nervous system.

No one likes being overaroused, HSP or not. A person feels out of control, and the whole body warns that it is in trouble. Overarousal often means failing to perform at one's best. Of course, it can also mean danger. An extra dread of overarousal may even be built into all of us. Since a newborn cannot run or fight or even recognize danger, it is best if it howls at anything new, anything arousing at all, so that grown-ups can come and rescue it.

Like the fire department, we HSPs mostly respond to false alarms. But if our sensitivity saves a life even once, it is a trait that has a genetic payoff. So, yes, when our trait leads to overarousal, it is a nuisance. But it is part of a package deal with many advantages.

More About Stimulation

Stimulation is anything that wakes up the nervous system, gets its attention, makes the nerves fire off another round of the little electrical charges that they carry. We usually think of stimulation as coming from outside, but of course it can come from our body (such as pain, muscle tension, hunger, thirst, or sexual feelings) or as memories, fantasies, thoughts, or plans.

Stimulation can vary in intensity (like the loudness of a noise) or in duration. It can be more stimulating because it is novel, as when one is startled by a honk or shout, or in its complexity, as when one is at a party and hearing four conversations at once plus music.

Often we can get used to stimulation. But sometimes we think we have and aren't being bothered, but suddenly feel exhausted and realize why: We have been putting up with something at a conscious level while it was actually wearing us down. Even a moderate and familiar stimulation, like a day at work, can cause an HSP to need quiet by evening. At that point, one more "small" stimulation can be the last straw.

Stimulation is even more complicated because the same stimulus can have different meanings for different people. A crowded shopping mall at Christmastime may remind one per-

---

VALUING YOUR SENSITIVITY

Think back to one or more times that your sensitivity has saved you or someone else from suffering, great loss, or even death. (In my own case, I and all my family would be dead if I had not awakened at the first flicker of firelight in the ceiling of an old wooden house in which we were living.)

---

son of happy family shopping excursions and create a warm holiday spirit. But another person may have been forced to go shopping with others, tried to buy gifts without enough money and no idea of what to purchase, had unhappy memories of past holidays, and so suffers intensely in malls at Christmas.

One general rule is that when we have no control over stimulation, it is more upsetting, even *more* so if we feel we are someone's victim. While music played by ourselves may be pleasant, heard from the neighbor's stereo, it can be annoying, and if we have previously asked them to turn it down, it becomes a hostile invasion. This book may even increase your annoyance a bit as you begin to appreciate that you are a minority whose rights to have less stimulation are generally ignored.

Obviously it would help if we were enlightened and detached from all of these associations so that nothing could arouse us. No wonder so many HSPs become interested in spiritual paths.

Is Arousal Really Different From Anxiety and Fear?

It is important not to confuse arousal with fear. Fear creates arousal, but so do many other emotions, including joy, curiosity, or anger. But we can also be overaroused by semiconscious thoughts or low levels of excitement that create no obvious emotion. Often we are not aware of what is arousing us, such as the newness of a situation or noise or the many things our eyes are seeing.

Actually, there are several ways to *be* aroused and still other ways to *feel* aroused, and they differ from time to time and from person to person. Arousal may appear as blushing, trembling, heart pounding, hands shaking, foggy thinking, stomach churning, muscles tensing, and hands or other parts of the body perspiring. Often people in such situations are not aware of some or all of these reactions as they occur. On the other hand, some people say they feel aroused, but that arousal shows up very little in any of these ways. Still, the term does describe something that all these experiences and physical states share. Like the word "stress," arousal is a word that really communicates something we all know about, even if that something varies a lot. And of course stress is closely related to arousal: Our response to stress is to become aroused.

Once we do notice arousal, we want to name it and know its source in order to recognize danger. And often we think that our arousal is due to fear. We do not realize that our heart may be pounding from the sheer effort of processing extra stimulation. Or other people assume we are afraid, given our obvious arousal, so we assume it, too. Then, deciding we must be afraid, we become even more aroused. And we avoid the situation in the future when staying in it and getting used to it might have calmed us down. We will discuss again the importance of not confusing fear and arousal in chapter 5 when we talk about "shyness."

Your Trait Really Does Make You Special

There are many fruits growing from the trait of sensitivity. Your mind works differently. Please remember that what follows is *on the average*; nobody has all these traits. But compared to non-HSPs, most of us are:

- Better at spotting errors and avoiding making errors.
- Highly conscientious.
- Able to concentrate deeply. *(But we do best without distractions.)*
- Especially good at tasks requiring vigilance, accuracy, speed, and the detection of minor differences.
- Able to process material to deeper levels of what psychologists call "semantic memory."

- Often thinking about our own thinking.
- Able to learn without being aware we have learned.
- Deeply affected by other people's moods and emotions.

Of course, there are many exceptions, especially to our being conscientious. And we don't want to be self-righteous about this; plenty of harm can be done in the name of trying to do good. Indeed, all of these fruits have their bruised spots. We are so skilled, but alas, when being watched, timed, or evaluated, we often cannot display our competence. Our deeper processing may make it seem that at first we are not catching on, but with time we understand and remember more than others. This may be why HSPs learn languages better (although arousal may make one less fluent than others when speaking).

By the way, thinking more than others about our own thoughts is not self-centeredness. It means that if asked what's on our mind, we are less likely to mention being aware of the world around us, and more likely to mention our inner reflections or musings. But we are no less likely to mention thinking about other people.

Our bodies are different too. Most of us have nervous systems that make us:

- Specialists in fine motor movements.
- Good at holding still.
- "Morning people." *(Here there are many exceptions.)*
- More affected by stimulants like caffeine unless we are very used to them.
- More "right-brained" (less linear, more creative in a synthesizing way).
- More sensitive to things in the air. *(Yes, that means more hay fever and skin rashes.)*

Overall, again, our nervous systems seem designed to react to subtle experiences, which also makes us slower to recover when we must react to intense stimuli.

But HSPs are not in a more aroused state all the time. We are not "chronically aroused" in day-to-day life or when asleep. We are just more aroused by new or prolonged stimulation.

(Being an HSP is *not* the same as being "neurotic"—that is, constantly anxious for no apparent reason).

How to Think About Your Differences

I hope that by now you are seeing your trait in positive terms. But I really suggest trying to view it as neutral. It becomes an advantage or disadvantage only when you enter a particular situation. Since the trait exists in all higher animals, it must have value in many circumstances. My hunch is that it survives in a certain percentage of all higher animals because it is useful to have at least a few around who are always watching for subtle signs. Fifteen to 20 percent seems about the right proportion to have always on the alert for danger, new foods, the needs of the young and sick, and the habits of other animals.

Of course, it is also good to have quite a few in a group who are not so alert to all the dangers and consequences of every action. They will rush out without a whole lot of thought to explore every new thing or fight for the group or territory. Every society needs both. And maybe there is a need for more of the *less* sensitive because more of them tend to get killed! This is all speculation, of course.

Another hunch of mine, however, is that the human race benefits more from HSPs than do other species. HSPs do more of that which makes humans different from other animals: We imagine possibilities. We humans, and HSPs especially, are acutely aware of the past and future. On top of that, if necessity is the mother of invention, HSPs must spend far more time trying to invent solutions to human problems just because they are more sensitive to hunger, cold, insecurity, exhaustion, and illness.

Sometimes people with our trait are said to be less happy or less capable of happiness. Of course, we can seem unhappy and moody, at least to non-HSPs, because we spend so much time thinking about things like the meaning of life and death and how complicated everything is—not black-and-white thoughts at all. Since most non-HSPs do not seem to enjoy thinking about such things, they assume we must be unhappy doing all that pondering. And we certainly don't get any happier having them tell us we are unhappy (by *their* definition of happy) and that we are a problem for them because we seem unhappy. All those accusations could make *anyone* unhappy.

The point is best made by Aristotle, who supposedly asked, "Would you rather be a happy pig or an unhappy human?" HSPs prefer the good feeling of being very conscious, very human, even if what we are conscious of is not always cause for rejoicing.

The point, however, is *not* that non-HSPs are pigs! I *know* someone is going to say I am trying to make an elite out of us. But that would last about five minutes with most HSPs, who would soon feel guilty for feeling superior. I'm just out to encourage us enough to make more of us feel like equals.

Heredity and Environment

Some of you may be wondering if you really inherited this trait, especially if you remember a time when your sensitivity seemed to begin or greatly increase.

In most cases, sensitivity is inherited. The evidence for this is strong, mainly from studies of identical twins who were raised apart but grew up behaving similarly, which always suggests that behavior is at least partly genetically determined.

On the other hand, it is not always true that both separated twins show the trait, even if they are identical. For example, each twin will also tend to develop a personality quite like the mother raising that twin, even though she is not the biological mother. The fact is, there are probably no inherited traits that cannot also be enhanced, decreased, or entirely produced or eliminated by enough of certain kinds of life experiences. For example, a child under stress at home or at school only needs to be born with a slight tendency to be sensitive and he or she will withdraw. Which may explain why children who have older brothers and sisters are more likely to be HSPs—and that would have nothing to do with genes. Similarly, studies of baby monkeys traumatized by separation from their mothers have found that these monkeys in adulthood behave much like monkeys born innately sensitive.

Circumstances can also force the trait to disappear. Many

children born very sensitive are pushed hard by parents, schools, or friends to be bolder. Living in a noisy or crowded environment, growing up in a large family, or being made to be more physically active may sometimes reduce sensitivity, just as sensitive animals that are handled a great deal will sometimes lose some of their natural caution, at least with certain people or in specific situations. That the underlying trait is entirely gone, however, seems unlikely.

What About You?

It is difficult to know for any particular adult whether you inherited the trait or developed it during your life. The best evidence, though hardly perfect, is whether your parents remember you as sensitive from the time you were born. If it is easy to do so, ask them, or whoever was your caretaker, to tell you all about what you were like in the first six months of life.

Probably you will learn more if you do *not* begin by asking if you were sensitive. Just ask what you were like as a baby. Often the stories about you will tell it all. After a while, ask about some typical signs of highly sensitive babies. Were you difficult about change—about being undressed and put into water at bath time, about trying new foods, about noise? Did you have colic often? Were you slow to fall asleep, hard to keep asleep, or a short sleeper, especially when you were overtired?

Remember, if your parents had no experience with other babies, they may not have noticed anything unusual at that age because they had no one to compare you to. Also, given all the blaming of parents for their children's every difficulty, your parents may need to convince you and themselves that all was perfect in your childhood. If you want, you can reassure them that you know they did their best and that all babies pose a few problems but that you wonder which problems you presented.

You might also let them see the questionnaire at the front of this book. Ask them if they or anyone else in your family has this trait. Especially if you find relatives with it on both sides, the odds are very good your trait is inherited.

But what if it wasn't or you aren't sure? It probably does not matter at all. What *does* is that it is *your* trait now. So do not struggle too long over the question. The next topic is far more important.

Learning About Our Culture—
What You Don't Realize WILL Hurt You

You and I are learning to see our trait as a neutral thing—useful in some situations, not in others—but our culture definitely does not see it, or any trait, as neutral. The anthropologist Margaret Mead explained it well. Although a culture's newborns will show a broad range of inherited temperaments, only a narrow band of these, a certain type, will be the ideal. The ideal personality is embodied, in Mead's words, in "every thread of the social fabric—in the care of the young child, the games the children play, the songs the people sing, the political organization, the religious observance, the art and the philosophy." Other traits are ignored, discouraged, or if all else fails, ridiculed.

What is the ideal in our culture? Movies, advertisements, the design of public spaces, all tell us we should be as tough as the Terminator, as stoic as Clint Eastwood, as outgoing as Goldie Hawn. We should be pleasantly stimulated by bright lights, noise, a gang of cheerful fellows hanging out in a bar. If we are feeling overwhelmed and sensitive, we can always take a painkiller.

If you remember only one thing from this book, it should be the following research study. Xinyin Chen and Kenneth Rubin of the University of Waterloo in Ontario, Canada, and Yuerong Sun of Shanghai Teachers University compared 480 schoolchildren in Shanghai to 296 in Canada to see what traits made children most popular. In China "shy" and "sensitive" children were among those most chosen by others to be friends or playmates. (In Mandarin, the word for shy or quiet means good or well-behaved; sensitive can be translated as "having understanding," a term of praise.) In Canada, shy and sensitive children were among the least chosen. Chances are, this is the kind of attitude you faced growing up.

Think about the impact on you of not being the ideal for your culture. It has to affect you—not only how others have treated you but how you have come to treat yourself.

SHEDDING THE MAJORITY'S RULE

1. *What was your parents' attitude toward your sensitivity?* Did they want you to keep it or lose it? Did they think of it as an inconvenience, as shyness, unmanliness, cowardice, a sign of artistic ability, cute? What about your other relatives, your friends, your teachers?

2. *Think about the media, especially in childhood.* Who were your role models and idols? Did they seem like HSPs? Or were they people you now see you could never be like?

3. *Consider your resulting attitude.* How has it affected your career, romantic relationships, recreational activities, and friendships?

4. *How are you as an HSP being treated now by the media?* Think about positive and negative images of HSPs. Which predominate? (Note that when someone is a victim in a movie or book, he or she is often portrayed as by nature sensitive, vulnerable, overaroused. This is good for dramatic effect, because the victim is visibly shaken and upset, but bad for HSPs, because "victim" comes to be equated with sensitivity.)

5. *Think about how HSPs have contributed to society.* Look for examples you know personally or have read about. Abraham Lincoln is probably a place to start.

6. *Think about your own contribution to society.* Whatever you are doing—sculpting, raising children, studying physics, voting—you tend to reflect deeply on the issues, attend to the details, have a vision of the future, and attempt to be conscientious.

Psychology's Bias

Psychological research is gaining valuable insights about people, and much of this book is based on those findings. But psychology is not perfect. It can only reflect the biases of the culture from which it comes. I could give example after example of research in psychology that reflects a bias that people I call HSPs are less happy and less mentally healthy, even less creative and intelligent (the first two are definitely *not* true). However, I will save these examples for reeducating my colleagues. Just be careful about accepting labels for yourself, such as "inhibited," "introverted," or "shy." As we move on, you'll understand why each of these *mis*labels you. In general, they miss the essence of the trait and give it a negative tone. For example, research has found that most people, quite wrongly, associate introversion with poor mental health. When HSPs identify with these labels, their confidence drops lower, and their arousal increases in situations in which people thus labeled are expected to be awkward.

It helps to know that in cultures in which the trait is more valued, such as Japan, Sweden, and China, the research takes on a different tone. For example, Japanese psychologists seem to expect their sensitive subjects to perform better, and they do. When studying stress, Japanese psychologists see more flaws in the way that the nonsensitive cope. There is no point in blaming our culture's psychology or its well-meaning researchers, however. They are doing their best.

Royal Advisors and Warrior Kings

For better and worse, the world is increasingly under the control of aggressive cultures—those that like to look outward, to expand, to compete and win. This is because, when cultures come in contact, the more aggressive ones naturally tend to take over.

How did we get into this situation? For most of the world, it began on the steppes of Asia, where the Indo-European culture was born. Those horse-riding nomads survived by expanding their herds of horses and cattle, mainly by stealing the herds and lands of others. They entered Europe about seven thousand years ago, reaching the Middle East and South Asia a little later. Before their arrival there was little or no warfare, slavery, monarchy, or domination of one class by another. The newcomers made serfs or slaves out of the people they found, the ones without horses, built walled cities where there had been peaceful settlements, and set out to expand into larger kingdoms or empires through war or trade.

The most long-lasting, happy Indo-European cultures have

always used two classes to govern themselves—the warrior-kings balanced by their royal or priestly advisors. And Indo-European cultures have done well for themselves. Half of the world speaks an Indo-European language, which means they cannot help but think in an Indo-European way. Expansion, freedom, and fame are good. Those are the values of the warrior-kings.

For aggressive societies to survive, however, they always need that priest-judge-advisor class as well. This class balances the kings and warriors (as the U.S. Supreme Court balances the president and his armed forces). It is a more thoughtful group, often acting to check the impulses of the warrior-kings. Since the advisor class often proves right, its members are respected as counselors, historians, teachers, scholars, and the upholders of justice. They have the foresight, for example, to look out for the well-being of those common folks on whom the society depends, those who grow the food and raise the children. They warn against hasty wars and bad use of the land.

In short, a strong royal advisor class insists on stopping and thinking. And it tries, I think with growing success in modern times, to direct the wonderful, expansive energy of their society away from aggression and domination. Better to use that energy for creative inventions, exploration, and protection of the planet and the powerless.

HSPs tend to fill that advisor role. We are the writers, historians, philosophers, judges, artists, researchers, theologians, therapists, teachers, parents, and plain conscientious citizens. What we bring to any of these roles is a tendency to think about all the possible effects of an idea. Often we have to make ourselves unpopular by stopping the majority from rushing ahead. Thus, to perform our role well, we have to feel very good about ourselves. We have to ignore all the messages from the warriors that we are not as good as they are. The warriors have their bold style, which has its value. But we, too, have *our* style and our own important contribution to make.

The Case of Charles

Charles was one of the few HSPs I interviewed who had known he was sensitive his whole life and always saw it as a good thing. His unusual childhood and its consequences are a fine demonstration of the importance of self-esteem and of the effect of one's culture.

Charles is happily married for the second time and enjoys a well-paid and admirable academic career of service and scholarship. In his leisure time he is a pianist of exceptional talent. And he has a deep sense that these gifts are more than sufficient to give meaning to his life. After hearing all of this at the outset of our interview, I was, naturally, curious about his background.

Here is Charles's first memory. (I always ask this in my interviews—even if inaccurate, what is recalled usually sets the tone or provides the theme of the whole life.) He is standing on a sidewalk at the back of a crowd that is admiring a window filed with Christmas decorations. He cries out, "Everyone away, I want to see." They laugh and let him come to the front.

What confidence! This courage to speak up so boldly surely began at home.

Charles's parents were delighted by his sensitivity. In their circle of friends—their artistic, intellectual subculture—sensitivity was associated with particular intelligence, good breeding, and fine tastes. Rather than being upset that he studied so much instead of playing games with other boys, his parents encouraged him to read even more. To them, Charles was the ideal son.

With this background, Charles believed in himself. He knew he had absorbed excellent aesthetic tastes and moral values at an early age. He did not see himself as flawed in any way. He did eventually realize he was unusual, part of a minority, but his entire subculture was unusual, and it had taught him to see that subculture as superior, not inferior. He had always felt confident among strangers, even when he was enrolled in the best preparatory schools, followed by an Ivy League university, and then took a position as a professor.

When I asked Charles if he saw any advantages of the trait, he had no trouble reciting many. For example, he was certain it contributed to his musical ability. It had also helped him deepen his self-awareness during several years of psychoanalysis.

As for the disadvantages of the trait and his way of making

peace with them, noise bothers him a great deal, so he lives in a quiet neighborhood, surrounding himself with lovely and subtle sounds, including a fountain in his backyard and good music. He has deep emotions that can lead to occasional depression, but he explores and resolves his feelings. He knows he takes things too hard but tries to allow for that.

His experience of overarousal is mainly of an intense physical response, the aftermath of which can prevent him from sleeping. But usually he can handle it in the moment through self-control, by "comporting myself a certain way." When matters at work overwhelm him, he leaves as soon as he is not needed and "walks it out" or plays the piano. He deliberately avoided a business career because of his sensitivity. When he was promoted to an academic position that stressed him too much, he changed positions as soon as he could.

Charles has organized his life around his trait, maintaining an optimal level of arousal without feeling in any way flawed for doing so. When I asked, as I usually do, what advice he would give others, he said, "Spend enough time putting yourself out there in the world—your sensitivity is not something to be feared."

A Reason for Great Pride

This first chapter may have been very stimulating! All sorts of strong, confusing feelings could be arising in you by now. I know from experience, however, that as you read and work through this book, those feelings will become increasingly clear and positive.

To sum it up again, you pick up on the subtleties that others miss and so naturally you also arrive quickly at the level of arousal past which you are no longer comfortable. That first fact about you could not be true without the second being true as well. It's a package deal, and a very good package.

It's also important that you keep in mind that this book is about both your personal innate physical trait and also about your frequently unappreciated social importance. You were born to be among the advisors and thinkers, the spiritual and moral leaders of your society. There is every reason for pride.

• **Working With What You Have Learned** •

Reframing Your Reactions to Change

At the end of some chapters I will ask you to "reframe" your experiences in the light of what you now know. Reframing is a term from cognitive psychotherapy which simply means seeing something in a new way, in a new context, with a new frame around it.

Your first reframing task is to think about three major changes in your life that you remember well. HSPs usually respond to change with resistance. Or we try to throw ourselves into it, but we still suffer from it. We just don't "do" change well, even good changes. That can be the most maddening. When my novel was published and I had to go to England to promote it, I was finally living a fantasy I had cherished for years. Of course, I got sick and hardly enjoyed a minute of the trip. At the time, I thought I must be neurotically robbing myself of my big moment. Now, understanding this trait, I see that the trip was just too exciting.

My new understanding of that experience is exactly what I mean by reframing. So now it is your turn. Think of three major changes or surprises in your life. Choose one—a loss or ending—that seemed bad at the time. Choose one that seems as if it should have been neutral, just a major change. And one that was good, something to celebrate or something done for you and meant to be kind. Now follow these steps for each.

1. *Think about your response to the change and how you have always viewed it.* Did you feel you responded "wrong" or not as others would have? Or for too long? Did you decide you were no good in some way? Did you try to hide your upset from others? Or did others find out and tell you that you were being "too much"?

Here's an example of a negative change. Josh is thirty now, but for more than twenty years he has carried a sense of shame from when, in the middle of third grade, he had to go to a new elementary school. He had been well enough liked at his old school for his drawing ability, his sense of humor, his funny choices of clothes and such. At the new school these same qualities made him the target of bullying and teasing. He acted as if he didn't care, but deep inside he felt awful. Even at thirty, in the back of his mind he wondered if he hadn't deserved to be so "unpopular." Maybe he really was odd and a "weakling." Or else why hadn't he defended himself better? Maybe it was all true.

2. *Consider your response in the light of what you know now about how your body automatically operates.* In the case of Josh I would say that he was highly aroused during those first weeks at the new school. It must have been difficult to think up clever kid stuff to say, to succeed in the games and classroom tasks by which other children judge a new student. The bullies saw him as an easy target who could make them appear tougher. The others were afraid to defend him. He lost confidence and felt flawed, not likable. This intensified his arousal when he tried anything new while others were around. He could never seem relaxed and normal. It was a painful time but nothing to be ashamed of.

3. *Think if there's anything that needs to be done now.* I especially recommend sharing your new view of the situation with someone else—provided they will appreciate it. Perhaps it could even be someone who was present at the time who could help you continue to fit details into the picture. I also advocate writing down your old and new views of the experience and keeping them around for a while as a reminder.

2

Digging Deeper
Understanding Your Trait
for All That It Is

Now let's rearrange your mental furniture and make it impossible for you to doubt the reality of your trait. This is important, for the trait has been discussed so little in the field of psychology. We'll look at a case history as well as scientific evidence, most of it from studying children's temperaments, which makes it all the more fitting that the case history is a tale of two children.

Observing Rob and Rebecca

About the time I began studying high sensitivity, a close friend gave birth to twins—a boy, Rob, and a girl, Rebecca. From the first day one could sense a difference between them, and I understood exactly what it was. The scientist in me was delighted. Not only would I watch a highly sensitive child growing up, but Rob came with his own "control group," or comparison, his sister, Rebecca, born into exactly the same environment.

A particular benefit of knowing Rob from birth was that it dispelled any doubts I had about the trait being inheritable. While it is true that he and his sister were also treated differently from the start, at first that was largely because of his sensitivity, a difference he brought into the world. (Being different genders, Rob and Rebecca are fraternal twins, not identical, which means that their genes are no more similar than are those of any brother's and sister's.)

To add frosting to this psychologist's cake, the genders associated with sensitivity were switched. The boy, Rob, was the sensitive one; the girl, Rebecca, was not. The stereotypes were also reversed in that Rob was smaller than Rebecca.

As you read about Rob, don't be surprised if you experience an emotional response. The whole point of my description is that some of it may also apply to you. Thus, vague memories, or feelings from before you can remember what the feelings were attached to, may return. Be easy about such feelings. Just observe them. In fact, it might be helpful to write them down. It will be useful information as you read and work through the next few chapters

Sleep Troubles

In the first few days after Rob and Rebecca were born, the differences in temperament were greatest when the infants were tired. Rebecca would fall asleep easily and not wake up. Especially as a result of some change—visitors, travel—Rob would stay awake and cry. Which would mean that Mom or Dad would have to walk, rock, sing, or pat him, trying to bring him to a peaceful state.

With a slightly older sensitive child, current advice is to put the child to bed and let the quiet and dark gradually temper the overstimulation that is the true cause of the crying. HSPs know all about being "too tired to sleep." They are actually too *frazzled* to sleep.

Leaving a newborn to scream for an hour, however, is more than most parents can bear, probably because it is not really very wise to do so. A newborn is usually best soothed by motion. In Rob's case, his parents finally found that an electric swing induced sleep best.

Then came the problem of his remaining asleep. There are always points in anyone's sleep cycle that make it very easy or difficult to be awakened, but sensitive children seem to have fewer periods of deep, imperturbable sleep. And once awake, they have greater difficulty going back to sleep. (Remember, this was probably also true of you, whether you remember or not.) My own solution, with our highly sensitive child, was to use blankets to cover his crib. In his little tent all was quiet and cozy, especially if we were laying him down in an unfamiliar place. Sometimes sensitive children really force their parents to be both empathic and creative.

One Night, Two Kids

When Rob and Rebecca were almost three, their little brother was born. My husband and I visited for the night and slept in the bed of their parents, who were at the hospital. We had been warned that Rob might wake up at least once, frightened by a bad dream. (He had many more of them than his sister—HSPs often do.)

As expected, at five in the morning Rob wandered in, crying softly. When he saw the wrong people in his parents' bed, his sleepy moans became screams.

I have no idea what his mind envisioned. Perhaps "Danger! Mother is gone! Horrible beings have taken her place!"

Most parents agree that everything gets easier once a child can understand words. This is so much more true with a highly sensitive child, caught up in his own imagination. The trick was to slip some quick, soothing words of mine in between his sobs.

Fortunately, Rob has a great sense of humor. So I reminded him of a recent evening when I had baby-sat and served the two of them cookies as "appetizers," *before* dinner.

He gulped and stared, then smiled. And somewhere in his brain, I moved from the category of Monster Who Has Taken Mother to Silly Elaine.

I asked him if he wanted to join us, but I knew he would choose his own bed. Soon he was back there, sleeping soundly.

In the morning Rebecca came in. When she saw that her parents were gone, she smiled and said, "Hi, Elaine. Hi, Art," and walked out. That is the difference in the non-HSP.

It is painful to imagine what would have happened if I had

been the sort to have shouted at Rob to shut up and get back to bed. He probably would have done just that, feeling abandoned in a dangerous world. But he would not have slept. His intuitive mind would have elaborated on the experience for hours, including probably deciding he was somehow to blame. With sensitive children, physical blows or traumas aren't required to make them afraid of the dark.

Rounding Out Our Picture of Rob

By day, when the twins went out with their parents during that first year, the mariachi band at the Mexican restaurant fascinated Rebecca; it made Rob cry. In their second year, Rebecca was delighted by ocean waves, haircuts, and merry-go-rounds; Rob was afraid of them, at least at first, just as he was on the first day of nursery school and with the stimulation accompanying each birthday and holiday. Furthermore, Rob developed fears— of pinecones, of figures printed on his bedspread, of shadows on the wall. The fears were strange and unrealistic to us, but they were certainly real to him.

In short, Rob's childhood has been a little difficult for him and for his caring, stable, competent parents. Actually, unfair as it is, the difficult aspects of any temperament are displayed more when the home environment is sound. Otherwise, in order to survive, an infant will do whatever he or she must to adapt to the caretakers, with temperament going underground to resurface in some other way later, perhaps in stress-related physical symptoms. But Rob is free to be who he is, so his sensitivity is out there for all to see. He can express his feelings, and as a result he can learn what does and does not work.

For example, during his first four years, when Rob was overwhelmed, he would often burst into angry tears. At these times, his parents would patiently help him contain his feelings. And with every month he seemed better able to not become overwhelmed. When watching a movie with scary or sad sequences, for example, he learned to tell himself what his parents would say: "It's just a movie," or, "Yeah, but I know it ends okay." Or he would close his eyes and cover his ears or leave the room for a little while.

Probably because he is more cautious, he has been slower to learn some physical skills. With other boys he is less comfortable with wilder, rougher play. But he wants to be like them and tries, so he is accepted. And thanks to careful attention to his adjustment, thus far he likes school a great deal.

There are some other points about Rob that are not surprising, given his trait: He has an extraordinary imagination. He is drawn to everything artistic, especially music (true for many HSPs). He is funny and a great ham when he feels at home with his audience. Since he was three he has "thought like a lawyer," quick to notice fine points and make subtle distinctions. He is concerned about the suffering of others and polite, kind, and considerate—except, perhaps, when he is overcome by too much stimulation. His sister, meanwhile, has her own numerous virtues. One is that she is a steady sort, the anchor in her brother's life.

What makes Rob and Rebecca so very different from each other? What makes you answer yes to so many items on the self-test at the beginning of this book when most people would not?

You Are Truly a Different Breed

Jerome Kagan, a psychologist at Harvard, has devoted much of his career to the study of this trait. For him it is as observable a difference as hair or eye color. Of course, he calls it other names—inhibitedness, shyness, or timidity in children—and I cannot agree with his terms. But I understand that from the outside, and especially in a laboratory setting, the children he studies do seem mainly inhibited, shy, or timid. Just remember as I discuss Kagan that sensitivity is the real trait and that a child standing still and observing others may be quite *un*inhibited inside in his or her processing of all the nuances of what is being seen.

Kagan has been following the development of twenty-two children with the trait. He is also studying nineteen who seemed to be very "uninhibited." According to their parents, as infants the "inhibited" children had had more allergies, insomnia, colic, and constipation than the average child. As young children, seen in the laboratory for the first time, their heartbeat rates are generally higher and under stress show less change. (Heart rate can't change much if it is already high.) Also when under stress, their pupils dilate sooner, and their vocal cords are more tense, making their voice change to a higher pitch. (Many HSPs are relieved to know why their voice can become so strange sounding when they are aroused.)

The body fluids (blood, urine, saliva) of sensitive children show indications of high levels of norepinephrine present in their brains, especially after the children are exposed to various forms of stress in the laboratory. Norepinephrine is associated with arousal; in fact, it is the brain's version of adrenaline. Sensitive children's body fluids also contain more cortisol, both when under stress and when at home. Cortisol is the hormone present when one is in a more or less constant state of arousal or wariness. Remember cortisol; it comes up again.

Kagan then studied infants to see which ones would grow into "inhibited" children. He found that about 20 percent of all babies are "highly reactive" when exposed to various stimuli: They pump and flex their limbs vigorously, arch their backs as if irritated or trying to get away, and frequently cry. A year later, two-thirds of the study's reactive babies were "inhibited" children and showed high levels of fear in new situations. Only 10 percent showed low levels. So the trait is roughly observable from birth, as was the case with Rob.

All of this suggests what I have already said—that sensitive children come with a built-in tendency to react more strongly to external stimuli. But Kagan and others are discovering the details that make that so. For example, Kagan found that babies who later showed this trait also had cooler foreheads on the right side of their head, which indicates greater activity on the right side of the brain. (The blood is drawn away from the surface toward the activity.) Other studies have also found that many HSPs have more activity in the right hemisphere of the brain, especially those who stay sensitive from birth into childhood—that is, were clearly born that way.

Kagan's conclusion is that persons with the trait of sensitivity or inhibitedness are a special breed. They are genetically quite different, although still utterly human, just as bloodhounds and border collies are quite different, although both are still definitely dogs.

My own research also points to the idea of a distinct genetic "breed" of sensitive people. In my telephone survey of three hundred randomly selected people, I found both a distinct group and also a continuum. On a scale of one to five, about 20 percent felt they were "extremely" or "quite a bit" sensitive. An additional 27 percent said "moderately." Together, those three categories seemed like a continuum. But then there was a sharp break. A measly 8 percent were "not." And a whopping 42 percent said they were "*not at all*" sensitive, as if we were asking Laplanders about coconuts.

My sense of HSPs from meeting them is that they are indeed a distinct group, separate from the nonsensitive. Yet among them there is also a wide range in sensitivity. This may be due to there being several different causes of the trait, leading to different kinds, or "flavors," of sensitivity, some of them stronger than others, or to some people being born with two kinds, three kinds, and so on. And there are so many ways that humans can increase or decrease their sensitivity through experience or conscious choice. All of these effects could cause a blurring of the boundary of what is still basically a separate group.

There is no denying the sense that Rob and Rebecca are two different sorts of humans. You are, too. Your differences are very real.

The Brain's Two Systems

A number of researchers think that there are two systems in the brain and that it is the balance of these two that creates sensitivity. One system, the "behavioral activation" (or "approach," or "facilitation," system) is hooked up to the parts of the brain that take in messages from the senses and send out orders to the limbs to get moving. This system is designed to move us toward things, especially new ones. It is probably meant to keep us eagerly searching for the good things in life, like fresh food and companionship, all of which we need for survival. When the activation system is operating, we are curious, bold, and impulsive.

The other system is called the "behavioral inhibition" (or "withdrawal," or "avoidance," system). (You can already tell by the names which is the "good" one according to our culture.) This system is said to move us away from things, making us attentive to dangers. It makes us alert, cautious, and watchful for signs. Not surprisingly, this system is hooked up to all the parts of the brain Kagan noted to be more active in his "inhibited" children.

But what does this system really do? It takes in everything about a situation and then automatically compares the present to what has been normal and usual in the past and what should be expected in the future. If there is a mismatch, the system makes us stop and wait until we understand the new circumstance. To me this is a very significant part of being intelligent. So I prefer to give it a more positive name: the automatic pause-to-check system.

But now consider how one might have a more active pause-to-check system. Imagine Rob and Rebecca coming to school one morning. Rebecca sees the same classroom, teacher, and children as were there yesterday. She runs off to play. Rob notices that the teacher is in a bad mood, one of the children is looking angry, and some bags are in the corner that were not there before. Rob hesitates and may decide that there is reason for caution. So sensitivity—the subtle processing of sensory information—is the real difference once again. Notice how psychology has described the two systems as having opposing purposes. How like the opposition I described in the last chapter between the warrior-king class and the royal-advisor class.

This two-system explanation of sensitivity also suggests two different types of HSPs. Some might have only an average-strength pause-to-check system but an activation system that is even weaker. This kind of HSP might be very calm, quiet, and content with a simple life. It's as if the royal advisors are monks who rule the whole country/person. Another kind of HSP could potentially have an even stronger pause-to-check system but an activation system that is also very strong—just not quite as strong. This kind of HSP would be both very curious and very cautious, bold yet anxious, easily bored yet easily overaroused. The optimal level of arousal is a narrow range. One could say there is a constant power struggle between the advisor and the impulsive, expansive warrior within the person.

I think Rob is this type. Other young children, however, are described as so quiet and uncurious that they are in danger of being ignored and neglected.

What type are you? Does your pause-to-check/advisor system rule alone, thanks to a quiet activator/warrior-king system? That is, is it easy for you to be content with a quiet life? Or are the two branches that govern you in constant conflict? That is, do you always want to be trying new things even if you know that afterward you will be exhausted?

You Are More Than Genes and Systems

Let's not forget that you are a complicated being. Certain investigators, such as Mary Rothbart of the University of Oregon, are adamant that temperament is quite a different matter when you study adult humans, who can reason, make choices, and exert willpower to follow through on their choices. Rothbart believes that if psychologists study children and animals too much, they will overlook the role of human thinking and a lifetime's experience.

Let's go over your development, and Rob's, as Rothbart sees it, and how being sensitive would differ at each stage.

At birth, an infant's only reaction is negative—irritability, discomfort. Sensitive babies like you and Rob were mainly different in being more irritable and uncomfortable—what Kagan called "highly reactive."

At about two months the behavioral-activation system becomes functional. Now you showed an interest in new things in case they might satisfy your needs. Along with that came a new feeling—anger and frustration when you did not get what you wanted. So positive emotions and anger were possible, and how much you felt them depended on the strength of your activation system. Rob, having both systems strong, became an easily angered baby. But sensitive babies with a low activation system would be placid and "good" at this age.

At six months your superior automatic pause-to-check system came on line. You could compare present experiences with those of the past, and if the present ones were upsetting, as those in the past, you would experience fear. But again, you saw more subtle differences in each experience. For you there was more that was unfamiliar and possibly frightening.

At this point, six months, every experience becomes very important for HSPs. One can see how a few bad experiences when approaching new things could turn the pause-to-check system into a pause-and-do-nothing system, a true inhibition system. The best way to avoid bad things would seem to be avoiding everything. And, of course, the more the world is avoided, the newer everything will seem. Imagine how frightening the world could have seemed to you.

Finally, around ten months, you began to develop the ability to shift your attention, to decide how to experience something, or to stop a behavior. Only at this point could you start to handle conflicts between the two systems. A conflict would be *I want to try that, but it seems so strange.* (At ten months we might not use those words, but that would be the idea.) But now you could make some choices about which emotion to obey. One could almost see Rob doing it: *Okay, it's unfamiliar, but I'll go ahead, anyway.*

You probably had favorite methods of overriding the pause-to-check system if it slowed you too long or often. One way might have been to imitate those with less of it. You just went ahead and got some good things, too, like them, in spite of your caution. Another might have been the recategorizing of the stimulation to make it familiar. The growling wolf in the movie "is just a big dog." But most of your help probably came from others who wanted you to feel safe, not afraid.

Social help with fears involves yet another system that Rothbart believes is highly developed in adult humans. It also arrives at about ten months. With it, a child begins to connect with others, to enjoy them. If these social experiences are positive and supportive, another physiological system develops for which humans are biologically prepared. One could call this the loving system. It creates endorphins, the "good feeling" neurochemicals.

How much could you overcome your fears by trusting others to help? Who was around whom you could rely on? Did you act as if *Mother is here so I'll try?* Did you learn to imitate her calming words and deeds, applying them to yourself? "Don't be afraid, it'll be okay." I have seen Rob using all of these methods.

Now you might spend a moment thinking about yourself and your childhood, and we will do more of this in the next two chapters. I know you don't really remember, but judging from what facts you have, what was that first year *probably* like? How does your thinking and self-control affect your sensitivity now? Are there times when you can control your arousal? Who taught you to do so? Who were your role models? Do you think you were taught to control your cautiousness too much so that you dare to do more than your body can handle? Or does it seem that your lesson was that the world is unsafe and over-arousal is uncontrollable?

How Trust Becomes Mistrust and the Unfamiliar Becomes Dangerous

Most researchers on temperament have studied short-term arousal. It's easy to study, for it's quite apparent from the higher levels of heartbeat, respiration, perspiration, pupil dilation, and adrenaline.

There is another system of arousal, however, that is governed more by hormones. It goes into action just as quickly, but the effect of its main product, cortisol, is most noticeable after ten to twenty minutes. An important point is that when cortisol is present, the short-term arousal response is also even more likely. That is, this long-term type of arousal makes us even more excitable, more sensitive, than before.

Most of the effects of cortisol occur over hours or even days. They are mainly measured in the blood, saliva, or urine, so studying long-term arousal is less convenient. But psychologist Megan Gunnar of the University of Minnesota thought that the whole point of the pause-to-check system might be to protect the individual from this unhealthy, unpleasant, long-term arousal.

Research shows that when people first encounter something new and potentially threatening, the short-term response always comes first. Meanwhile, we start to consider our resources. What are our abilities? What have we learned about this sort of situation from past experiences? Who is around who might help out? If we think we or those with us can cope with the situation, we stop seeing it as a threat. The short-term alert dies out, and the long-term alarm never goes off.

Gunnar demonstrated this process in an interesting experiment. She set up a threatening situation much like those Kagan uses to identify "inhibited" children. But first, the nine-month-old babies were separated from their mothers for a half hour. Half were left with a very attentive baby-sitter who responded to all of the child's moods. The other half were left with a baby-sitter who was inattentive and unresponsive unless the child actually fussed or cried. Next, while alone with the baby-sitter, each nine-month-old was exposed to something startlingly new.

What is so important here is that only the highly sensitive babies with the inattentive baby-sitters showed more cortisol in their saliva. It was as if those with the attentive sitter felt they had a resource and had no need to make a long-term stress response.

Suppose the caretaker is your own mother? Psychologists observing babies with their mothers have discovered certain signs that tell them if a child feels "securely attached." A secure child feels safe to explore, and new experiences are not usually seen as a threat. Other signs indicate that a child is "insecurely attached." The mothers of these children are either too protective or too neglectful (or even dangerous). (We will discuss "attachment" more in chapters 3 and 4.) Research on sensitive children facing a novel, startling situation in the company of their mothers has found that these children do show their usual, strong short-term response. But if a sensitive child is securely attached to Mom, there is no long-term cortisol effect from the stress. Without secure attachment, however, a startling experience will produce long-term arousal.

One can see why it is important that young HSPs (and older ones, too) stay out in the world, trying things rather than retreating. But their feelings about their caretakers have to be secure and their experiences have to be successful or their reasons not to approach will only be proved true. And all of this gets started before you can even talk!

Many intelligent, sensitive parents provide all the needed experiences almost automatically. Rob's parents are constantly praising his successes and encouraging him to test his fears to see if they are realistic while offering help if he needs it. With time, his idea of the world will be that it is not as frightening as his nervous system was telling him it was during that first year or two. His creative traits and intuitive abilities, all the advantages of being sensitive, will flourish. The difficult areas will fade.

When parents do nothing special to help a sensitive child feel safe, whether the child becomes truly "inhibited" probably depends on the relative strength of the activation and pause-to-check systems. But remember that some parents and environments can make matters much worse. Certainly repeated frightening experiences will strongly reinforce caution, especially experiences of failing to be calmed or helped, of being punished for active exploring, and of having others who should be helpful become dangerous instead.

Another important point is that the more cortisol in an infant's body, the less the child will sleep, and the less sleep, the more cortisol. In the daytime, the more cortisol, the more fear, the more fear, the more cortisol. Uninterrupted sleep at night and timely naps all reduce cortisol in infants. And remember, lower cortisol also means fewer short-term alarms. It was easy to see that this was a constant problem with Rob. It may have been for you, too.

Furthermore, if sleep problems beginning in infancy are not controlled, they may last into adulthood and make a highly sensitive person almost unbearably sensitive. So get your sleep!

Into the Depths

There is another aspect of your trait that is harder to capture in studies or observations—except when strange fears and nightmares visit the sensitive child (or adult). To understand this very real aspect of the trait, one leaves the laboratory and enters the consulting room of the depth psychologist.

Depth psychologists place great emphasis on the unconscious and the experiences imbedded there, repressed or simply preverbal, that continue to govern our adult life. It is not surprising that highly sensitive children, and adults, too, have a hard time with sleep and report more vivid, alarming, "archetypal" dreams. With the coming of darkness, subtle sounds and shapes begin to rule the imagination, and HSPs sense them more. There are also the unfamiliar experiences of the day—some only half-noticed, some totally repressed. All of them swirl in the mind just as we are relaxing the conscious mind so that we can fall asleep.

Falling asleep, staying asleep, and going back to sleep when awakened require an ability to soothe oneself, to feel safe in the world.

The only depth psychologist to write explicitly about sensitivity was one of the founders of depth work, Carl Jung, and what he said was important—and exceptionally positive, for a change.

Way back when psychotherapy began with Sigmund Freud, there was controversy about how much innate temperament shaped personality, including emotional problems. Before Freud, the medical establishment had emphasized inherited constitutional differences. Freud tried to prove that "neurosis" (his specialty) was caused by traumas, especially upsetting sexual experiences. Carl Jung, Freud's follower for a long time, split with him finally on the issue of the centrality of sexuality. Jung decided that the fundamental difference was an inherited greater sensitivity. He believed that when highly sensitive patients had experienced a trauma, sexual or otherwise, they had been unusually affected and so developed a neurosis. Note that Jung was saying that sensitive people not traumatized in childhood are not inherently neurotic. One thinks of Gunnar's finding that the sensitive child with a secure attachment to his or her mother does not feel threatened by new experiences. Indeed, Jung thought very highly of sensitive people—but then he was one himself.

That Jung wrote about HSPs is a little-known fact. (I did not know this when I began my work on the trait.) For example, he said that "a certain innate sensitiveness produces a special prehistory, a special way of experiencing infantile events" and that "events bound up with powerful impressions can never pass off without leaving some trace on sensitive people." Later, Jung began to describe introverted and intuitive types in similar ways, but even more positively. He said they had to be more self-protective—what he meant by being introverted. But he also said that they were "educators and promoters of culture . . . their life teaches the other possibility, the interior life which is so painfully wanting in our civilization."

Such people, Jung said, are naturally more influenced by their unconscious, which gives them information of the "utmost importance," a "prophetic foresight." To Jung, the unconscious contains important wisdom to be learned. A life lived in deep communication with the unconscious is far more influential and personally satisfying.

But such a life is also potentially more difficult, especially if in childhood there were too many disturbing experiences without a secure attachment. As you saw from Gunnar's research and as you will see in chapter 8, Jung was exactly right.

So It's Real and It's Okay

Rob, Jerome Kagan, Megan Gunnar, and Carl Jung should have you well convinced now that your trait is utterly real. You *are* different. In the next chapter, you will consider how you may need to live differently from others if you are going to be in healthy harmony with your quite different, highly sensitive body.

By now you may be seeing a somewhat dark picture too— one of fear, timidity, inhibitedness, and distressed overarousal. Only Jung spoke of the trait's advantages, but even then it was in terms of our connection to the depths and darkness of the psyche. But remember that this sort of negativity is, once again, largely a sign of our culture's bias. Preferring toughness, the culture sees our trait as something difficult to live with, something to be cured. Do not forget that HSPs differ mainly in their sensitive processing of subtle stimuli. This is your most basic quality. That is a positive and accurate way to understand your trait.

• **Working With What You Have Learned** •

Your Deeper Response

This is something to do right now, just as you have finished reading this chapter. Your intellect has taken in some ideas, but your emotions may be having some deeper reactions to what you have been reading.

To reach these deeper reactions, you need to reach the deeper parts of the body, of your emotions, of the more fundamental, instinctual sort of consciousness that Jung called the unconscious. This is where the ignored or forgotten parts of yourself dwell, areas that may be threatened or relieved or excited or saddened by what you are learning.

Read all of what is here: then proceed. Begin by breathing very consciously from the center of your body, from your abdomen. Make certain that your diaphragm stays involved—at first blow out through your mouth fairly hard, as if blowing up a balloon. Your belly will tighten as you do this. Then, when you inhale, the breath will be taken in from the level of your stomach, very automatically. Your breathing in should be automatic and easy. Only your breathing out should be extended. That, too, can become less forceful and no longer out through your mouth once you are settled into breathing from your center, your belly, and not from high up in your chest.

Once settled, you need to create a safe space within your imagination where anything at all is welcome. Invite any feeling to enter awareness there. It might be a bodily feeling—an ache in the back, a tension in your throat, an unsettled stomach. Let the sensation grow and let it tell you what it is there to show you. You also might see a fleeting image. Or hear a voice. Or observe an emotion. Or a series of these—a physical feeling might become an image. Or a voice might express an emotion you begin to feel.

Notice all that you can in this quiet state. If feelings need to be expressed—if you need to laugh, cry, or rage—try to let yourself do that a little.

Then, as you emerge from that state, think about what happened. Note what stirred the feelings you had—what it was in what you read, what it was in what you thought or remembered while you read. How were your feelings related to being sensitive?

Afterward, put into words some of what you have learned— think about it for yourself, tell someone else, or write it down. Indeed, keeping a journal of your feelings while you read this book will be very helpful.

3

General Health and Lifestyle for HSPs
Loving and Learning From Your Infant/Body Self

In this chapter you'll learn to appreciate your highly sensitive body's needs. Since this is often surprisingly difficult for HSPs, I have learned to approach it through a metaphor—treating the body as you would an infant. It is such a good metaphor, as you will see, that it may not be one at all.

Six Weeks of Age: How It May Have Been

A storm threatens. The sky turns metallic. The march of clouds across the sky breaks apart. Pieces of sky fly off in different directions. The wind picks up force, in silence. . . . The world is disintegrating. Something is about to happen. Uneasiness grows. It spreads from the center and turns into pain.

The above is a moment of growing hunger as experienced by a hypothetical six-week-old infant called Joey, as imagined by developmental psychologist Daniel Stern in his charming book *Diary of a Baby*. A tremendous amount of recent research on infancy informs Joey's diary. For example, it is now thought that infants cannot separate inner from outer stimulation or sort out the different senses or the present from a remembered experience that has just happened. Nor do they have a sense of themselves as the one who is experiencing it all, the one to whom it is happening.

Given all of the above, Stern found that weather is a good analogy for an infant's experience. Things just happen, varying mostly in intensity. Intensity is all that disturbs, by creating a storm of overarousal. HSPs take note: Overarousal is the first and most basic distressing experience of life; our first lessons about overarousal begin at birth.

Here is how Stern imagines Joey feeling after he has nursed and eased his hunger:

> All is remade. A changed world is waking. The storm has passed. The winds are quiet. The sky is softened. Running lines and flowing volumes appear. They trace a harmony and, like shifting light, make everything come alive.

Stern sees infants as having the same needs as adults for a moderate level of arousal:

> A baby's nervous system is prepared to evaluate immediately the intensity of . . . anything accessible to one of his senses. How intensely he feels about something is probably the first clue he has available to tell him whether to approach it or to stay away . . . if something is moderately intense . . . he is spellbound. That just-tolerable intensity arouses him. . . . It increases his animation, activates his whole being.

In other words, it is no fun to be bored. On the other hand, the infant/body self is born with an instinct to stay away from whatever is highly intense, to avoid the state of overarousal. For some, however, it's harder to do.

Six Weeks and Highly Sensitive

Now I will try my own hand at this new literary genre of infant diary, with the experience of an imaginary, highly sensitive infant, Jesse.

The wind has been blowing incessantly, sometimes gusting into a howling gale, sometimes falling to an edgy, exhausting moan. For a seeming eternity clouds have swirled in random patterns of blinding light and glowering dark. Now an ominous dusk is descending, and for a moment the wind seems to ebb with the light.

But the darkness is disorienting in itself, and the howling wind begins to shift directions indecisively, as it might in the region of tornadoes. Indeed, out of this rising chaos the veerings do take a shape, gaining energy from one another, until a cyclonic fury emerges. A hellish hurricane is happening in deepest night.

There is some place or time where this awfulness stops, but there is no way to find that haven, for this weather has neither up nor down, east nor west—only round and round toward the fearful center.

I imagined the above happening after Jesse had gone with his mother and two older sisters to the shopping mall, riding in his car seat, then a stroller, then back home in the car seat. It was a Saturday, and the mall was jammed. On the way home his two sisters had a fight about which radio station to listen to, each of them turning the volume louder. There was considerable traffic, many stops and starts. They returned home late, long after Jesse's usual nap time. When offered a chance to nurse, he only cried and fussed, too overwhelmed to attend to his vaguer sense of hunger. So his mother tried putting him down to sleep. That is when the hurricane finally hit.

We should not forget that Jesse was hungry, too. Hunger is yet another stimulus, from inside. Besides arousing one further, it produces a diminution of the biochemical substances necessary for the usual, calmer functioning of the nervous system. My research indicates that hunger has an especially strong effect on HSPs. As one put it, "Sometimes when I'm tired it's like I regress to this age where I can almost hear myself saying, 'I *must* have my milk and cookies, *right now.*'" Yet once overaroused, we may not even notice hunger. Taking good care of a highly sensitive body is like taking care of an infant.

Why the Infant/Body Self?

Think of what the infant and the body have in common. First, both are wonderfully content and cooperative when they are not overstimulated, worn out, and hungry. Second, when babies and sensitive bodies really are exhausted, both are largely helpless to correct things on their own. The baby-you relied on a caretaker to set limits and satisfy your simple, basic needs, and your body relies on you to do it now.

Both also cannot use words to explain their troubles; they can only give louder and louder signals for help or develop a symptom so serious it cannot be ignored. The wise caretaker knows that much woe is avoided by responding to the infant/body at the first sign of distress.

Finally, as we noted in the last chapter, caretakers who think newborn babies or bodies can be spoiled and should be "left to cry" are wrong. Research demonstrates that if a small infant's crying is responded to promptly (except at those times when responding just adds to the overstimulation), that infant will cry less, not more, when older.

This infant/body self is an expert on sensitivity. She has been sensitive from the day she was born. She knows what was hardest then, what is hard now. He knows what you lacked, what you learned from your parents and other caretakers about how to treat him, what he needs now, and how you can take care of him in the future. By starting here, we make use of the old adage "Well begun is half-done."

You and Your Caretaker

About half or a little more than half of all infants are raised by adequate parents, and thus become what is called "securely attached" children. The term is taken from biology. All newborn primates hang on to Mom, and most moms want their infants to hang on tight, securely.

As the infant gets a little older, when feeling safe he or she can begin to explore and try to do things independently. The mother will feel pleased about that—watchful and ready if there is trouble but otherwise glad that her little one is growing up. But there will still be a kind of invisible attachment. The moment there is danger, their bodies will reunite and become attached again. Secure.

Now and then, for various reasons usually having to do with how the mother or father was raised, a primary caretaker may give one of two other messages, creating an insecure attachment. One is that the world is so awful, or the caretaker is so preoccupied or vulnerable, that the infant must hang on very, very tight. The child does not dare to explore very much. Maybe the caretaker does not want exploring or would leave the infant behind if he or she did not hang on. These babies are said to be anxious about, or preoccupied with, their attachment to their caretaker.

The other message an infant may receive is that the caretaker is dangerous and ought to be avoided or values more highly a child who is minimal trouble and very independent. Perhaps the caretaker is too stressed to care for a child. And there are those who at times, in anger or desperation, even want the infant to disappear or die. In that case the infant will do best not to be attached at all. Such infants are said to be avoidant. When separated from their mothers or fathers, they seem quite indifferent. (Sometimes, of course, a child is securely attached to one parent and not to the other.)

From our first attachment experiences we tend to develop a rather enduring mental idea of what to expect from someone we are close to and depend on. While that may seem to make for rigidity and lost opportunities, meeting your first caretaker's desires about how you attached was important for your survival. Even when it ceases to be a matter of survival, the program is still there and very conservative. Sticking to whichever plan works—to be secure, anxious, or avoidant—protects against making dangerous mistakes.

Attachment and the Highly Sensitive Body

Remember in the last chapter the highly sensitive children who did not have long-term arousal in unfamiliar situations? They were the ones with responsive caretakers or mothers with whom they had secure relationships. This suggests that you HSPs who grew up feeling securely attached knew that you had good resources and could handle overstimulation fairly well. Eventually, you learned to do for yourself what your good caretakers had been doing for you.

Meanwhile, your body was learning not to respond as if threatened by each new experience. And in the absence of a response, the body did not experience distressing, long-term arousal. You found that your body was a friend to trust. At the same time, you were learning that you had a special body, a sensitive nervous system. But you could handle things by learning when to push yourself a little, when to take your time, when to back off entirely, when to rest and try later.

Like the remainder of the population, however, about half of you had parents who were less than ideal. It is painful to think about, but we'll take up this issue slowly, returning to it several times later. But you do need to face what you may have missed. Having an inadequate parent had to have more of an impact because you were sensitive. You needed understanding, not special problems.

Those of you with an insecure childhood also need to face it so that you can be more patient with yourself. Most important, you need to know what was not done so you can be a different sort of parent to your infant/body. Chances are that you are not taking good care of yourself—either neglecting your body or being too overprotective and fussy. It is almost surely because you are treating your body as your not-so-great first caretaker once took care of you/it (including overreacting in the opposite way to that experience).

So let's see exactly what a good caretaker and not-so-good caretaker of an infant/body is like. We start with the care of the newborn—or with your body at those times now in your life when it feels as tiny and helpless as a newborn's. A good description of what is needed comes from the psychologist Ruthellen Josselson:

> Enfolded in arms, we have a barrier between ourselves and whatever might be hurtful or overwhelming in the world. In arms, we have an extra layer of protection from

the world. We sense that buffer even though we may be unclear what part of it comes from ourselves and what from outside.

A good-enough mother, in her holding function, manages things so that her baby is not overstimulated. She senses how much stimulation is welcomed and can be tolerated. An adequate holding environment leaves the baby free to develop in a state of being; the infant does not always have to react. In the state of optimal holding, the self can come into existence free of external intrusion.

When holding is not adequate, when the infant/body is intruded upon or neglected—or worse, abused—stimulation is too intense for the infant/body self. Its only recourse is to stop being conscious and present, thereby developing a habit of "dissociating" as a defense. Overstimulation at this age also interrupts self-development. All energy must be directed toward keeping the world from intruding. The whole world is dangerous.

Now let's consider a little later age, when you were ready to explore *if* you felt safe. This equates with those times now when your body is ready to explore and be out in the world *if* it feels safe. At this stage an overprotective caretaker probably becomes a greater problem for a sensitive infant/body than a neglectful one. During infancy or when we are feeling very delicate, constant intruding and checking on the infant/body are sources of overstimulation and worry. At this stage anxious overprotection inhibits exploring and independence. An infant/body constantly watched cannot function freely and confidently.

For example, just a little time feeling hunger and crying or feeling cold and fussing helps an infant/body know his or her own wants. If the caretaker is feeding the infant/body before it is even hungry, it loses contact with its instincts. And if the infant/body is kept from exploring, it does not get used to the world. The caretaker/you is reinforcing the impression that the world is threatening and the infant/body cannot survive out there. There are no opportunities to avoid, manage, or endure overarousal. Everything remains unfamiliar and overarousing. In terms of the previous chapter, the infant/body does not have enough successful approach experiences to balance the strong, inherited pause-to-check system that can take over and become too inhibiting.

If this is your style with your infant/body, you may want to think back to its source. Perhaps you had an overprotective, needy caretaker who really wanted a child very dependent and never able to leave. Or the caretaker's own sense of strength or self-worth was bolstered by being stronger and so needed. If your caretaker had several children, being the most sensitive made you ideal for these purposes. Note that there were probably many times, too, that this sort of caretaker really was not available, whatever you were told—such a caretaker was tuned into her or his needs, not yours.

The point of all this is that how others took care of you as an infant/body has very much shaped how you take care of your infant/body now. Their attitude toward your sensitivity has shaped your attitude toward it. Think about it. Who else could have taught as deep a lesson? Their care for you and their attitude toward your body directly affects your health, happiness, longevity, and contributions to the world. So unless this section of the chapter is distressing you, stop and take some time to think about your infant/body's first caretaker and the similarities between that early caretaking and how you care for yourself now.

If you do feel distressed, take a break. If you think you might need some professional (or perhaps nonprofessional) emotional support and company while you look at your insecure attachment and its affects on you now, get that help.

Out Too Much, In Too Much

Just as there are two kinds of problem caretakers—underprotective and overprotective—there are two general ways that HSPs fail to care properly for their bodies. You may push yourself *out too much*—overstimulate yourself with too much work, risk taking, or exploring. Or you may keep yourself *in too much*—overprotecting yourself when you really long to be out in the world like others.

By "too much," I mean more than you would really like,

YOUR INFANT/BODY'S FIRST CARETAKER
AND THE ONE WHO CARES FOR IT NOW

Thinking about what you know about your first two years, make a list of the sorts of words or phrases that your parents might have used to describe you as a baby. Or you can ask them. Some examples:

A joy. Fussy. Difficult. No trouble. Never slept. Sickly. Angry. Easily tired. Smiled a lot. Difficult to feed. Beautiful. Can't recall anything about your infancy. Walked early. Mostly reared by a series of caretakers. Rarely left with baby-sitters or at a child care center. Fearful. Shy. Happiest alone. Always into things.

Watch for the phrase that was almost your "middle name"—the one they would put on your gravestone if given half a chance. (Mine was "She never caused anybody any trouble.") Watch for the phrases that stir up emotion, confusion, conflict in you. Or the phrases that seem too strongly emphasized, so much so that the opposite is even more true if you think about it. An example would be an asthmatic child being described as "no trouble."

Now, think about the parallels between how your caretakers viewed your infant/body and how you do now. Which of their descriptions of you are really true for you? Which were really their worries and conflicts that you could shed now? For example, "sickly." Do you still see yourself as sickly? Were you and are you now really more sickly than others? (If so, do learn the details of your childhood illnesses—your body remembers and deserves your sympathy.)

Or how about "walked early." Are achievements and milestones how people earned attention in your family? If your body fails to achieve to your satisfaction, can you love it, anyway?

more than feels good, more than your body can handle. Never mind what others have told you is "too much." Some of you may be people who, at least for a period of your lives, truly belong in or out almost all the time. It feels right. Rather, I am referring to the situation where you sense you are overdoing it one way or the other and would like to change but cannot.

Furthermore, I do not mean to imply that those who were anxiously attached, with overprotective or inconsistent caretakers, are always overprotective of the infant/body self. Or that those with neglectful or abusive caretakers always neglect or abuse their infant/body self. It's not that simple. First, our minds are such that we can as easily overreact or compensate and do the opposite. Or, more likely, we'll swing back and forth between the two extremes or apply them in different areas of life (e.g., overdo at work, protect too much in intimate relationships; neglect mental health but overattend to physical health). Finally, you may have overcome all of this and be treating your body just fine.

On the other hand, you who were securely attached may be wondering why you are struggling with these same two extremes. But our circumstances, culture, subculture or work culture, friends, and our own other traits can all also make us go too far either way.

If you are unsure about which you do, review the box "Are You Too Out? Too In?"

The Problem of Being In Too Much

Some HSPs, perhaps all of us at times, get sidelined because of thinking that there is no way an HSP can be out in the world and survive. One feels too different, too vulnerable, perhaps too flawed.

I heartily agree that you will not be able to be involved in the world in the style of the nonsensitive, bolder sorts of folks you may be comparing yourself to. But there are many HSPs who have found a way to be successful on their terms, in the world, doing something useful and enjoyable, with plenty of time for staying home and having a rich, peaceful inner life, too.

ARE YOU TOO OUT? TOO IN?

For each statement, put a 3 for *very true*, 2 for *somewhat true* or *equally true and not true*, depending on the situation, or 1 for *hardly ever true*.

— 1. I often experience the brief effects of being over-aroused, overstimulated, or stressed—things like blush-ing, heart pounding, or my breath becoming more rapid or shallow, my stomach tensing, my hands sweating or trembling, or suddenly feeling on the verge of tears or panic.

— 2. I am bothered by the long-term effects of arousal—the sense of distress or anxiety, upset digestion or loss of appetite, or not being able to fall, or stay, asleep.

— 3. I try to face situations that make me overaroused.

— 4. In a given week, I stay home more than I go out. (Take the time to figure this out carefully, adding up only the available hours, *excluding* sleep and a couple of hours for dressing, undressing, bathing, etc.)

— 5. In a given week, I spend more time alone than with oth-ers. (Figure as above.)

— 6. I push myself to do things I fear.

— 7. I go out even when I don't feel like it.

— 8. People tell me I work too much.

— 9. When I notice I have overdone it physically, mentally, or emotionally, I immediately stop and rest and do what-ever else I know I need to do for myself.

— 10. I add things to my body—coffee, alcohol, medications, and the like—to keep myself at the right level of arousal.

— 11. I get sleepy in a dark theater and/or during a lecture unless I'm quite interested.

— 12. I wake in the middle of the night or very early in the morning and can't go back to sleep.

— 13. I don't take time to eat well or to exercise regularly.

Add up your answers to all of the questions, *excluding* 4, 5, and 9. Then add up 4, 5, and 9, and subtract these from the total of the others. The most "out" score possible would be 27. Most "in" would be a 1. A moderate score would be 14. Especially if you scored 10 or under, do reflect on what I have to say about *The Problem of Being In Too Much*. If you scored over 20, better take to heart what I have written in the next section, *On Being Too Out in the World*.

It may help to consider your behavior from the viewpoint of your infant/body. If it wants to try new things but is afraid, you need to help it, not reinforce the fear. Otherwise, you are telling it that it really is all wrong about its desires, that it is not fit to survive out there. That is a crippling message to give a child. You'll want to think long and hard about who gave you this feeling in childhood, and why, rather than helping you get out and learn to do things your way.

As you reparent your body, the first thing to realize is that the more it avoids stimulation, the more arousing the remaining stimulation becomes. A teacher of meditation once told the story of a man who wanted nothing to do with the stress of life, so he retreated to a cave to meditate day and night for the rest of his life. But soon he came out again, driven to overwhelming distress by the sound of the dripping of water in his cave. The moral is that, at least to some extent, the stresses will always be there, for we bring our sensitivity with us. What we need is a new way of living with the stressors.

Second, it is often the case that the more your body acts—looks out the window, goes bowling, travels, speaks in public—the less difficult and arousing it becomes. This is called habituation. If it is a skill, you also become better at it. For example, traveling alone in a foreign country can seem utterly overwhelming to an HSP. And you may always choose to avoid some aspects of it. But the more you do it, the easier it becomes and the more you know about what you do and do not like.

The way to come to tolerate and then enjoy being involved in the world is by being in the world.

I do not say any of this lightly, however. I was someone who mostly avoided the world until midlife, when I was more or less forced to change by powerful inner events. Since then I have had to face some fear, overarousal, and discomfort almost every day. This is serious business and isn't fun. But it really can be done. And it feels wonderful to be out there, succeeding, calling out to the world, "Look at me! I can do it, *too!*"

On Being Too Out in the World

If the root of being in too much is a belief that the infant-body is defective, the root of being out too much is equally negative. It suggests that you love the child so little that you are willing to neglect and abuse it. Where did you get *that* attitude?

It doesn't necessarily all come from parents. Our culture has an idea of competition in the pursuit of excellence that can make anyone not striving for the top feel like a worthless, nonproductive bystander. This applies not only to one's career but even to one's leisure. Are you fit enough, are you progressing in your hobby, are you competent as a cook or gardener? And family life—is your marriage intimate enough, your sexual life optimal, have you done all that you can do to raise excellent children?

The infant/body rebels under all this pressure, signaling its distress. In response, we find ways to toughen it or to medicate it into silence. So the chronic stress-related symptoms arise, like digestion problems, muscle tension, constant fatigue, insomnia, migraine headaches; or a weak immune system makes us more susceptible to the flu and to colds.

Stopping the abuse first requires admitting it is just that. It also helps to find what part of you is the abuser. The part that has bought into society's script of perfection? That needs to outdo a brother or sister? That has to prove that you really are not flawed or "too sensitive"? That wants to win your parents' love or even just a glance your way for once? That needs to prove you're as gifted as they think? Or that the world cannot survive without you? Or that you can control everything and are perfect and immortal? There is often some arrogance in there somewhere, even if it is the arrogance of another about you.

There is one other reason HSPs drive their bodies too hard, and that is their intuition, which gives some of them a steady stream of creative ideas. They want to express them all.

Guess what? You cannot. You will have to pick and choose. Doing anything else is arrogance again and cruel abuse of your body.

I had a dream about this once—about headless, glowing, unstoppable beings out to get me—which in the morning brought to mind Disney's animation of *The Sorcerer's Apprentice*. Mickey Mouse plays the apprentice and uses sorcery to bring to life a broom to do the chore his master wants done: the filling of a cistern. This is not just laziness—Mickey is too arrogant to do something so lowly, working slowly within the limits of his own body. But Mickey has started something he cannot end. When the water is flooding the room and the broom still will not stop, Mickey chops it up, and soon hundreds of headless brooms are carrying water, drowning Mickey in the fulfillment of his own bright ideas.

That is the lively revenge you can expect from your body when you treat it like a lifeless broom, all in the service of too many bright ideas.

The choice of Mickey to be the apprentice was a good one—he is usually so representative of the average guy in our culture—upbeat, energetic. That energy has its good side; it promotes the belief that as individuals and as a people we can do anything if we work hard enough and are clever enough. Anyone can be president or rich and famous. But the "shadow" or dangerous side of that virtue (all virtues have a shadow) is that it makes life an inhuman competition.

The Balancing Act

How much you are out in the world or how much you avoid it must be answered individually and will change with time. I realize, too, that for most people a lack of time and money make the balancing act very difficult. We are forced to make choices and set priorities, but being very conscientious, HSPs often put themselves last. Or at least we give ourselves no more time off or opportunity to learn new skills than anyone else. In fact, however, we need more.

If you are in too much, the evidence is clear that you and your subtle sensitivity are needed in the world. If you are out too much, the evidence is equally clear that you will perform any responsibility far better if you obtain adequate rest and recreation.

Here is the wise advice of one HSP I interviewed:

> You need to learn all about this sensitivity. It will be an obstacle or an excuse only if you allow it to be. For myself, when I am too withdrawn, I would like to stay home for the rest of my life. But it is self-destructive. So I go out to meet the rest of the world, then come back to incorporate them. Creative people need time without people. But they can't go too long. When you retreat, you lose your sense of reality, your adaptability.
>
> Getting older can also take you out of touch with reality, cause you to lose your flexibility. You need to stay out there more as you age. But as you age, grace develops, too. Your basic traits become stronger, especially if you develop all of yourself, not just your sensitivity.
>
> Be in tune with your body. It is a great gift you can use, this sensitivity to your body. It can guide you, and your opening to it will make it better. Of course, sensitive people want to *shut* the doors to the world and to their bodies. They become fearful. You can't do that. Self-expression is the better way.

Rest

Infants need a lot of rest, don't they? So do highly sensitive bodies. We need all kinds of rest.

First, we need sleep. If you have trouble sleeping, make this your first priority. Research on chronic sleep loss has found that when people are allowed to sleep as much as they need, it can take two weeks for them to reach the point where they show no signs of sleep deprivation (dropping off to sleep abnormally quickly or in any darkened room). If you are showing signs of "sleep debt," you need to plan some vacation time periodically that allows you to do nothing but sleep as much as you want. You will be surprised by how much that will be.

HSPs do worse than others working night shifts or mixed shifts, and they recover more slowly from jet lag. Sorry, but it goes with the territory. Better not to plan, or at least not to plan to enjoy, brief trips across many time zones.

If insomnia is a problem, you can find plenty of advice on that in other sources. There are even centers for treating it. But here are some points that may apply especially to HSPs. First, respect your natural rhythms and retire when you first become sleepy. For a morning person, that means going to bed early in the evening. For a night person, the ones with the more difficult problem, it means sleeping late as often as possible.

Sleep researchers tend to advise people to associate their bed only with sleeping and to get up if they cannot sleep. But I find HSPs sometimes do better if they promise themselves to stay in bed for nine hours with their eyes closed without worrying if they are actually sleeping. Since 80 percent of sensory stimulation comes in through the eyes, just resting with your eyes closed gives you quite a break.

The problem with staying in bed while awake, however, is that some people begin to worry or otherwise overarouse themselves with their thoughts and imaginings. If this happens, it might be better to read. Or get up and think through the issue on your mind, write down your ideas or solutions, then go back to bed. Sleep problems are one of those many areas where we each are unique and must find what works for ourselves.

We need other kinds of rest, too, however. HSPs tend to be very conscientious and perfectionistic. We cannot "play" until all the details of our work are done. The details are like little needles of arousal poking us. But that can make it difficult to relax and have some fun. The infant/body wants play, and play creates endorphins and all the other good changes that undo stress. If you are depressed, overly emotional in other ways, not sleeping, or showing other signs of being out of balance, force yourself to plan more play.

But what is fun? Be careful not to let the non-HSPs in your world define that for you. For many HSPs, fun is reading a good book or gardening a little bit, at their own pace, or a quiet meal at home, prepared and eaten slowly. In particular, squeezing in a dozen activities by noon may not be your idea of fun at all. Or it may be okay in the morning but not by afternoon. So always plan a way to bail out. If you are with someone, be sure to warn them ahead of time so that they will not feel insulted or hurt when you drop out.

Finally, when planning a vacation, consider the cost in terms of airline tickets or deposits if you decide you want to come home early or stop traveling and stay in one place. Then be mentally prepared ahead of time to pay that cost.

Besides sleep and recreation, HSPs also need plenty of "downtime" just for unwinding and thinking over the day. Sometimes we can do this while performing our daily tasks—driving, washing dishes, gardening. But if you have found ways to eliminate some of those tasks, you still need that downtime. Take it.

Yet another form of rest, perhaps the most essential, is "transcendence"—rising above it all, usually in the form of meditation, contemplation, or prayer. At least some of your transcendent time should be aimed at taking you out of all ordinary thinking, into pure consciousness, pure being, pure unity, or oneness with God. Even if your transcendence falls short of this, when you return you will have a bigger, fresher perspective on your life.

Sleep takes you out of your narrow state of mind, too, of course, but the brain is in a different state when asleep. Indeed, it is in a different state for each type of activity—sleep, play, meditation, prayer, yoga—so a mixture is good. But do include some meditation that has the goal of experiencing pure consciousness and involves no physical activity and no concentration or effort. This state is undoubtedly the one that provides the most deep rest while the mind is still alert. Research on Transcendental Meditation, which does create this state, has very consistently found that meditators show less of the distressing long-term arousal described in the previous chapter. (Cortisol in meditators' blood decreases.) It is as if their meditations give them some of the needed feeling of security and inner resources.

Of course, you also want to pay attention to what you eat and to get enough exercise. But that is a very individual matter, and there are plenty of other books to advise you on that. Do learn about the foods that tend to calm the body or take the edge off, helping you to sleep. And get enough of the vitamins and minerals—for example, magnesium—that affect stress and overarousal.

If you are used to caffeine, it probably does nothing special to arouse you unless you drink a little more than usual. It is a powerful drug for HSPs, however. Be careful about using it just now and then, thinking it will improve your performance the way it does for those around you. For example, if you are a morning person and do not usually drink caffeine and then drink it one morning before an important exam or interview, it could actually make you perform worse by overarousing you.

Strategies for Overarousal

A good caretaker develops many strategies for soothing his or her infant. Some are more psychological; some, more physical. Either approach will change the other. Choose according to your intuition. Any approach requires taking action—getting up, going to the infant, doing something.

For example, you walk into New York's Pennsylvania Station, are overwhelmed, and begin to feel afraid. Psychologically or physically you need to do something to keep the infant/body from getting upset. In this case it might be a good idea to work through the fear and upset psychologically: This is *not* a noisy hell filled with dangerous strangers. It is just a larger version of many train stations you have dealt with, overflowing with normal people trying to get where they want to go, with plenty who would help you if you asked.

Here are some other psychological methods useful in handling overarousal:

- Reframe the situation.
- Repeat a phrase, prayer, or mantra that, through daily practice, you have come to associate with deep inner calm.

- Witness your overarousal.
- Love the situation.
- Love your overarousal.

In *reframing*, notice what is familiar and friendly, what you have successfully dealt with that is similar. When *repeating a mantra or prayer*, if your mind races back to what is over-arousing it, it is important not to get discouraged and stop. You will still be calmer than you would be without it.

When *witnessing*, imagine standing to one side, watching yourself, perhaps talking about yourself with a comforting imaginary figure. "There's Ann again, so overwhelmed she's falling to pieces. I really feel for her. When she's like this, of course, she can't see beyond right now. Tomorrow, when she's rested, she'll be all excited again about her work. She just has to take some rest now no matter what seems to need to be done. Once she's rested, it will go smoothly."

Loving the situation sounds pretty flippant, but it's important. An expanded, loving mind, one that is open to the whole universe, is the opposite of a tightly constricted, overaroused mind. And if you cannot love the situation, it is vitally important and even more essential that you *love yourself in your state* of not being able to love the situation.

Finally, do not forget the power of music to change your mood. (Why do you think armies have bands and buglers?) But beware that most HSPs are strongly affected by music, so the right choice is essential. When you are already aroused, you do not want to stir yourself up more with emotional pieces or something associated with important memories (the music most people, being underaroused, cannot get enough of). Sobbing violins are out at such times. And, of course, since any music increases stimulation, use it only when it seems to soothe you. Its purpose is to distract you. Sometimes you need to be distracted; at other times, you need to attend carefully.

But since we are dealing with the body, it can be an equally good idea to try a physical approach.

Here's a list of some purely physical strategies:

- Get out of the situation!
- Close your eyes to shut out some of the stimulation.

- Take frequent breaks.
- Go out-of-doors.
- Use water to take the stress away.
- Take a walk.
- Calm your breathing.
- Adjust your posture to be more relaxed and confident.
- Move!
- Smile softly.

It's amazing how often we forget to take action simply to get out of a situation. Or take a break. Or take the situation—task, discussion, argument—out of doors. Many HSPs find nature deeply soothing.

Water helps in many ways. When overaroused, keep drinking it—a big glass of it once an hour. Walk beside some water, look at it, listen to it. Get into some if you can, for a bath or a swim. Hot tubs and hot springs are popular for good reasons.

Walking is also one of those basic comforts. The familiar rhythm is soothing. So is the rhythm of slow breathing, especially from your stomach. Exhale slowly with a little extra effort, as if blowing out a candle. You will automatically inhale from your stomach. Or merely attend to your breathing—this old friend will settle you down.

The mind often imitates the body. For example, you may notice that you have been walking around leaning forward slightly, as if rushing toward the future. Balance yourself over your center instead. Or your shoulders may be rounded, your head down, as if under a burden. Straighten up, throw off the burden.

Tucking your head between raised shoulders may be your favorite position both in sleep and while awake, an unconscious attempt at self-protection from blows of stimulation and waves of overarousal. Instead, uncurl. When standing, raise your head, pull your shoulders back, center your upper body over your torso and feet so that the weight feels most effortlessly balanced. Feel the solid ground through your feet. Bend your knees a little and breathe deeply from your stomach. Feel your body's strong center.

Try to create the moves as well as the posture of someone

calm, in command. Lean back, relax. Or get up and move toward what appeals to you. Get the "approach system" on line. Or move like someone angry, disdainful. Shake a fist. Scowl. Gather your things and prepare to walk out. Your mind will imitate your body.

It is crucial to hold yourself and move in the manner you want to feel. Overaroused HSPs tend to substitute "freeze" for the "fight or flight" response. Relaxed posture and free movement can break that numb tension. Or stop moving if you are just being frantic or jittery.

Smiling? Maybe it is a smile just for yourself. Why you are smiling does not matter.

The Containers in Your Life

Another way to understand all of this advice is to remember how we began this chapter, by appreciating that your infant/body's earliest and still most basic need is to be held and protected from overstimulation. On that strong basis, you can go out and explore, feeling secure about that safe harbor of the good caretaker's arms.

If you think about it, your life is filled with such safe containers. Some are concrete—your home, car, office, neighborhood, a cottage or cabin, a certain valley or hilltop, a forest or bit of shoreline, certain clothing, or certain beloved public places, such as a church or library.

Some of the most important containers are the precious people in your life: spouse, parent, child, brother or sister, grandparent, close friend, spiritual guide, or therapist. Then there are the even less tangible containers: your work, memories of good times, certain people you cannot be with anymore but who live on in memory, your deepest beliefs and philosophy of life, inner worlds of prayer or meditation.

The physical containers may seem the most reliable and valuable, especially to the infant/body self. It is the intangible ones, however, that are really the most reliable. There are so many accounts of people who maintained their sanity by retreating into such containers while under extreme stress or danger. Whatever happened, nothing and no one could take from them their private love, faith, creative thinking, mental practice, or spiritual exercise. Part of maturing into wisdom is transferring more and more of your sense of security from the tangible to the intangible containers.

Perhaps the greatest maturity is our ability to conceive the whole universe as our container, our body as a microcosm of that universe, with no boundaries. That is more or less enlightenment. But most of us will need more finite containers for a while, even if we are beginning to learn to make do with intangible ones in a pinch. Indeed, as long as we are in bodies, enlightened or not, we need some bit of tangible safety, or at least a sense of sameness.

Above all, if you do lose a container (or worse, several), accept that you will feel especially vulnerable and overwhelmed until you can adjust.

Boundaries

Boundaries are obviously an idea closely related to containers. Boundaries should be flexible, letting in what you want and keeping out what you don't want. You want to avoid shutting everyone out all the time indiscriminately. And you want to control any urges to merge with others. It would be nice, but it just doesn't work for long. You lose all of your autonomy.

Many HSPs tell me that a major problem for them is poor boundaries—getting involved in situations that are not really their business or their problem, letting too many people distress them, saying more than they wanted, getting mired in other people's messes, becoming too intimate too fast or with the wrong people.

There's one essential rule here: *Boundaries take practice!* Make good boundaries your goal. They are your right, your responsibility, your greatest source of dignity. But do not become too distressed when you slip up. Just notice how much better you are getting at it.

Besides all the other reasons to have good boundaries, you can use them to keep out stimulation when you have had all that you can take. I have met a few HSPs (one in particular raised in an overcrowded urban housing project) who can, at will, shut out almost all stimulation in their environment. Quite a handy skill. "At will" is important, however. I am not referring to involuntary dissociation or "spacing out." I am talking about choosing to shut out the voices and other sounds around you, or at least decreasing their impact on you.

So, want to practice? Go sit by a radio. Imagine yourself with some kind of boundary around yourself that keeps out what you don't want—maybe it is light, energy, or the presence of a trusted protector. Then turn on the radio but keep out the radio's message. You will probably still hear the words, but refuse to let them in. After a while, turn the radio off and think about what you experienced. Could you give yourself permission to shut out the broadcasting? Could you feel that boundary? If not, practice it again someday. It will improve.

The Infant/Body's Message

1. Please don't make me handle more than I can. I am helpless when you do this, and I hurt all over. Please, please, protect me.

2. I was born this way and can't change. I know you sometimes think something awful must have made me this way, or at least made me "worse," but that ought to give you even more sympathy for me. Because either way I can't help it. Either way, *don't blame me for how I am.*

3. What I am is wonderful—I let you sense and feel so much more deeply. I am really one of the best things about you.

4. Check in on me often and take care of me right at that moment if you possibly can. Then, when you can't, I can trust that you are at least trying and I won't have long to wait.

5. If you must make me wait for my rest, please ask me nicely if it's okay. I'm only more miserable and troublesome if you get angry and try to force me.

6. Don't listen to all the people who say you spoil me. You know me. You decide. Yes, sometimes I might do better left alone to cry myself to sleep. But trust your intuition. Sometimes you *know* I am too upset to be left alone. I do need a pretty attentive, regular routine, but I'm not easily spoiled.

7. When I'm exhausted, I need sleep. Even when I seem totally wide awake. A regular schedule and a calm routine before bed are important to me. Otherwise, I will lie awake in bed all stirred up for hours. I need a lot of time in bed, even if I'm lying awake. I may need it in the middle of the day, too. Please let me have it.

8. Get to know me better. For example, noisy restaurants seem silly to me—how can anybody eat in them? I have a lot of feelings about such things.

9. Keep my toys simple and my life uncomplicated. Don't take me to more than one party in a week.

10. I might get used to anything in time, but *I don't do well with a lot of sudden change*. Please plan for that, even if the others with you can take it and you don't want to be a drag. Let *me* go slow.

11. But I don't want you to coddle me. I especially don't want you to think of me as sick or weak. I'm wonderfully clever and strong, in my way. I certainly don't want you hovering over me, worried about me all day. Or making a lot of excuses for me. I don't want to be seen as a nuisance, to you or to others. Above all, I count on you, the grown-up, to figure out how to do all of this.

12. Please don't ignore me. Love me!

13. And like me. As I am.

• **Working With What You Have Learned** •

Receiving Your First Advice
From Your Infant/Body Self

Pick a time when you are not rushed and will not be interrupted, when you are feeling solid and in the mood for self-exploration. What follows can bring up strong feelings, so if you start to feel overwhelmed, take it slow or just stop. What follows can also just be difficult to do because of resistances that cause the mind to wander, the body to become uncomfortable or sleepy. If that happens, it's natural and fine. Try a little of this on several occasions and appreciate whatever happens.

PART I

Read all of these instructions first, so that, as much as possible, you can do without looking back at them as you proceed.

1. Curl up like a baby or lie on your stomach or back—find the position you think was yours.

2. Shift from thinking in your head to feeling emotionally from your body, as a baby does. To help with that, for a full three minutes breathe very consciously from the center of your body, your stomach.

3. After the breathing, become yourself as an infant. You think you cannot remember, but your body will. Start with an image of weather, like the example at the start of this chapter. Is it mostly fair or stormy?

Or begin with your earliest conscious memory, even if it was from a little later age. It is all right to be an infant with a slightly older child's understanding. For example, this slightly older child may be certain that it is better not to cry for help. Alone is best.

4. Be especially aware that you are a *highly sensitive* infant.

5. Be aware of what you most need.

PART II

Now or at a later time ... Again, read all of the instructions first, so that you will not need to refer back to them so much that it's distracting.

1. Imagine a very beautiful baby who is about six weeks old. Really tiny. Admire the sweetness, the delicateness. Notice that you would do almost anything to protect this child.

2. Now realize that this wonderful baby is your infant/body self. Even if this baby is more like some infant you have recently seen, this is your imagination's baby.

3. Now watch as you start to whimper and fuss. Something is the matter. Ask this baby, "What can I do for you?" And listen well. This is your infant/body speaking.

Do not worry that you are "just making this up." Of course, you are, but your infant/body self will be involved somewhere in the "making up."

4. Answer back, start a dialogue. If you foresee difficulties meeting this infant's needs, talk about it. If you are sorry for something, apologize. If you get angry or sad, that's something also good to know about your relationship with the baby.

5. Do not hesitate to do either part of this exercise again or to do it differently. For example, next time just open your mind to the infant/body self, at whatever age and in whatever setting she or he wants to appear.

4

Reframing Your Childhood and Adolescence
Learning to Parent Yourself

In this chapter we'll begin to rethink your childhood. As you read about typical experiences of sensitive children, memories of yourself as a child will return. But you'll see them freshly through the lens of your new knowledge about your trait.

These experiences matter. Like a plant, the kind of seed that goes into the ground—your innate temperament—is only part of the story. The quality of soil, water, and sun also deeply affects the grown plant that is now you. If the growing conditions are very poor, the leaves, flowers, and seeds barely appear. Likewise, as a child, you did not expose your sensitivity if your survival required different behavior.

When I began my research, I discovered "two kinds" of HSPs. Some reported difficulty with depression and anxiety; some reported very little of these feelings. The separateness of the two groups was quite clear. Later, I discovered that the depressed and anxious HSPs almost all had troubled childhoods. Non-HSPs with troubled childhoods do not show nearly as much depression and anxiety. But neither do HSPs with healthy childhoods. It is important that we and the public not confuse high sensitivity with "neuroticism," which includes certain types of intense anxiety, depression, overattachment, or avoidance of intimacy, and are usually due to a troubled childhood. True, some of us were dealt both hands in life—high sensitivity *and* neuroticism—but the two things are not at all the same. This confusion of sensitivity with neuroticism and the effects of childhood trauma is one reason for some of the negative stereotypes of HSPs (that we are by nature always anxious, depressed, and so on). So let's all work to keep it straight.

It is easy to understand why a troubled childhood might affect HSPs more than non-HSPs.

HSPs are prone to see all the details, all the implications, of a threatening experience. But it is easy to underestimate the impact of childhood, since so much that is important occurs before we can remember. Moreover, some of what is important was just too distressing and deliberately forgotten. If someone caring for you became angry or dangerous, the conscious mind buried that information as too awful to acknowledge, even while your unconscious developed a deeply mistrustful attitude.

The good news is that we can work on any negative effects. I have seen HSPs who have done just that and been freed of much of their depression and anxiety. But it takes time.

Even if your childhood was wonderful, however, it was probably difficult being highly sensitive. You felt different. And your parents and teachers, even if excellent in most respects, did not know how to handle a sensitive child. There simply was not much information on the trait, and there was so much tension about making you "normal," like the ideal.

A final point to remember: Sensitive boyhoods and girlhoods are quite different from each other. In this chapter, therefore, I will pause often to point out how your experience probably differed with your gender.

Marsha, a Wisely Avoidant Little Girl

Marsha, an HSP in her sixties, saw me in psychotherapy for several years, hoping to understand some of her "compulsions." In her forties she had become a poet and photographer and at sixty her work was gaining considerable respect.

While some of her story is distressing, her parents basically did their best. And she has dealt well with her past and continues to learn from it, both inwardly and through her art. I think if you were to ask today if she is happy, she would say yes. But what matters most is her steady growth in wisdom.

Marsha was the youngest of six children born to immigrant parents struggling to make ends meet in a small midwestern town. Marsha's older sisters recall their mother sobbing at the news of each of her pregnancies. Marsha's aunts recall her mother, their sister, as deeply depressed. But Marsha has no memory of her mother ever being slowed down by grief, depression, fatigue, or hopelessness. She was an impeccable German housekeeper and devout churchgoer. Similarly, Marsha's father "worked, ate, slept."

The children did not feel unloved. Their parents simply had no time, energy, or money for affection, conversation, vacations, helping with homework, imparting wisdom, or even giving gifts. This brood of six chicks, as Marsha sometimes described herself and the others, mostly raised themselves.

Of the three styles of attachment that you read about in the previous chapter—secure, anxious, and avoidant—Marsha's early childhood required her to be avoidant. She had to be a child who did not need anyone, who caused as little trouble as possible.

Little Marsha, HSP, in Bed With the Big Beasts

During the first two years of Marsha's life, the household sleeping arrangements placed her in the same bed with three older brothers. Alas, they used their baby sister to experiment sexually, in the way that unsupervised children sometimes do. After two years, she was moved to her sisters' rooms. All she recalls is that "finally I felt a little bit safe at night." But she remained the target of cruel, overt sexual harassment from one of her older brothers until she was twelve.

Marsha's parents never noticed all of this, and she believed that if she told on her brothers, her father would kill them. Killing was a part of life. It seemed that it could happen. Marsha recalled being stunned by the regular beheading of chickens in the backyard and the casual, callous attitude toward this necessity of life. So there is extra meaning in her seeing the children of her family as a brood of chicks.

Besides the sexual torment, her brothers loved to tease and frighten Marsha, as if she were their personal toy. More than once they caused her to faint from fear. (HSPs make such good targets because we react so strongly.) However, no cloud lacks its silver. As their special plaything, she was also taken places and tasted freedoms that girls usually missed in those days. Her brothers, who possessed a tough independence that she preferred to her mother's and sisters' passivity, were her role models—and this was in some ways a valuable experience for a sensitive girl.

For Marsha, the best attachment was with an older sister, but that sister died when Marsha was thirteen. Marsha recalls lying on her parents' bed, staring into space, waiting for news of her sister. She had been told that if her parents did not call in an hour, it would mean that her sister had died. When the clock struck the hour, Marsha recalls picking up a book and going back to reading. Here was yet another lesson in not attaching.

Marsha as a Tiny Fairy, Marsha in the Chicken Coop

Marsha's first memory is of lying naked in the sunlight watching dust motes, awed by the beauty—a memory of her sensitivity as a source of joy. It has been that way all her life, especially now that it can be expressed in her art.

Notice that no other person is in her first memory. In a similar way, her poetry and photography tend to be about things, not people. There are often images of houses—with closed windows and doors. The haunting emptiness of some of her work speaks to the private experiences of all of us, especially those whose early childhoods taught us to avoid closeness.

In one photo, produced during her therapy, chickens are in the foreground, in clear focus. (Recall the significance of chickens for Marsha.) The chicken wire and door frame of a jail-like chicken coop are fainter. Faintest of all, in the darkened door of the coop, is the ghostly image of a group of ragged children. Another important image of her art came from a dream about a bright, angry little fairy who lived in a secret garden and would allow no one in.

Marsha has used food, alcohol, and various drugs compulsively—in amounts that bordered on excessive. But she was too smart to go over the edge, having a very practical streak and an IQ of over 135. In one dream she was wheeling a starving, angry infant through a banquet hall filled with food, but it wanted none of it. We discovered that the baby was starved, in a greedy, desperate way, for love and attention. Like hungry chickens, when we cannot be fed what we need, we feed ourselves what we can find.

HSPs and Attachment

In the previous chapters we learned about the importance of your attachment to your caretaker, usually your mother. An insecure attachment style will persist throughout life unless one has an unusually secure one with someone in adulthood, such as a mate or during long-term psychotherapy. Alas, non-therapy relationships sometimes can't withstand the task of undoing childhood-based insecurity (the avoidance of intimacy or the compulsion to merge and fear of being abandoned). Also, while you go out into the world unconsciously seeking that long-desired security, without extensive experience with what you seek, you often repeat the same old mistakes, choosing again and again the same familiar sort of person who makes you feel insecure.

While I found a slight tendency for more HSPs than non-HSPs to show one of the nonsecure attachment styles as adults, that does not mean the trait creates the situation. It probably reflects the way a sensitive child is more aware of the subtle cues in any relationship.

As an HSP, some of your most important lessons about the other was whether to expect help with overarousal or an extra dose of it. Every day was a lesson.

In his *Diary of a Baby* (described in chapter 2), Stern gives the example of a "face duet" between mother and the imaginary Joey. Mother coos and brings her face close, then withdraws. Joey smiles, laughs, encourages the game. But eventually it becomes too intense. At these moments of overarousal, Stern's imaginary Joey breaks eye contact and looks away, in effect stopping the arousal. To describe this face duet, Stern again uses the weather analogy, the mother being the wind which plays over the child. So when Joey is overwhelmed, Stern imagines this diary entry:

> Her next gust is rushing towards me, whipping up space and sound. It is upon me. It strikes me. I try to meet its force, to run with it, but it jolts me through and through. I quake. My body stalls. I hesitate. Then I veer off. I turn my back to her wind. And I coast into quiet water, all alone.

This should all be familiar to you now—Joey is trying for that optimal level of arousal described in chapter 1. Those taking care of babies usually sense this. When a baby is restless and bored, they invent games like the face duet or something more arousing, like making weird faces or reaching slowly toward the child while saying, "I'm gonna get you." The squeals of delight are a great reward to the adult. And there may be a sense that being pushed to the limit is good for the child's confidence and flexibility. When the child shows distress, however, most adults stop.

Now consider our imaginary, highly sensitive Jesse. The face duet is probably not much different except that it is a little quieter and briefer. Jesse's mother will have adjusted her playing in order to keep Jesse within his comfort range.

But what about those times when others get their hands on Jesse? Suppose his older sister or Grandpa makes the duet a little more intense? What if, when Jesse averts his gaze, his way of taking a time-out, his sister moves so close that they are face-to-face again. Or she turns Jesse's face back.

Maybe Jesse closes his eyes.

Maybe his sister puts her mouth by Jesse's ear and screams.

Maybe Grandpa takes him and tickles him or tosses him up in the air a few times.

Jesse has lost all control over his arousal level. And each howl of Jesse's brings a fresh rationalization: "He loves it, he loves it—he's just scared a little."

The Confusing Issue—Do You "Love It"?

Have you imagined yourself in Jesse's place? What a confusing situation. The source of your arousal is utterly out of your control. Your intuition tells you that the other, usually so helpful, is now anything but help. Yet the other is laughing, having fun, expecting you to.

Here is a reason why you may find it hard even now to know what you do and do not like, separate from what others like to do to you or with you or think you should like.

I remember once watching two dog owners taking their small pups into the surf and throwing them out into deep water. The dogs swam desperately to their owners' waiting arms even though it meant that the treatment would be repeated. Not only was it probably the only alternative to drowning, but these arms were the ones that provided all the safety and food the pups had ever known. So they wagged their tails wildly, and I suppose their owners believed what they wanted and thought the pups loved the "game." Maybe even the pups were unsure after a while.

Then there was the HSP whose earliest memory was of being the imaginary "dough" in a family-reunion skit of "patty-cake, patty-cake." In spite of crying and pleading with her parents, this two-year-old was passed in a circle from stranger to stranger. Reliving the long-repressed feelings that went with this memory, she realized that it (and other situations she had probably repressed completely) left her with a sense of helpless terror about being picked up, about being controlled physically in any way, and about her parents not protecting her.

The bottom line is that in those first years you either learned to trust the other, and the outer world generally, or you didn't. If you did, your sensitivity remained, but you were rarely threatened into distressing long-term arousal. You knew how to handle it; it seemed under your control. If you asked others to stop doing something, they did. You knew you could trust them to help you rather than overburden you. On the other hand, one way that chronic shyness, anxiety, or social avoidance can begin is if your early experiences did not build that trust. It is not inborn but learned.

This either-or effect is not rigid—you probably learned to trust in some situations more than others. But it is also true that in the first two years the child adapts an overall strategy or mental representation of the world which can be quite enduring.

HSPs With Good Childhoods

There are, by the way, some reasons to expect many HSPs to have had unusually good childhoods. Gwynn Mettetal is a psychologist at Indiana University studying how best to help parents of the "temperamentally at risk." She notes that most parents try hard to understand their children and raise them correctly. A sensitive child's realization of these good intentions can provide a stronger than usual feeling of being loved.

Parents of a highly sensitive child often develop an especially intimate bond with their child. The communication is more subtle, and the triumphs in the world are more significant. "Look, Mom—I scored a goal!" takes on all new meaning to parents and coaches when the soccer-player is an HSP. And since the trait is inborn, there is a good chance that one or both of your parents understood you very well.

Research at the University of California Medical School in San Francisco found that children who were "highly sensitive to stress" had more injuries and illnesses if they were under stress but actually had fewer when not under stress. Since stress is greatly influenced by the security of a child's attachment and family life, I think it's safe to assume that highly sensitive children enjoying a secure attachment style also enjoy unusually good health. Isn't that interesting to know?

Finally, even if your parents practiced benign neglect, you may have received enough love and been allowed sufficient space to grow up fine on your own. Perhaps imaginary figures, characters in books, or nature itself calmed and supported you enough; your trait may have made you happier than other children with this solitude. Or your intuition and many good attributes may have brought you into other, healthier close relationships, with a relative or teacher. Even a little time with the right person can make all the difference.

If your family was unusually difficult, you should also be

aware that your trait may have protected you from being quite as involved in or confused by the chaos as another child might have been. And when you start to heal, your intuition will help you in that process. Those who study attachment find that most of the time we impart to our children the same experience we had, but there are definitely exceptions, and they are the adults who have healed their worst childhood hurts. If you make the admittedly painful effort, you can be one of those, too. We will return to this in chapter 8.

New Fears Out in the World

As you approached school age, there were new tasks and new ways your sensitivity could help or hinder you. Like Rob in chapter 2, your exposure to the big, wide world would have further stimulated your imagination, produced a heightened awareness of everything that escaped others, and given you great joy and appreciation of the smallest beauties in life. As your sensitivity encountered a bigger world, it also probably gave rise to new "unreasonable" fears and phobias.

Fears can increase at this age for many reasons. First, there is simple conditioning: Whatever was around when you were overaroused became associated with overarousal and so became something more to be feared. Second, you may have realized just how much was going to be expected of you, how little your hesitations would be understood. Third, your sensitively tuned "antenna" picked up on all the feelings in others, even those emotions they wanted to hide from you or themselves. Since some of those feelings were frightening (given that your survival depended on these people), you may have repressed your knowledge of them. But your fear remained and expressed itself as more "unreasonable" fear.

Finally, being sensitive to the discomfort, disapproval, or anger of others probably made you quick to follow every rule as perfectly as possible, afraid to make a mistake. Being so good all the time, however, meant ignoring many of your normal human feelings—irritation, frustration, selfishness, rage. Since you were so eager to please, others could ignore your needs when, in fact, yours were often greater than theirs. This would only fuel your anger. But such feelings may have been so frightening that you buried them. The fear of their breaking out would become yet another source of "unreasonable" fears and nightmares.

Finally, for many of you, the patience your parents showed about your sensitivity in the first three years now ran thin. They had hoped you would outgrow it. But as it came time to send you to school, they knew the world was not going to treat you gently. They may have begun to blame themselves for overprotecting you, to launch a campaign of pushing you harder. Maybe they even sought professional help, giving you an even stronger message that something was wrong with you. All of this also could have added to your anxiety at this age.

The Problem of Sensitive Little Boys

There appear to be just as many males as females born as HSPs. But then your culture gets hold of you. Cultures have strong ideas about how little men and women ought to behave.

The issue is so important to us that it is almost funny. A colleague told me about this informal social psychological experiment: A new baby was left in a park with an attendant who, when asked by passersby, would claim to have agreed to sit with the child for a few moments and did not know if it was a boy or girl. Everyone stopping to admire the infant was quite distressed at not being able to know the child's gender. Some even offered to undress the child to find out. Other studies explain why gender matters so much: people tend to treat baby boys and girls quite differently.

It is fascinating how extensively gender is confused with sensitivity. Men should not be sensitive, women should be. And it all begins at home. Research shows that little boys who are "shy" are not liked as well by their mothers, which, according to the researchers, "can be interpreted as a consequence of the value-system of the mother." What a start on life. Shy boys get negative reactions from others, too, especially when the boy is also mild-tempered at home.

Sensitive Little Girls—Mothers' Special Companions

In contrast to shy boys, girls seen as shy get along well with their mothers; they are the good ones. The problem here is that sensitive girls can be overprotected. In the sensitive daughter a mother may find the child she dreams of, the one who will not, should not, and cannot leave home—all of which dampens the sensitive little girl's natural urge to explore and overcome her fears.

Girls at every age show more negative effects (including withdrawal from the world) from any negative attitudes their mother has toward them—criticism, rejection, coldness. This is probably far more true for sensitive girls. Moreover, fathers often forget to help their daughters overcome their fears. Finally, overall, little girls are more affected by both parents, for better or worse.

Having read all of this, it is time to think about the ways in which you need to be a different kind of parent to yourself now. To begin, do the self-assessment of "How You Cope With Threats of Overarousal."

Being a Different Kind of Parent to Yourself

Some situations are overstimulating because they are too intense or long. The child in you cannot bear the fireworks, cannot take another hour at the carnival. Reading the previous chapter should have helped you to take your infant/body seriously when it has had enough. But sometimes it is doing fine but afraid of what is coming, of the very idea of seeing the fireworks or riding the Ferris wheel. When new situations produce overstimulation because they are unfamiliar, and unfamiliar things in the past have turned out to be upsetting, then naturally we reject everything new without trying it. That means we can miss out on a lot.

In order to be willing to try new things, you need plenty of experiences in facing new situations and doing okay. For an HSP, doing well in new circumstances is never automatic. Parents who understand their highly sensitive kids develop a "step-by-step" strategy. Then the children themselves eventually learn

HOW YOU COPE WITH THREATS
OF OVERAROUSAL

Do not hesitate to check several of the statements below, even if they seem inconsistent. Just check the items that apply to you, making each answer independent of the one before.

When I am afraid of trying something new or am on the verge of being overstimulated or overaroused, I usually

— Try to escape the situation.
— Look for ways to control the stimulation.
— Expect to be able to endure it in some way.
— Feel a rising sense of fear that everything may go wrong now.
— Seek out someone I can trust to help me or at least keep that person in mind.
— Get away from everyone so that at least no one can add to the problem.
— Try to be with others—friends, family, a group I know well—or go to church, take a class, get out in public somewhere.
— Vow to try even harder to avoid it and everything like it no matter how much I miss out on.
— Complain, get angry, do whatever I must to get those responsible to stop distressing me.
— Focus on calming down and trying to take things one step at a time.

Your own methods: _____

All of these have their place—even fear, which can mobilize us to act. But some are obviously better suited to some situations than others, so flexibility is the key. If you use fewer than three, you should look at the list again and think about adopting more.

Who taught you these methods? What might have happened to prevent you from using more of them? Recognizing these childhood sources of your coping responses can help you see what is still useful, what is no longer necessary.

to apply it to themselves. If your parents did not teach you step by step, it is time you learned to teach yourself this style of meeting the unfamiliar.

I have adapted here some of the advice on the "shy child" from Alicia Lieberman's *Emotional Life of the Toddler,* to be used by grownups when we feel afraid to enter new situations:

1. Just as a parent does not send a toddler into a new situation alone, do not do that to yourself. Take someone else along.

2. Just as a parent begins by talking about the situation with the child, talk to the fearful part of yourself. Focus on what is familiar and safe.

3. Just as a parent keeps the promise that the child can leave if he or she becomes too upset, allow yourself to go home if you need to.

4. Just as a parent is confident the child will be okay after a while, expect the part of yourself that is afraid to be okay after some time to adjust to all the unfamiliar stimulation.

5. Just as a parent is careful not to respond to a child's fear with more concern than is justified by the situation, if the part that is fearful needs help, respond with no more anxiety than the braver part of you thinks is justified.

Remember, too, that overarousal can be mistaken for anxiety. A good parent to yourself might say, "There sure is a lot going on here; it makes your heart pound with excitement, doesn't it?"

Weighing "Special Needs" Against the Risk of Lasting Discouragement

Perhaps the most difficult task is deciding how much to protect yourself, how much to gently push yourself forward. It is the problem all parents of sensitive children face. You probably know how to put pressure on yourself; you do it just the way your parents, teachers, and friends did. Few HSPs escape the pressure to be a good sport, normal, or pleasing to others, and even when those others are long gone, you keep on trying to please them. You imitate their failure to accept your special need to be buffered. In the terms of the last chapter, you tend to be "out" too much.

Or you may have imitated overprotection, which may have been nothing but a failure to help you when you were both afraid and eager to try something within your ability. In that case, you may be "in" too much.

How discouraging to watch your friends enjoying something you are too afraid to try. Do not underestimate such discouragement. It can be just as present in adulthood as you see friends taking on careers, travel, moves, and relationships that you would fear. Yet deep inside you also know you have the same or more talent, desire, and potential.

Envy can wake us up to one of two truths: We want something and better do something about it while we still can, or we want something and just cannot have it. As you saw in chapter 2, in Rotherbart's description of how we develop, adult humans are capable of directing attention, using willpower, and deciding to overcome a fear. If your envy is strong and you decide you want to do something, you probably can.

Another, equally important part of growing up is no longer pretending we will be able to do absolutely everything. Life is short and filled with limits and responsibilities. We each get a piece of the "good" to enjoy, just as we each contribute a piece of that good to the world. But none of us can have it all for ourselves or do it all for others.

I have noticed that not all HSPs feel discouraged by not being able to do everything their peers do. They have little envy. They appreciate their trait and know it gives them much that others lack. I think the discouragement, like the failure to buffer ourselves, comes from attitudes learned in early childhood.

It's Never Too Late to Overcome Discouragement

While it is wise to accept what we cannot change about ourselves, it is also good to remember that we are never too old to replace discouragement with bits and pieces of confidence and hope.

As a child, I had a special sensitivity to falling, which spiraled into overarousal and a loss of coordination whenever I was up high or relying on my own balance. Thus, I never insisted on being taught things like riding a bicycle, roller skating, or ice skating—which I think only relieved my mother. Thus, I have always been more of an envious observer than a participant in physical activities, but there have been glowing exceptions, such as what happened at the end of a summer-solstice celebration I attended in California, on a 'ranch in the foothills of the Sierras.

The women at the event were of all ages. But in the evening, when they had found a swing, they became a group of young girls. The swing was on a long rope and swept out over a slope. In the twilight, it was like flying to the stars. Or so they said. Everyone had tried it except me.

When the others had wandered indoors, I stayed, looking at the swing and feeling that old shame of being the scaredy-cat, even though probably no one had noticed.

Then a woman much younger than I appeared and offered to show me how to use the swing. I said no, I didn't want to. But she ignored that. She promised she would never push me harder than I wanted. And she held out the swing.

It took some time. But somehow I felt safe with her, and I built up the courage to swing out toward the stars like the others.

I never saw that young woman again, but I will always be grateful not only for the experience but for the respect and understanding she showed as she taught me how—one gentle swing at a time.

Your School Years

Marsha's memories of her school years were typical of HSPs. She excelled in school and was even a kind of leader when it came to plans and ideas. She was also bored. Her restless imagination led her to read books during lessons. Still, she was "usually the smartest."

At the same time that she was bored, the overstimulation of school always bothered her. She recalls best just the noise. It did not frighten her, but especially if the teacher left the room, the noise was unbearable. The racket at home, eight people in a tiny house, also made her miserable. In good weather she hid in trees or under the porch and read books. In bad weather she just learned to tune everything out while she read.

At school, however, overarousal can be harder to avoid. One day the teacher read aloud some newspaper accounts of the horrible tortures of certain prisoners of war. Marsha passed out.

When you started school, like Marsha, you encountered the wider world. The first shock may have been the separation from home. But even if you were prepared for that by going to preschool, your senses could never be prepared for the long, noisy day in the average primary-grade classroom. At best, your teachers maintained a range of stimulation that worked for the average child's optimal level of arousal. For you it was almost always excessive.

Probably at first you dealt with school by withdrawing and just observing. I recall well my son's first day in school. He went to the corner and stared as if dumbstruck. But silent watching is not "normal." The teacher says, "The others are playing—why don't you?" Rather than displeasing the teacher or being seen as odd, maybe you overcame your reluctance. Or maybe you simply could not. In which case, more and more attention came your way—just what you did not need.

Jens Asendorpf of the Max Plank Institute for Psychology in Munich has written on how normal it is for some children to prefer to play alone. At home parents usually sense that doing so is just part of their child's personality. But at school things are different. By second grade, playing alone causes a child to be rejected by other children and an object of concern for teachers.

For some of you, all this overarousal and shame led to poor classroom performance. Most of you, however, being fond of reading and quiet study, excelled in schoolwork. It was the development of social or physical skills that was hampered by your overarousal. To handle that, perhaps you found a close friend to play with. And perhaps you had the reputation of being the one who thought up the best games, wrote the best stories, and painted the best pictures.

Indeed, if you had entered school with confidence about

yourself and your trait, as did Charles in chapter 1, you may have been a real leader. If not, as one sensitive friend of mine, a physicist, said, "Can you think of anyone really great who had an easy time of it in school?"

Schoolboys, Schoolgirls

In my research I found that by school age most male HSPs were introverts. This makes sense, since a sensitive boy is not "normal." They had to be careful in groups or with strangers to see how they were going to be treated.

Sensitive girls, like sensitive boys, often rely on one or two friends throughout their school years. But some of them are fairly extroverted. Unlike the boys, if they display some over-arousal or emotion, they are doing what is expected of them. It may even help them to be accepted by the other girls.

The negative side of this permission to be emotional, however, can be that a sensitive girl is never forced to put on the armor that sensitive boys have to don to survive. Girls may have little practice in emotional control and feel helpless in the face of emotional overarousal. Or they may use their emotions to manipulate others, including to protect themselves from over-arousal. "If we have to play that game again, I'm going to cry." The straightforward self-assertion needed in adulthood is not expected or wanted from them.

Giftedness

If you were labeled gifted, your childhood may have been easier. Your sensitivity was understood as part of a larger trait that was more socially accepted. There existed better advice to teachers and parents concerning gifted children. For example, one researcher reminds parents that such children cannot be expected to blend well with their peers. Parents will not produce a spoiled freak if they give their child special treatment and extra opportunities. Parents and teachers are firmly told to allow gifted children to just be who they are. This is good advice for children with *all* traits that miss the average and ideal, but gift-edness is valued enough to permit deviation from the norm.

There is some good and bad in everything, however. Parents or teachers may have pressured you. Your self-worth may have been entirely contingent upon your achievements. Meanwhile, if you were not with gifted peers, you would be lonely and possibly rejected. There are now some better guidelines for raising gifted children. I have adapted them for reparenting your gifted self.

Reparenting Your "Gifted" Self

1. Appreciate yourself for being, not doing.
2. Praise yourself for taking risks and learning something new rather than for your successes; it will help you cope with failure.
3. Try not to constantly compare yourself to others; it invites excessive competition.
4. Give yourself opportunities to interact with other gifted people.
5. Do not overschedule yourself. Allow time to think, to daydream.
6. Keep your expectations realistic.
7. Do not hide your abilities.
8. Be your own advocate. Support your right to be yourself.
9. Accept it when you have narrow interests. Or broad ones.

About this last point—maybe you just want to study neutrinos and nothing else. Or maybe you just want to read, travel, study, or talk until you figure out the meaning of human life on this planet. It takes both types to make a world. (Besides, you will probably change at another stage in life.) More will be said about giftedness in adults (a neglected topic) in chapter 6.

The Highly Sensitive Adolescent

Adolescence is a difficult time for anyone. But my research has found that on the average HSPs report their high school years as the most difficult of all. There are mind-boggling biological changes and the rapid addition of one adult responsibility after another: driving, vocational or college choices, the proper use of alcohol and drugs, potential parenthood, being trusted with children in jobs as baby-sitters or camp counselors, and little things like keeping track of ID, money, and keys. Then there is the big one, the awakening of sexual feelings and the painful self-consciousness that it brings. Sensitive youths seem bound to feel uneasy with the sexual roles of victim or aggressor that the media imply they are expected to play.

It is also possible, however, to displace energy or anxiety onto sex because the real source of the anxiety is harder to face. Think of the pressure to make choices that will determine your entire life, with no idea of the outcome; the expectation that you'll leave the home you've always known and do so gladly or at least resolutely; the fear that now your "fatal flaw" will reveal itself fully as you fail to make the expected transition to independent living.

It is not surprising that many sensitive adolescents meet the crisis by destroying their budding self so they will not have to watch it fail to bloom "right." And there are plenty of ways to self-destruct: marrying or having a baby in a way that imprisons one in a narrow, prescribed role; abusing drugs or alcohol; becoming physically or mentally incapacitated; joining a cult or organization that offers security and answers; or suicide. It is not that all of these behaviors are caused by being sensitive (or that the self, tough plant that it is, will not survive some of them and be a late bloomer). But these escapes, available to all adolescents, are used by some HSPs as well.

Of course, for many the duties of adulthood are postponed by going to college. (Then there may be graduate school, a postdoctorate, an internship.) Or one finds another way to assume life's duties very gradually. Delaying, as opposed to avoidance, is a fine tactic, another form of the method of learning I call step-by-step. Never feel bad about using it for a while.

Maybe you delayed leaving home. You lived with parents for a few years, worked for them for a while, or moved in with hometown high school friends. Becoming a functioning adult step-by-step really works fine. Suddenly one day you are an adult, doing it all, and you never noticed how you got there.

Sometimes, however, we take too big a step. College can be that for some HSPs. I have known so many HSPs who dropped out after the first term (or after their first return home, often at Christmas). Neither they nor their parents nor their counselors understand the real problem, overstimulation from a whole new life—new people, new ideas, new life plans, plus living in a noisy dorm and staying up all night talking or partying, plus probably experimenting with sex, drugs, and alcohol (or nursing your friends through the aftereffects of *their* experiments).

Even when the sensitive student would rather withdraw and rest, there is that pressure to do what others do, be normal, keep up, make friends, satisfy everyone's expectations. Whatever trouble you had in college should be reframed. It was not some personal failure.

Not surprisingly, a good home life helps all adolescents a great deal, even at the time for leaving the nest. The enduring influence of the home is especially strong for HSPs. By adolescence your family had taught you a great deal about how you can and should behave in the real world.

When Sensitive Boys and Girls Become Men and Women

As highly sensitive adolescents become adults, the differences between the genders increase. Like tiny variations in direction at the start of a trip, differences in upbringing can cause sensitive men and women to arrive at very different destinations.

In general, men have higher self-esteem then women. When parents appreciate their sensitive boy, as in the case of Charles in chapter 1, then, as an adult, he will have great self-confidence. At the other extreme, I found many highly sensitive men who were filled with self-loathing—not surprising, given the rejections they had experienced.

A study of men who had been shy since childhood (I assume that most were HSPs) found that they married an average of three years later than other men, had their first child four years later, and began a stable career three years later, which in turn tended to lead to lower professional achievement. This could reflect cultural prejudice against shy men or lower self-confidence. It could also indicate the kind of caution and delaying that is healthy for an HSP or the valuing of other things beside family and career—perhaps spiritual or artistic goals. At any rate, if you have been slow to take these steps, you have plenty of company.

In contrast, the same study found that shy women went through the traditional stages of life right on time. A shy woman was far less likely to have worked at all or to have continued working when she married, as if availing herself of the patriarchal tradition of going from her father's house to her husband's without having to learn to support herself.

Yet in high school these same women tended to have a "quiet independence, an interest in things intellectual, a high aspiration level, and an inner-directedness." One can only imagine the tension in these women's lives created by that "quiet independence," the need to follow their inner direction, and their sense that the only safe, quiet oasis for them was a traditional marriage.

Many of the women I interviewed felt that their first marriages were mistakes, attempts to deal with their sensitivity through adding another person to their life or by assuming a safe role. I do not know if their divorce rate is any higher, but their reasons might be different from those of other women. It seems that they are eventually forced both to face the world alone and to find outlets for their strong intuition, creativity, and other talents. If their first marriages did not allow room for that growth, it became a stepping-stone from home to greater independence when they were finally ready.

Marsha was certainly one such woman. She married young and waited until her forties to develop the creative and intellectual abilities so evident in her school years. For Marsha (and about a third of the women I interviewed) there may have been more to this hesitancy about the world than simple sensitivity. These women had had upsetting sexual experiences—Marsha with her brothers. Even without overt sexual abuse, all young women are known to experience a descent into low self-esteem at puberty, probably as they realize their role as sexual objects. The highly sensitive girl will sense all the implications even more and make self-protection a higher priority. Some overeat to become unattractive, some overstudy or overtrain so they have no free time, some pick one boy early and hang on to him for protection.

Marsha reported that her leadership and classroom brilliance ended in junior high school, as soon as her breasts developed (with above-average fullness). Suddenly she was drawing constant attention from boys. She wore an overcoat to school in all weather and became as inconspicuous as she could. Besides, as she put it, the leaders now were the "dumb, giggly boy chasers." She could not or would not be one of them.

She was often accosted by boys, anyway. One day a pair chased her and stole a kiss. She went home horrified, stepped into the house, and saw an actual or visionary rat—she never knew which—hurtling down the stairs at her. For years after that, whenever she kissed a boy, she saw that rat.

At sixteen she fell in love for the first time, but broke it off when they seemed to be getting too close. She remained a virgin until twenty-three, when she was date-raped. After that she gave herself to anyone who persisted—"except the boys I really loved." Then came an abusive marriage, the long wait for the courage to divorce that man, and the beginning of her artistic career.

In sum, once again there is the gender difference in how sensitivity is manifested. As sensitive boys become men, they must fall out of step with other men in the timing and the nature of their lives. Being sensitive is not "normal" for men. Meanwhile, for women sensitivity is expected. Sensitive girls find it all too easy to take the path of traditional values without first learning how to be in the world.

Growing Up's Bottom Line: We Grow Into a Highly Social World

We are at the end of a chapter but possibly the start of a life's work: learning to see your childhood in the light of your trait and reparenting yourself when necessary.

Looking back, you will notice how much this chapter about growing up highly sensitive has been concerned with you and your relationships with others—with parents, relatives, peers, teachers, strangers, friends, dating partners, spouses. Humans are very social animals, even we HSPs! It seems to be time to turn to the HSP's social life and to this word which keeps coming up, this state of mind called "shy."

The heart of this chapter and perhaps of this book is the reframing of your life in terms of your sensitivity. It is the task of seeing your failures, hurts, shyness, embarrassing moments, and all the rest in a new way, one that is both more coolly accurate and warmly compassionate.

List the major events you remember from childhood and adolescence, the memories that shaped who you are. These might be single moments—a school play or the day your parents told you they were divorcing. Or they might be whole categories—the first day of school each year or being sent to camp each summer. Some memories will be negative, even traumatic and tragic. Being bullied or teased. Some will have been positive but still perhaps overwhelming: Christmas morning, family vacations, successes, honors.

Choose one event and go through the steps for reframing introduced in chapter 1:

1. *Think about your response to the event and how you have always viewed it.* Did you feel you responded "wrong" or not like others would have? Or for too long? Did you decide you were no good in some way? Did you try to hide your upset from others? Or did others find out and tell you that you were being "too much"?

2. *Consider your response in the light of what you know now about how your body automatically operates.* Or imagine me, an author, explaining it to you.

3. *Think if there's anything that needs to be done about it now.* If it seems right, share your new view of the situation with someone else. Perhaps it could even be someone who was present at the time who could help you continue to fit details into the picture. Or write down your old and new view of the experience and keep it around for a while as a reminder.

If this is helpful, reframe another major childhood event in a few days, until you have gone through the list. Do not rush the process. Allow a few days for each. A major event deserves time to be digested.

5

Social Relationships
The Slide Into "Shy"

"You're too shy." Did you hear that often? You will think about it differently after reading this chapter, which discusses where shyness usually happens most: in your nonintimate social relationships. (The close ones are discussed in chapter 7.) Many of you are gifted socially—that's a fact. But since there is no point in fixing something that's not broken, I'll focus here on a problem that typically needs fixing—what others call "shyness," social "avoidance," social "phobia." But we will approach it, and a few other common issues for HSPs, in a very different way.

Again, by focusing on problems I don't mean to imply that HSPs necessarily have a difficult social life. But even the president of the United States and the queen of England must sometimes worry about what others are thinking about them. So you probably worry about that, too, sometimes. And worry makes us overaroused, our special Achilles heel.

Also, we often are told, "Don't worry; no one is judging you." But being sensitive, you may be noticing that people really are watching and judging; people usually do. The nonsensitive are often happily oblivious of it. So your task in life is much harder: to *know* about those glances, those silent judgments, and still not let them affect you too much. It's not easy.

If You Have Always Considered Yourself Shy

Most people confuse sensitivity with shyness. That is why you heard "You're too shy." People say a certain dog, cat, or horse was born "shy" when it really has a sensitive nervous system (unless it has been abused; then it would be more accurate to say it's "afraid"). Shyness is the fear others are not going to like or approve of us. That makes it a response to a situation. It is a certain *state*, not an always-present trait. Shyness, even chronic shyness, is not inherited. Sensitivity is. And while chronic shyness does develop more in HSPs, it needn't. I have met many HSPs who are almost never shy.

If you often feel shy, there is a good explanation for how you or anyone else probably got that way, non-HSPs included. Sometime in your past you entered a social situation (usually overstimulating to begin with) and felt that you failed. Others said you did something wrong or did not seem to like you, or you failed to meet your own standards in the situation. Maybe you were already overaroused, having used your excellent imagination to envision all that might go wrong.

Usually one failure is not enough to make anyone chronically shy, although it can happen. Usually it happens that the next time you were in the same situation, you were more aroused because you feared a repeat of the previous time. And being more aroused made failure more likely. By the third time, you were being very brave, but you were also impossibly aroused. You couldn't think of anything to say, you acted inferior and were treated that way, and so forth. You can see how this pattern could repeat and repeat into a downward spiral. It can also spread to other situations that are even a little similar, like all situations with people present!

HSPs, being more easily aroused, are more likely to enter that spiral. But you were not born shy, just sensitive.

Ridding "Shyness" From Your Self-Concept

There are three problems with accepting the label "shy." First, it is totally inaccurate. It misses the real you, your sensitivity to subtlety and your difficulty with overarousal. Remember, overarousal is not always due to fear. Thinking it is fear can make you feel shy when you are not, as we will see.

This confusion of your trait with the state of mind called shyness is natural, given that 75 percent of the population (at least in the United States) are very socially outgoing. When they see that you look overaroused, they do not realize that it could be due to too much stimulation. That is not *their* experience. They think you must be afraid of being rejected. You're shy. You fear rejection. Why else would you not be socializing?

Sometimes you *are* afraid of rejection. Why not? Your style is not the cultural ideal, after all. But as an HSP, sometimes you just don't want the extra arousal. When others are treating you as if you're shy and afraid, it can be hard to realize that you've simply chosen to be alone, at least at first. You are the one rejecting. You are not being rejected. (Besides not understanding because they were born needing more arousal than you to be comfortable, non-HSPs also can project their own fear of rejection onto you—that is, attributing to you something they do not want to admit in themselves.)

If you are spending less time in crowds or meeting strangers, when you do have to be in such situations, you are almost bound to be less skilled. It is not your specialty. But again, to assume you are shy or afraid is inaccurate. When people set out to help you, they are usually starting from the wrong premise. For example, they think you lack confidence and reassure you that you are likable. In effect, however, that is telling you there is something the matter with you—low self-esteem. Not knowing your underlying trait, they give you the wrong reason for your being less sociable and cannot give you the many real reasons you should feel fine about yourself.

Calling Yourself Shy Is Negative

Unfortunately, the term shy has some very negative connotations. It does not have to; shy can also be equated with words such as discreet, self-controlled, thoughtful, and sensitive. But studies have shown that most people on first meeting those I would call HSPs considered them shy and equated that with anxious, awkward, fearful, inhibited, and timid. Even mental health professionals have rated them, more often than not, this way and also as lower on intellectual competence, achievement, and mental health, which, in fact, bear no association with shyness. Only people who knew the shy people well, such as their spouses, chose the positive terms. Another study found that the tests used by psychologists to measure shyness are replete with the same negative terms. Maybe that would be all right if the tests were of a state of mind, but they're often used to identify "shy people," who then bear a negative label. Beware of the hidden prejudice behind the word shy.

Calling Yourself Shy Is Self-Fulfilling

A rather charming psychological experiment involving shyness, done at Stanford University by Susan Brodt and Philip Zimbardo, demonstrates why you need to know that you are *not shy* but just an HSP who can become overaroused.

Brodt and Zimbardo found women students who said they were extremely "shy," especially with men, and others who were not "shy," to serve as a comparison group. In the study, which supposedly concerned the effects of loud noise, each woman spent time with a young man. The man, who was unaware of whether or not the woman was "shy," had been instructed to converse with each woman in the same style. The interesting twist was that some of the shy women were fooled into thinking that their overarousal—their pounding heart and racing pulse—was due to the loud noise.

The result was that those "shy" women who believed their overarousal had been caused by a loud noise talked just as much as the nonshy women. They even took charge, controlling the topic of conversation just as much as the nonshy women did. The other group of shy women, who had nothing else on which to blame their arousal, talked much less and allowed the man to control the conversation much more. After the experiment, the young man was asked to guess which women were shy. He could not distinguish nonshy women from shy women who had been led to believe their arousal was due to the noise.

These shy women became less shy by assuming that there

was no *social* reason for their overarousal. They also said they did not feel shy and truly enjoyed the experience. Indeed, when asked if they would prefer to be alone next time if they were again a participant in a "noise bombardment experiment," two-thirds said they would prefer not to be, compared to only 14 percent of the other shy women and 25 percent of the nonshy. Apparently these shy women had an especially fine time just because they thought their overarousal was caused by something besides shyness.

Remember this experiment the next time you feel over-aroused in a social situation. Your heart may be pounding for any number of reasons having nothing to do with the people you are with. There may be too much noise, or you may be worrying about something else you are only half aware of that has nothing to do with the person you are with. So go ahead, ignore the other causes (if you can), and have a good time.

I have given you three strong reasons not to call yourself shy anymore. It is inaccurate, negative, and self-fulfilling. And do not let others label you with it, either. Let's say it is your civic duty to eradicate this social prejudice. Not only is it unfair, but as discussed in chapter 1, it is dangerous because it helps to silence the thoughtful voices of HSPs by reducing their self-confidence.

How to Think About Your "Social Discomfort"

Social discomfort (the term I prefer to "shy") is almost always due to overarousal, which makes you act, speak, or appear not very socially skilled. Or it is the dread that you will become overaroused. You dread doing something awkward, not being able to think of what to say. But the dread itself is usually enough now to create the overarousal, once in the situation.

Remember, discomfort is temporary, and it gives you choices. Suppose you are uncomfortably cold. You can tolerate it. You can find a more congenial environment. You can create some heat—build a fire, turn up the thermostat—or ask those in charge to do it. You can put on a coat. The one thing you should not do is blame yourself for being inherently more sus-ceptible to a cold environment.

The same is true of a temporary social discomfort due to overarousal. You can put up with it, leave the situation, change the social atmosphere or ask others to, or do something else to make you more comfortable, like put on your "persona" (I'll discuss this later).

In all cases, you are consciously ridding yourself of the discomfort. So forget the idea that you are inherently uncomfortable in social situations.

Five Ways to Handle Overarousal in Social Situations

1. Remember that overarousal is not necessarily fear.
2. Find other HSPs to talk to, one on one.
3. Use your arousal-reducing skills.
4. Develop a good "persona" and consciously use it.
5. Explain your trait to others.

Never underestimate the power of simply acknowledging to yourself that you are overaroused, possibly by something having nothing to do with the people you are with. If you are judged for that, it is not the real you but the one temporarily flustered by overarousal. If and when they know the calm you, the you who is subtly aware, they will be favorably impressed. You know that is true because you have close friends who admire you.

When I went back to graduate school at midlife, on the very first day, in the first hour, in the breakfast room, I dropped a full glass of milk all over myself and the floor and several others in the vicinity. No one had bumped me. I just hit it against something. It happened in full view of all of my future fellow students and faculty, the people I most wanted to impress.

The pure shock added to my already almost unbearable overarousal. But thanks only to the research I was doing on HSPs like you and me, I knew all about why I had done it. My body's inability to even carry milk was predictable. The day was difficult, but I did not let the spilled milk add to my social discomfort.

As the day went by, I found other HSPs, and that helped a

great deal. We were all spilling milk, so to speak. In the average social situation there ought to be about 20 percent who are HSPs and another 30 percent who feel moderately sensitive. Studies of shyness find that on an anonymous questionnaire 40 percent call themselves shy. In a roomful of people, the odds are that there is at least one person with your trait or who is feeling social discomfort. Catch their eyes after you stumble, literally or metaphorically, and notice the look of deep sympathy. You have an instant friend.

Meanwhile, use all the points suggested in chapter 3 to reduce your arousal. Take breaks. Go for a walk. Breathe deeply. Move in some way. Consider your options. Maybe it's time to go. Maybe there's a better place to position yourself, by an open window, an aisle, or the door. Think in terms of containers—who or what quiet, familiar presence could hold you right now?

There were times on that first day of graduate school when I feared that the faculty would think something was seriously wrong with me. With the average non-HSP, being this over-aroused could only mean serious conflicts and instability. So I used all my tricks—walking, meditating, driving off campus at lunchtime, calling home for some comfort. And it worked well enough.

We often think our overarousal is more noticeable to others than it really is. You know that much of social life is one "persona" meeting another, with neither person looking too far beneath the surface. By behaving in a predictable way, talking the way others do even when you don't feel like it, no one will hassle you or draw the wrong conclusion that you're arrogant, aloof, plotting, and so forth. For example, research finds that "shy" students tend to see themselves as doing their best socially, but their roommates tend to think they're just not trying enough. That may be the fault of the culture for not understanding HSPs, but until we change it, you may want to make your life a little easier by acting a little more like everyone else does. Put on your persona; the term comes from the Greek word for mask. Behind the mask you can be whoever you want.

On the other hand, sometimes the best tactic is to explain your overarousal. I often do this when speaking or teaching in front of a group of strangers. I tell them that I know I sound a little strained but in a few minutes I'll be fine. In a group, explaining your trait may lead to a more intimate conversation about everyone's social discomfort, make it possible for you to go off alone without feeling guilty, or free you to take a break without being left out when you return. Perhaps there is someone who could lessen the stimulation you're experiencing—adjust the lighting or volume or let you pass when introductions are made.

Once you mention being highly sensitive, you'll arouse one of two stereotypes, depending on your choice of words. One stereotype, frankly, is of a passive victim, someone weak and troubled. The other is of a gifted, deep, powerful presence in the room. It takes practice bringing up the positive stereotype through the words you choose to explain your needs. We'll work on that in chapter 6.

When I have to be with a group of people for a whole day or weekend, I often explain that I need plenty of time alone. Often others do, too. But even if I'm the only one going to my room early and taking long walks alone, I've learned not to generate sympathy or pity but to leave behind an air of mystery. Members of the "royal advisor" class must consider these matters. Be a little cagey about your HSP "PR."

People, Arousal, and Introversion

Thus far we have attacked the "problem" by getting rid of the label shy and understanding what is going on as familiar overarousal. It is equally important that you appreciate that there's more than one right way to be social.

Your way of being social arises from a basic fact: For most of us, the majority of the arousing stimulation in the external world is created by other people, whether at home, at work, or in public. We're *all* social beings who enjoy and must depend on others. But many HSPs avoid people who come in the overstimulating packages—the strangers, the big parties, the crowds. For most HSPs, this is a smart strategy. In a highly stimulating, demanding world, everyone has to establish priorities.

Of course, no one can be an expert at dealing with the situations they choose to avoid. But most of you can manage or learn to. Just managing is an acceptable, smart way to save your energy for whatever else matters to you.

It's also true that some HSPs avoid strangers, parties, and other group situations because of having been rejected by peers and groups in the past. Because they didn't fit our culture's ideal of being outgoing, they've been judged harshly and avoid people they cannot be sure of. That seems reasonable, although sad, and is nothing to be ashamed of.

In all, 70 percent of HSPs tend to be socially "introverted." That does *not* mean you dislike people. It means you prefer to have a few close relationships rather than a large circle of friends and don't usually enjoy large parties or crowds. But even the most introverted person is sometimes an extravert and enjoys a stranger or a crowd. Even the most extraverted is sometimes an introvert.

Introverts are still social beings. In fact, their well-being is more affected by their social relationships than is the well-being of extraverts. Introverts just go for quality, not quantity.

(If you're not enjoying a sense of emotional well-being, however, a close relationship with someone does not always solve that problem. Many people, in fact, cannot have a good, close relationship until they develop a greater sense of well-being through some healing work in psychotherapy, in the broadest sense, as described in chapter 8.)

The Extraverted HSP

I want to emphasize that being an HSP is not the same as being socially introverted. In my studies I've found that 30 percent of us are socially extraverted. As an extravert, you have large circles of friends and tend to enjoy groups and strangers. Perhaps you were raised in a big, sociable, loving family or safe neighborhood and learned to see people as sources of safety rather than reasons to be on guard.

You still find other sources of arousal difficult, however, like a long work day or being in the city too much. When overaroused, you avoid socializing. (Extraverted non-HSPs actually relax better with people around.) While most of our attention here is on the habitually introverted, extraverts will probably find it useful, too.

Appreciating the Introverted Style

Avril Thorne, now of the University of California at Santa Cruz, sat down to watch how introverts actually interact. Using tests to identify highly introverted and highly extraverted women college students, she paired them either with the same sort of person or their opposite and videotaped the conversations.

The highly introverted women were serious and focused. They talked more about problems and were more cautious. They tended to listen, to interview, to give advice; they seemed to be concentrating on the other in a deep way.

In contrast, the highly extraverted women did more "pleasure" talk, sought more agreement, looked for similarities in background and experience, and paid more compliments. They were upbeat and expansive and liked being paired with either type, as if their main pleasure were in the talking.

When the extraverted were with someone who was highly introverted, they liked not having to be so cheerful. And the introverted found conversing with the extraverted "a breath of fresh air." The picture we gain from Thorne is that each type contributes something to this world that is *equally* important. But given the undervaluing of the introverted style, it will be good to spend some time focusing on the virtues of the introverted.

Carl Jung on the Introverted Style

Carl Jung saw introversion as a basic division among humans, causing the major battles of philosophy and psychology, most of which boil down to conflicts over whether the outer facts or the inner understanding of those facts are more important in comprehending any situation or subject.

Jung saw the two as attitudes toward life, which in most people alternate, like breathing in and out. But a few are more consistently in or out. Furthermore, to him the two attitudes had nothing directly to do with being sociable or not. To be introverted is simply to turn inward, towards the subject, the self, rather than outward toward the object. Introversion arises from a need and preference to protect the inner, "subjective" aspect of life, to value it more, and in particular not to allow it to be overwhelmed by the "objective" world.

One cannot emphasize enough the importance of introverts in Jung's view.

> They are living evidence that this rich and varied world with its overflowing and intoxicating life is not purely external, but also exists within ... Their life teaches more than their words. ... Their lives teach the other possibility, the interior life which is so painfully wanting in our civilization.

Jung knew the prejudice in Western culture against the introverted. He could tolerate it when it came from the extraverted. But he felt that the introverted who undervalue themselves are truly doing the world a disservice.

It Takes All Kinds

Sometimes we do need just to enjoy the world out there as it is and be glad for those who help us, the extraverted who can make even total strangers feel connected. Sometimes we need an inner anchor—that is, those who are introverted and give their full attention to the deepest nuances of private experience. Life is not just about the movies we have both seen and the restaurants we have both tried. Sometimes discussing the subtler questions is essential for the soul.

Linda Silverman, an expert on gifted children, found that the brighter the child, the more likely he or she will be introverted. Introverts are exceptionally creative even with something as simple as the number of unusual responses to a Rorschach inkblot test. They are also more flexible in a sense, in that sometimes they *must* do what extraverts do all the time, meet strangers and go to parties. But some extraverted people can avoid being introverted, turning inward, for years at a time. This greater versatility on the part of some introverts is especially important later in life, when one begins to develop what one has lacked up until midlife. Later in life, too, self-reflection becomes more important for everyone. In short, introverts may mature more gracefully.

So you're in good company. Ignore the barbs about "lightening up." Enjoy the levity of others and allow yourself your own specialty. If you are not good at chitchat, be proud of your silence. Equally important, when your mood changes and your extraverted self appears, let it be as clumsy or silly as it needs to be. We are all awkward doing our nonspecialty. You possess one piece of the "good." It would only be arrogance to think any of us should have it all.

Making Friends

Introverts prefer close relationships for many reasons. Intimates can understand and support each other best. A good friend or partner can also upset you more, but that forces inner growth, which is often a high priority for HSPs. And, given your intuition, you probably like to talk about complicated things like philosophy, feelings, and struggles. That is hard to do with a stranger or at a party. Finally, introverts possess traits that can make them good at close relationships; with intimates they can experience social success.

The extraverted are right, however, when they say that "a stranger is just a friend I haven't met yet." All your closest friends were once strangers. As those relationships change (or even end), you'll always want to meet new potential close friends. So you might think back over how you met your best friends.

The Persona and Good Manners

Especially if you are usually introverted, remember that in most social situations you at least need to meet minimal social expectations. HSPs can reduce all rules of etiquette to a four-word rule: Minimize the other's overarousal. (Or to two words: Be kind.) Dead silence, since it is not expected, can arouse another person. But so can being too outgoing, which is often the extravert's mistake. The goal is just to say something pleasant and unsurprising.

Yes, this may bore some people who are nonsensitive and enjoy lots of stimulation. But you want your short-term arousal when meeting a new person to settle down even if it is not a problem for the other. Then later on you can be as creative and surprising as you want. (But at that point you are taking calcu-

HOW YOU MET YOUR BEST FRIENDS

Write down the names of your best friends, one to a page of paper. Then answer the following questions about the beginning of each friendship.

Did circumstances force you to talk?

Did the other take the initiative?

Was there anything unusual about how you were feeling?

Were you being especially extraverted that day?

How were you dressed or feeling about your appearance?

Where were you? At school, at work, on vacation, at a party?

What was the situation? Who introduced you? Or were you thrown together by chance? Or did one of you happen to speak to the other about something? What happened?

What were the first moments and hours and days like?

When and how did you know this would be a friendship?

Now look for commonalities among these. For example, you may not like parties, but that was the setting for meeting two of your best friends. Are any of these common features, like going to school or working with others, absent from your life at present? Is there anything you want to do about what you have learned? Vow to go to one party a month? (Or to avoid parties from now on—they turned out not to be a source of friends, after all.)

lated risks, and any successes can be counted as extra credit points.)

Now you need a more advanced course on personas, or social roles. A good persona obviously involves good manners and predictable, nonarousing behavior. But it can be a bit more specialized, according to your needs. A banker wants to have a solid, practical persona. If there's an artist within, that is kept private. Artists, on the other hand, will do well to keep their banker sensibilities hidden from public view. Students are smart to appear a little humble; teachers need to appear authoritative.

The idea of a persona goes against North American culture's admiration of openness and authenticity. Europeans have a far better grasp of the value of not saying everything that one is thinking. Yet there are people who identify too much with their persona. We all know the type. Having nothing else underneath, it's hard to say they're being dishonest or unauthentic. But it's rare for an HSP to overidentify with a persona.

If you still think I'm asking you to be insincere, think of it as choosing the appropriate level of openness for that place and time. Take the example of when you've barely met someone who wants a friendship with you and you have decided not to pursue it. You probably don't reject the other's lunch invitation by saying, "I have come to realize that I don't want to be a close friend of yours." You say something about having a very busy schedule right now.

This response is honest at a certain level—if you had infinite time you might actually pursue such a relationship at least a step further. To tell the other person what put them low on your list of priorities is not, in my experience, morally correct. The best persona and good manners involve this sort of face-saving, compassionate level of honesty, especially with those you don't know particularly well.

Learning More Social Skills

There are two kinds of information about social skills, whether it comes packaged as a book, tape, article, lecture, or course. One kind comes from the experts on extraversion, social skills, sales, personnel management, and etiquette. These folks are often witty and upbeat. They talk about learning, not curing, so they do not lower your self-esteem by implying that you have a serious problem. If you turn to these pros, just understand that your goal is not to be exactly like them but to learn a few tips. Watch for titles like *How to Win Over a Crowd* and *What to Say in Every Possible Awkward Moment*. (I made these up; new ones are constantly appearing.)

The other kind of information comes from psychologists trying to help people with shyness. Their style is first to make you worried so you'll be motivated, then to take you step by step through some pretty sophisticated, well-researched methods of changing your behaviors. This approach can be very effective, but also has some problems for HSPs, although it may seem more suited to you. Talk about "curing" your shyness or "conquering your syndrome" cannot help but make you feel flawed, and it overlooks the positive side of your inherited trait.

Whatever advice you read or hear, remember that you do not have to accept how the extraverted three-quarters of the population defines social skills—working the room, always having a good comeback, never allowing "awkward" silences. You have your own skills—talking seriously, listening well, allowing silences in which deeper thoughts can develop.

It is also probably true that you already know much of what is covered by these experts. So I've taken the main points and put them into a short test to show you what you do know and teach you some of the rest.

DO YOU KNOW THE LATEST ON OVERCOMING SOCIAL DISCOMFORT?

Answer true or false; then check your answers on pages 113–115.

1. It helps to try to control negative "self-talk," such   T F
   as "He probably won't like me" or "I'll probably
   fail as I always do."

2. When people feel shy, it is obvious to those around   T F
   them.

3. You need to expect some rejections and not take   T F
   it personally.

4. It helps to have a plan for overcoming your social   T F
   discomfort—for example, trying to meet one new
   person a week.

5. When formulating your plan, the bigger the steps   T F
   you take, the faster you will achieve your goal.

6. It is best not to rehearse what you'll say with a   T F
   new person or in a new situation; it will make you
   sound stiff and unspontaneous.

7. Be careful about body language; the less it conveys, T F
the better.

8. When trying to get a conversation started or to T F
continue, ask questions that are a little bit personal
and that cannot be answered with one or two
words.

9. A way to show you are listening is to sit back T F
with your arms and legs crossed, keep your face
still, and don't meet the other person's eyes.

10. Never touch another person. T F

11. Don't read the newspaper before going out where T F
you will meet people—it will just upset you.

12. Self-disclosure is not important to conversation as T F
long as you are talking about something interesting.

13. Good listeners repeat back what they've heard, T F
reflecting the other's feelings, and then respond
with their own feelings, not ideas.

14. Don't tell other people interesting details about T F
yourself; it will only make them jealous.

15. To deepen a conversation or make it more T F
interesting to both of you, sometimes it works
to share your own flaws or problems.

16. Try not to disagree with the other person. T F

17. When a conversation is making you feel that you T F
want to spend more time with the other person,
it's best to say so.

Based on Jonathan Cheek, *Conquering Shyness* (New York: Dell, 1989) and M. McKay, M. Dewis, and P. Fanning, *Messages: The Communication Book* (Oakland, Calif.: New Harbinger Press, 1983.)

Don't Feel Bad If You Know What to Do But Don't Always Do It

Gretchen Hill, a psychologist at the University of Kansas, questioned shy and nonshy people about what was the appropriate behavior in twenty-five social situations. She found that the shy people knew equally well what was expected of them but said they were not capable of doing it. She hints that shy people lack self-confidence—the usual inner flaw attributed to us. So we are told to be more confident. Which we can't, of course. So we've failed again. But maybe we're sometimes justified in our lack of confidence, with so many experiences of being too aroused to behave appropriately. Naturally, some of us expect not to be able to do what we know to be socially correct. I think that simply telling ourselves to be more confident rarely helps. Stick to the twofold approach of this chapter: Work on the overarousal, appreciate your introverted style.

Another reason for not being able to put into practice what you know about social skills is that old patterns from childhood may be taking over and need to be faced. Or some feelings command your attention. One sure sign? You keep saying things like "I don't know why I did that—I knew better—that just wasn't like me." Or, "After all my efforts, nothing is working."

The Case of Paula

Paula was definitely born highly sensitive. Her parents had commented on her "shyness" from birth. She was always aware of having a greater sensitivity to sound and confusion than her friends. In her thirties, when I interviewed her, she was extremely capable in her profession, which involved organizing major events from behind the scenes. But she stood no chance of advancing because of her terror of public speaking and of people in general, which kept her from managing anything but the smallest team of coworkers. In fact, Paula had organized her life around the few times when her job demanded that she convene staff meetings. For these she needed to exercise for hours and perform various rituals in order to prepare herself emotionally.

Paula had read all the books on overcoming such fears and had used her considerable willpower to fight the feelings. But she realized that her fear was unusual, so she tried some longer, more intense therapy. There she found some reasons for the fear and started working through it.

As Paula was growing up, her father was a "rage-aholic" (He is now an alcoholic as well.) He had always been a smart man, analytic, helpful with his children's homework. Indeed, he was very involved with all of them and actually a little less cruel to Paula than he was to her brothers. But some of that attention may have been sexual, Paula was beginning to discover, and was certainly confusing. At any rate, his rage affected her the most.

Paula's mother was very nervous about other people and their opinions and was highly dependent on her iron-willed husband. She was also something of a martyr, building her life around her children. Yet she also disliked everything about raising them. Her explicit horror stories of childbirth and lack of fondness for babies make it seem likely that Paula's first attachment was anything but secure. Later, her mother made Paula her confidante, telling her far more than a child could handle, including a whole catalog of reasons to dislike sex. Indeed, both parents told her all about their feelings for each other, including their sexual intimacies.

Given this background, Paula's "fear of public speaking" was more akin to a basic distrust of other people. She was born sensitive and therefore easily overaroused, yes. But she was also insecurely attached as a child, which makes it far harder for a child to face threatening situations with confidence. Indeed, her mother felt and taught a general irrational fear of (rather than confidence in) people. Finally, Paula's early attempts at speaking her own mind had been met with rage from her father.

Perhaps a final reason for her fear of speaking in public was that she came to feel she knew too much—about her father's possibly incestuous feelings for her and both of her parents' private lives.

These are not easy issues to resolve, but they can be brought into one's consciousness and worked on with a competent therapist. The voices afraid to speak are finally freer. Specific training in social skills might still be needed afterward, but at that point they should really work.

Basic Social Advice for HSPs

Here are some suggestions about some situations that often cause HSPs social discomfort.

When you just have to chitchat. Decide whether you would rather talk or listen. If you want to listen, most people will be glad to talk. Ask a few specific questions. Or just ask, "So what do you do when you aren't at parties?" (Or conferences, weddings, concerts, etc.)

If you want to talk (which puts you in control and keeps you from being bored), plan ahead to plant the topic you enjoy and can go on and on about. Like, "Bad weather, isn't it? At least it makes it easier to stay in and work on my writing project." Of course, the other person will ask what you are writing. Or, "Bad weather—I couldn't train today." Or, "Bad weather—my snakes hate it."

Remembering names. You may forget a person's name because you were distracted and overaroused when you both first met. If you hear a name, try to make it a habit of using it in your next sentence. "Arnold, how nice to meet you." Then use it again within two minutes. Thinking back afterward about who you met might make it stick even longer. But trouble with names just goes with the territory.

Having to make a request. The small ones, for example, for information, ought to be easy. But sometimes we put them on our list of things to do and they just sit there, seeming big and difficult. If possible, make the requests the moment you realize you need to. Or make them in a bunch, when you are feeling in an outgoing mood. For slightly more important requests, make them small again. Think about how quickly it will be over and how little trouble it will be for the person you ask. For even more important requests, make a list of what you want to cover. Begin with being sure you're talking to the right person for your purpose. Making an important request should be rehearsed with someone, having the other person respond to you in every possible way. This does not make it much easier. But you will feel more prepared.

Selling. Frankly, it's not a usual HSP career. But even if you do not sell a commercial product, there are many times in life when we want to sell an idea, ourselves for a job, or maybe our creative work. And what if you believe something could truly help a person or the world at large? In its gentlest form, yours probably, selling is simply sharing with others what you know about something. Once they understand what you think is its value, you can let them make up their own mind.

When money is to be exchanged, HSPs often feel guilty that they're taking "so much" or anything at all. (And if we feel flawed, "What am I really worth, anyway?") Usually we cannot and should not give ourselves or our products away. We need money to continue to make available what we're offering. People understand that, just as you do when you purchase something.

Making a complaint. This can be difficult for an HSP even if it's legitimate. But it is worth practicing; the assertiveness is empowering for those who often feel put down just for being who they are (too young, too old, too fat, too dark-skinned, too sensitive, etc.).

You must be ready, however, for the other's response. Anger is the most arousing emotion for good reasons; it is meant to mobilize us to fight. It is arousing whether it is yours, theirs, or even that of someone you're just observing from a distance.

Being in a small group. Groups, classes, and committees can be a complicated business for HSPs. We often pick up on a great deal that others do not notice. But our desire not to add to our arousal level may keep us quiet. Eventually, though, someone will ask what *you* think. This is an awkward moment but an important one for the group. Habitually quiet HSPs often fail to allow for the fact that the silent person gains more and more influence with time. Besides wanting to give you a chance to speak, the group may unconsciously be worried. Are you in the group or out? Are you sitting there judging them? Are you unhappy and about to leave? If you left, they would be left with these fears, which is why quiet members eventually get so much attention. It may be out of politeness, too, but the fear is always there as well. If you do not join in with just the right enthusiasm, you will receive considerable attention. Then others may well find that their best defense is rejecting you before you reject them. If you do not believe me, try remaining silent in a new group just once and you'll see it all unfold.

Given this energy that always goes to the silent one, if you want to be quieter than others, you need to reassure them that you're not rejecting them or planning to leave the group. Tell them you feel part of the group just by listening. Tell them your positive feelings about the group, if you have any. Tell them you'll speak up when you're ready. Or ask them to ask you again.

You can also decide if you want to explain your sensitivity. But it means you'll have a label that will tend to become self-fulfilling.

Public speaking or performing. This is a natural for HSPs— yes, it is. (I leave you to think of all the reasons why it is *harder* for us.) First, we often feel we have something important to say that others have missed. When others are grateful for our contribution, we feel rewarded, and the next time is easier. Second, we *prepare.* In some situations, as when we go back to check if we turned off the toaster, we can seem "compulsive" to people not as determined as ourselves to prevent all unnecessary surprises (like a burned house). But anyone would be a fool not to "overprepare" for the extra arousal due to an audience. Having prepared best, we succeed most. (Those are two reasons why all the books on shyness can cite so many politicians, performers, and comics who "conquered their shyness, so you can, too.")

The key, again, is to prepare, prepare, prepare. You probably are not afraid to read out loud, so until you feel more comfortable, prepare exactly what you want to say and read it. If doing so is a bit unusual for the situation, explain confidently some good reasons for reading. Then do it with authority.

Reading well also requires preparation and practice. Be sure you use emphasis and can meet any time limits so that you can read slowly.

Later, you can graduate to notes. In a large group I always

make notes before I raise my hand to speak or ask a question just in case my mind goes blank when I'm called on. (I do the same in any situation that makes me overaroused, including doctors' offices.)

Above all, practice as much as possible in front of an audience, replicating, as much as possible, the performance situation. Use the same room at the same time of day, wear the clothes you'll wear, have the sound system set up, and so forth so that there will be fewer new elements to the situation. It is the greatest secret to getting the arousal under control. Once you do, you might just enjoy yourself up there.

I overcame my fear of public speaking by teaching—a good beginning for an HSP. You are giving, you are needed, so your conscientious side takes over. The audience is not expecting entertainment, so anything you can do to make the occasion enjoyable will be gratefully received. And you will find you have real insights once you become bold enough to express them.

Students can sometimes be callous, though. I was lucky to begin at a college where quiet politeness and open expressions of gratitude were the norm. If you can establish the same norms, it will help all of you in your classroom. Some of your students are also afraid to speak up. You can all learn together.

What if others are watching you? Are they really? Maybe you have created an inner audience that you fear. You can carry such an audience around and "project" it (see it where it is not, or at least is not to the degree you imagine).

If others really are watching, can you ask them not to watch? Can you refuse to be watched? Or can you take any pleasure in their watching?

Here is the story of my only belly-dancing lesson. Learning any physical skill in a group is almost impossible for me because the overarousal from being watched wrecks my coordination. I soon fall behind the others and perform even worse.

This time, however, I played a new role. I was the lovable and endearing (that part was important) absentminded woman professor whose head is always in the clouds and has entirely forgotten where she left her body. She has been set down in this hilarious situation to try to learn to belly dance, and everyone enjoys the lesson more by watching her struggles.

The result was that I knew they were watching me, but it was all right. They laughed, but I heard it as loving. Any progress I made was given inordinate praise and recognition. For me, it worked.

Next time you feel watched, try meeting the stares and labeling yourself for them with something you can enjoy. "We poets are never very good with adding" or "There's something about being a natural-born mechanic that makes it hard to draw pictures that don't look like the inside of a broken engine."

Sometimes a situation is awkward by anyone's standards. So you turn red and survive it. It is part of being human. It does not happen that often. Once I was standing in a line at a formal event, and my three-year-old son accidentally pulled my skirt off. Do you have one to top that? Sharing stories afterward is about all we can do.

• **Working With What You Have Learned** •
Reframing Your Shy Moments

Think of three occasions when you felt social discomfort. If possible, choose three rather different situations and ones that you recall in some detail. Reframe them, one at a time, in terms of the two main points of this chapter: (1) Shyness is not your trait—it is a state anyone can feel. (2) The introverted social style is every bit as valuable as the extraverted one.

1. *Think about your response to the event and how you have always viewed it.* Maybe you felt "shy" at a recent party. It was a Friday night after a hard day at work. Dragged along by people at your office, you were hoping to meet someone who would become a real friend. But the others went off, and you ended up in a corner, feeling conspicuous because you were not talking to anyone. So you left early and spent the rest of the night assessing your whole personality, your entire life, and feeling rotten.

2. *Consider your response in the light of what you now know about how your nervous system automatically operates.* Or imagine me explaining it to you: "Hey, give yourself a break! The crowded, noisy room after a busy day, being left alone by your friends, your past experiences with these sorts of parties—it was an avalanche waiting for a cuckoo clock. You like to be introverted. Sure, go to parties, but they should be small ones where you know people. Otherwise, pick out someone who appears as sensitive and deeply interesting as yourself and take off together as soon as possible. That's the HSP way to party. You are not shy or unlovable. You will definitely meet interesting people and have close relationships—you just have to pick and choose your situations."

3. *Is there anything you want to do about this now?* Perhaps there is a friend you could call and arrange to spend some time with, your way.

Answers to
Do You Know the Latest on Overcoming Social Discomfort?

If you were right on a dozen or more, sorry to have bored you. You should write your own book. Otherwise, these answers provide much of what you need to know!

1. *True.* "Negative self-talk" keeps you aroused and makes it hard to listen to the other person.

2. *False.* You, an HSP, may notice shyness in others, but most people don't.

3. *True.* People can reject you for all sorts of reasons having nothing to do with you. If it upsets you, feel that for a moment. Then try to let it go.

4. *True.* Decide to take so many specific, gradual steps per day or week no matter how nervous the first steps make you.

5 *False.* Big steps would be best if you could take those steps. But since you're a little afraid, and also afraid you will fail, you must promise the fearful part of yourself that you'll not go too fast, even as you're firm that the fear is going to be overcome eventually.

6. *False*. The more you rehearse, the less nervous you'll be—which means you'll be more, not less, relaxed and spontaneous.

7. *False*. Body language is always conveying something. A stiff, still body can be interpreted many ways, but most of them won't be positive. Better to let your body move and show some interest, caring, enthusiasm, or sheer liveliness.

8. *True*. It's okay to pry a little. Most people love to talk about themselves and will like your interest and slight boldness.

9. *False*. Stand or sit as close as is appropriate and comfortable, lean forward, uncross your arms and legs, and make frequent eye contact. If eye contact is too arousing, it's okay to look at the other person's nose or ear—people cannot tell the difference. Smile and use other facial expressions (being careful, of course, not to convey more interest than you want to).

10. *False*. Depending on the situation, of course, a brief touch on the shoulder, arm, or hand, especially at parting, just conveys warmth.

11. *False*. In general, a glance at the paper will give you some ideas for conversations and connect you up with the world. Just avoid the depressing stories.

12. *False*. Self-disclosure is important if your goal is to feel some connection and not just pass the time. This doesn't mean you have to reveal deep secrets. Too much self-disclosure too soon will create overarousal, besides seeming inappropriate. Be sure to ask for the other's opinion, too, of course.

13. *True*. For example, someone says they are excited about a new project. You can say, "Wow, I hear how excited you are. That must feel great." By taking the time to reflect that *feeling* before asking about the specifics of the project, you display one of your greatest assets, your sensitivity to feelings. You also encourage the other person to reveal more of his or her inner life, which you would probably prefer to talk about, anyway.

14. *False*. You don't want to gloat, of course. But everyone wants to be talking with someone worthwhile. Take the time to write out some of the best or most interesting things about yourself and think of how you might slip them into conversations. Not "I moved here because I like the mountains" but "I moved here because I am starting a mountain-climbing school"

or "I especially like mountain backdrops for my photographs of rare birds of prey."

15. *True*—with some cautions. When first meeting someone, you don't want to reveal too many needs or flaws. You don't want to seem self-effacing in a submissive way or unaware of appropriate behavior. But there is also something nice in admitting to your human nature if you can convey that you still feel good about yourself. (My favorite line from Captain Picard of *Star Trek: The Next Generation* is, "I have made some *fine* mistakes in my life." It is so humble, wise, and self-confident, all at once.) Certainly if the other person has revealed something painful or embarrassing, it will deepen the conversation considerably if you do the same.

16. *False*. Most people enjoy a *little* conflict. Moreover, maybe the point of the conflict is important to you or reveals something you should know about the other person.

17. *True*. Of course, take your time to be sure of what you feel and be ready for an occasional rejection.

6

Thriving at Work
Follow Your Bliss and Let Your Light Shine Through

Of all the topics I cover in my seminars, vocations, making a living, and getting along at work are the most urgent concerns of many HSPs, which makes sense in some ways, since we don't thrive on long hours, stress, and overstimulating work environments. But much of our difficulty at work, I believe, is our not appreciating our role, style, and potential contribution. This chapter therefore deals first with your place in society and your vocation's place in your inner life. Impractical as these may sound, they actually have great practical significance. Once you understand your true vocation, your own intuition will begin to solve your specific vocational problems. (No book can do that as well for you because none can address your unique situation.)

"Vocation" Is Not "Vacation" Misspelled

A vocation, or calling, originally referred to being called to the religious life. Otherwise, in Western culture one did as is done in most cultures: what one's parents did. In the Middle Ages one was a noble, serf, artisan, and so forth. Because in Christian Indo-European countries the "priestly royal advisor" class that I spoke of in chapter 1 was officially celibate, no one was born into that class. It was the only job to which one had to be called.

With the Renaissance and the rise of the middle class in the cities, people were freer to choose their work. But it is a very recent idea that there is one right job for each person. (It came at about the time of another idea, that there is one right person for each of us to marry.) At the same time, the number of possible vocations has increased greatly, as has the importance and difficulty of matching the right person to the right job.

The Vocation of All HSPs

As I said in chapter 1, the more aggressive cultures in the world, all Western societies included, stem from an original social organization that divided people into two classes, the impulsive and tough warriors and kings on the one hand and the more thoughtful, learned priests, judges, and royal advisors on the other. I also said that the balance of these two classes is important to the survival of such cultures and that most HSPs naturally gravitate to the royal advisor class.

Speaking now of vocation, I don't mean that all HSPs become scholars, theologians, psychotherapists, consultants, or judges, although these are classic royal-advisor-class careers. Whatever our career, we are likely to pursue it less like a warrior, more like a priest or royal counselor—thoughtfully, in all senses. Without HSPs in positions at the top in a society or organization, the warrior types tend to make impulsive decisions that lack intuition, use power and force abusively, and fail to take into account history and future trends. That's no insult to them; it is just their nature. (This was the whole point of Merlin's role in the King Arthur legends; similar figures are in most Indo-European epics.)

One practical implication of belonging to the advisory class is that an HSP can hardly ever have enough education and experience. (I add experience because sometimes HSPs pursue education at the cost of experience.) The greater the variety of our experiences, *within the range of what is reasonable for us* (hang gliding is not required), the wiser our counsel.

The education of HSPs is also important in order to validate our quieter, subtler style. I believe we need to stay well represented in our traditional professions—teaching, medicine, law, the arts, science, counseling, religion—which are increasingly becoming the domain of non-HSPs. That means that these social needs are being met in the warrior style, with expansion and profit the only concern.

Our "priestly" influence has declined partly due to our having lost self-respect. At the same time, the professions themselves are losing respect without our quieter, more dignified contribution.

None of which is meant to imply some terrible plot by the less sensitive. As the world becomes more difficult and stimulating, it is natural for the non-HSPs to thrive, at least at first. But they will not thrive long without us.

Vocation, Individuation, and the HSP

Now, what about your particular vocation? Following the thinking of Carl Jung, I see each life as an *individuation* process, one of discovering the particular question you were put on earth to answer. This question may have been left unfinished by an ancestor, although you must proceed with it in the manner of your own generation. But the question is not easy, or it would not take a lifetime. What matters is that working through it deeply satisfies the soul.

This individuation process is what the scholar of mythology Joseph Campbell referred to when he would exhort students struggling with their vocation to "follow your bliss." He always made it clear that he didn't mean doing whatever is easy or fun at the moment; he meant engaging in work that feels right, that calls you. To have such work (and if we are very fortunate, to be paid for it, too) is one of life's greatest blessings.

The individuation process requires enormous sensitivity and intuition in order to know when you are working on the right question in the right way. As an HSP, you are built for this as a racing yacht is designed to catch the wind. That is, the HSP's vocation in the larger sense is being careful to pursue well his or her vocation in the personal sense.

Jobs and Vocation

But then there is the problem of who will pay HSPs for pursuing our bliss. I usually agree with what Jung always insisted: It is a big mistake to financially support our type. If an HSP is not forced to be practical, he will lose all touch with the rest of the world. She will become an empty windbag no one listens to. But how can one make money and still follow a calling?

One way is to seek the point where the path directed by our greatest bliss crosses that directed by the world's greatest need—that is, what it is willing to pay for. At this intersection you will earn money for doing what you love.

Actually, the relation of a person's vocation to his or her paying job can be quite varied and will change over a lifetime. Sometimes your job is just the way to make money; the vocation is pursued in your spare time. A fine example is Einstein's developing the theory of relativity while he was a clerk in a patent office, happy to have mindless work so he could be free to think about what mattered to him. At other times, we can find or create a job that fulfills our vocation, and the pay will be at least adequate. There may be many possible jobs that do that, or the job that will serve the purpose will change as experience grows and the vocation deepens.

Vocation and the Liberated HSP

Individuation is, above all, about being able to hear your inner voice or voices through all the inner and outer noise. Some of us get caught up in demands from others. These may be real responsibilities or may be the common ideas of what makes for success—money, prestige, security. Then there are the pressures others can bring to bear on us because we are so unwilling to displease anyone.

Eventually, many, if not most, HSPs are probably forced into what I call "liberation," even if it doesn't happen until the second half of life. They tune in to the inner question and the

---

REFRAMING THE CRITICAL POINTS
IN YOUR VOCATIONAL AND WORK HISTORY

Now might be a good time for you to pause and do some re-framing, as you did in previous chapters. Make a list of your major vocational steps or job changes. Write down how you've always understood those events. Perhaps your parents wanted you to be a doctor but you knew it was not for you. Having no better explanation, maybe you accepted the idea that you were "too soft" or "lacked motivation." Now write down what you understand in light of your trait. In this case, that most HSPs are utterly unsuited for the inhuman grind required, unfortunately, by most medical schools.

Does your new understanding suggest something you need to do? In the example, this new understanding of medical school might need to be discussed with one's parents if they still insist on their negative views. Or it might mean finding a medical school that is more humane or studying a related subject, such as physiology or acupuncture, that allows for a different style of professional education.

---

inner voices rather than the questions others are asking them to answer.

Being so eager to please, we're not easy to liberate. We're too aware of what others need. Yet our intuition also picks up on the inner question that must be answered. These two strong, conflicting currents may buffet us for years. Don't worry if your progress toward liberation is slow, for it's almost inevitable.

I don't, however, want to develop some idealized image of a certain kind of HSP you must become. That is precisely *not* liberation. It is finding who you are, not what you think someone else wants you to become.

Knowing Your Own Vocation

Some of you may be struggling with discovering your vocation and feeling a little frustrated that your intuition is not helping you more. Alas, intuition can also stand in your way because it makes you aware of too many inner voices speaking for too many different possibilities. Yes, it would be desirable just to serve others, thinking little of my material gain. But that rules out a lifestyle with time to pursue the finer things in life. And both exclude the actualizing of my artistic gifts. And I have always admired the quiet life, centered in family. Or should it be centered in the spiritual? But that is so up in the air when I admire a life close to the earth. Perhaps I would be happiest working for ecological causes. But then, the needs of humans are so great.

All the voices are strong. Which one is right? If you're flooded with such voices, you will probably have trouble with decisions of all sorts; very intuitive people usually do. But you'll need to develop your decision-making skills for whatever vocation you choose. So start now paring down the choices to two or three. Maybe make a rational list of the pros and cons. Or pretend you have made up your mind definitely one way and live with that for a day or two.

Another problem for HSPs who are very intuitive and/or introverted is that we may not be well informed about the *facts*. We let our hunches guide us. We don't like to *ask*. But gathering concrete information from real people is part of the individuation process for introverted or intuitive people especially.

If you feel you "just cannot," you are revealing the third obstacle to knowing your vocation: low self-confidence. Deep inside you probably know what you really want to do. Of course you may have selected something you cannot possibly succeed at in order to avoid moving along and doing the possible. But maybe you're still confused about what you can and cannot do.

As an HSP you may have great difficulty with certain tasks which, by your culture's standards, are crucial to success in most vocations—perhaps public speaking or performance, perhaps tolerating noise, meetings, networking, office politics, travel. But now you know the specific cause of your difficulty with these and can explore ways around the overarousal they create. So there's really very little that you can't do if you find a way to do it in your own style.

Low self-confidence is very understandable in HSPs however. Many of you have felt flawed. You may have tried so hard to please others that you've been little more than a bridge on other peoples' paths and have been treated just like that, like something underfoot. However, how will you feel going to your grave without having tried?

You say you're afraid of failing. Which inner voice says that? A wise one that protects you? Or a critical one that paralyzes you? For the sake of getting going, assume the voice is right and you'll fail. Forget about the people who tried and succeeded, the theme of so many movies. I know people who have tried and failed. Many of them. They may be out megabucks and megatime, but they're still happier for having tried. Now they're moving on to other goals, wiser for what they learned about themselves and the world. And really, since no effort amounts to a total failure, they're much more confident about themselves than when they were sitting on the sidelines.

Finally, in finding your vocation, do use the excellent books and services on vocational choice. Just keep your sensitivity always in your awareness as an important factor which most vocational counselors don't address.

What Other HSPs Are Doing

Perhaps it would help to hear about the kinds of careers other HSPs have chosen. Of course, we bring our own flair to everything. In my telephone survey, I found, for example, that not many HSPs were salespersons, but one was—of fine wines. Another sold real estate, saying that she used her intuition to match people with homes.

One can imagine other HSPs shaping other jobs—almost any job—into something quiet, thoughtful, and conscientious, as when HSPs said they were teachers, hair stylists, mortgage brokers, pilots, flight attendants, professors, actors, early childhood educators, secretaries, doctors, nurses, insurance agents, professional athletes, cooks, and consultants.

Other jobs seemed obviously suited to HSPs: cabinetmaker, pet groomer, psychotherapist, minister, heavy-equipment operator (noisy but no people), farmer, writer, artist (lots of these), X-ray technician, meteorologist, tree trimmer, scientist, medical transcriber, editor, scholar in the humanities, accountant, and electrician.

While some research has found that so-called shy people make less money, I certainly found plenty of HSPs in positions that sounded well paid—administrators, managers, bankers. Maybe other studies found that their so-called shy respondents were poorly paid because of a quirk in their data similar to mine: Twice as many HSPs as non-HSPs in my study called themselves homemaker, housewife, or full-time parent. (Not all were women.) If you counted them as not earning money, this would certainly lower their income average as a group. But, of course, these people add income to their family by performing services which, if paid for, would be expensive.

HSP "homemakers" find a good niche for themselves, provided they can ignore the culture's undervaluing of their work. In fact, the culture benefits greatly. Research on parenting, for example, continually finds the elusive quality of "sensitivity" to be the key in raising children well.

Turning Vocation Into a Job That Pays

There are good books written just on the topic of turning what you love into what pays you a salary, so as usual I will focus on the aspects especially relevant to us. To make a paying job out of your true vocation often requires creating an entirely new service or profession, and that may mean starting your own business or creating a new job where you already work. That can seem daunting unless you remember to do it in the style of an HSP.

First, throw out the image of everyone getting their work done through networking, knowing the right people, and the like. Some networking is always needed, but there are ways that are effective enough and far more pleasant for an HSP—letters, e-mail, staying in touch with one person who stays in touch with many, taking out to lunch and "debriefing" your extraverted colleague who goes to every conference.

Second, you need to trust some of your advantages. With your intuition, you can study trends and perceive needs or markets before others. If you are excited about something, there is a good chance others are, or could be, once they heard your reasons. If your interest is not too unusual, it should fit into existing jobs. If it is very unusual, you are probably the leading expert, and someone somewhere will need you soon, especially once you share your vision.

Years ago an HSP with a passion for film and video took a job as a librarian and convinced her university that they should have a state-of-the-art film and video department. She saw that these media would be the cutting edge in education, especially continuing education of the public. Everyone sees that now, and her film and video library is the finest in the country.

Self-employment (or being granted full autonomy within a larger organization) is a logical route for HSPs. You control the hours, the stimulation, the kinds of people you will deal with, and there are no hassles with supervisors or coworkers. And, unlike many small or first-time entrepreneurs, you will probably be conscientious about research and planning before you take any risks.

You will have to watch, however, for certain tendencies. If you are a typical HSP, you can be a worry-prone perfectionist. You may be the most hard-driving manager you have ever worked for. You also may have to overcome a certain lack of focus. If your creativity and intuition give you a million ideas, at some point, early, you will have to let most of them go, and you will have to make all kinds of difficult decisions.

If you are an introvert also, you will have to make an extra effort to stay in touch with your public or market. You can always bring in an extravert as a partner or assistant. Indeed, having partners or hiring others to absorb all sorts of excess stimulation is a good idea. But with them as a buffer between you and the world, your intuition will not receive direct input unless you plan for some real contact with those you serve.

Art as Vocation

Almost all HSPs have an artistic side they enjoy expressing. Or they deeply appreciate some form of art. But some of you will pursue the arts as your vocation or even your livelihood. Almost all studies of the personalities of prominent artists insist that sensitivity is central. Unfortunately, that sensitivity is also linked with mental illness.

The difficulty, I believe, is that normally we artists work alone, refining our craft and our subtle creative vision. But withdrawal of any kind increases sensitivity—that is part of why one withdraws. So we are extrasensitive when the time comes to show our work, perform it, explain it, sell it, read reviews of it, and accept rejection or acclaim. Then there's the sense of loss and confusion when a major work is done or a performance is over. The stream of ideas surging up from the unconscious no longer has an outlet. Artists are more skilled at encouraging and expressing that force than understanding its sources or its impact if acted upon.

It is not surprising that artists turn to drugs, alcohol, and medications to control their arousal or to recontact their inner self. But the long-term effect is a body further off balance. Moreover, it is part of the myth or archetype of the artist that any psychological help will destroy creativity by making the artist too normal.

But a highly sensitive artist in particular had better think deeply about the mythology surrounding the artist. The troubled, intense artist is one of the most romantic figures in our culture, now that saints, outlaws, and explorers are on the wane. I recall a creative-writing teacher once listing nearly every famous author on the blackboard and asking us what they had in common. The answer was attempted suicide. I'm not sure the class saw it as a tragedy so much as a romantic aspect of their chosen career. But as a psychologist as well as an artist, I saw a deadly serious situation. How often the value of artists' works has increased once they were declared insane or had committed suicide. While the life of the artistic hero-adventurer especially calls to the young HSP, it can also be a trap quite unconsciously laid by those with mundane lives who allow no time for the artist within and want someone else to be the artist for them, displaying all the craziness they repress in themselves. Much of the suffering of sensitive artists could be prevented by understanding the impact of this alternating of the low stimulation of creative isolation with the increased stimulation of public exposure which I have described. But I am not sure that this understanding will be widely applied until the myth of the unstable artist and the need for it have also been understood.

Service to Others as a Vocation

HSPs tend to be enormously aware of the suffering of others. Often their intuition gives them a clearer picture of what needs to be done. Thus, many HSPs choose vocations of service. And many "burn out."

But to be helpful to others you do not have to work at a job that burns you out. Many HSPs insist on working on the front lines, so to speak, receiving the most stimulation. They would feel guilty staying behind, sending others out to do what to them seems so onerous. But by now I think you can see that some people are, in fact, perfectly suited to the front lines and love it there. So why not let them satisfy their urges? People are also needed behind the front lines, developing strategy from a lookout above the battlefield.

To put it another way, some people like to cook, and some like to wash dishes. For years I could not let others take on the chore of cleaning up after I had enjoyed cooking, one of my favorite pastimes. Then I finally, truly, heard someone when he insisted he *really liked* to clean up—and detested cooking.

One summer I toured Greenpeace's *Rainbow Warrior* and listened to some of the crew's adventures, such as their having been dropped in front of the bow of huge whaling-factory ships or having been in the sights of torpedoes and machine guns for days at a time. For all my love of whales, I would be more trouble than help in those sorts of circumstances. But I knew I could support the effort in other ways.

In short, you do not have to take the job that will create excessive stress and overarousal. Someone else will take it and flourish in it. You do not have to work long hours. Indeed, it may be your duty to work shorter ones. It may be best not to advertise it, but keeping yourself healthy and in your right range of arousal is the first condition for helping others.

A Lesson From Greg

Greg was a highly sensitive schoolteacher who was much loved and respected by his students and colleagues. Yet he came to me to discuss why he was quitting the only profession he had ever wanted, expecting me to verify that teaching was no profession for HSPs. I agreed it was a tough one. But I also think good, sensitive teachers are essential to every sort of happiness and progress, for individuals and society. I could not bear to see such a gem leave the field.

Thinking about it with me, he agreed that teaching was a very logical vocation for a sensitive, caring person. Teaching jobs ought to be designed for them, but in fact the pressures are making it hard for HSPs to stay in teaching. His task, he realized, was to change the job description. Indeed, it was his ethical duty. He would do far more good by refusing to overwork himself than by quitting.

Beginning the very next day, Greg never worked after four in the afternoon. It required applying much of his creativity just to find the right shortcuts. Many were not ideal and truly distressed his conscientious soul. He felt he had to hide his new work habits from his colleagues and principal, although in time they caught on. (The principal approved, seeing that Greg was doing the essential tasks well and feeling happier.) Some of his colleagues copied him; some envied and resented him but could not change their ways. Ten years later, Greg is still a highly successful teacher, and a happy, healthy one.

It is true that even when exhausted you still are providing something to those you serve. But you are out of touch with your deepest strengths, role-modeling self-destructive behavior, martyring yourself, and giving others cause for guilt. And in the end you will want to quit, like Greg, or be forced to by your body.

HSPs and Social Responsibility

None of the above is meant to take more HSPs out of the battle for social justice and environmental sanity. On the contrary, we need to be out there, but in our way. Perhaps some of what goes wrong in government and politics is not so much a product of the Left or Right but the lack of enough HSPs making everyone pause to check the consequences. We have abdicated, leaving things to the more impulsive, aggressive sorts, who do happen to thrive on running for political office and then on running everything else.

The Romans had a great general named Cincinnatus. The legend is that he had wanted to live quietly on his farm but was persuaded twice to return to public life to save his people from military disasters. The world needs to coax more such folks into public positions. But if they don't coax us, we had better volunteer now and then.

HSPs in the World of Business

The business world is undoubtedly undervaluing its HSPs. People who are gifted and intuitive yet conscientious and determined not to make mistakes ought to be treasured employees. But we are less likely to fit into the business world when the metaphors for achievement are warfare, pioneering, and expansion.

Business can also be seen as a work of art requiring an artist, a task of prophecy requiring a visionary, a social responsibility requiring a judge, a job of growing requiring skills like those of a farmer or parent, a challenge of educating the public requiring skills like those of a teacher, and the like.

Companies do vary. Be alert to corporate culture when you take a position or have the chance to influence the corporate culture you are in. Listen to what is said but also use your intuition. Who is admired, rewarded, and promoted? Those who foster toughness, competitiveness, and insensitivity? Creativity and vision? Harmony and morale? Service to the customer? Quality control? HSPs should feel at home in varying degrees in all but the first.

The Gifted HSP in the Workplace

In my opinion, all HSPs are gifted because of their trait itself. But some are unusually so. Indeed, one reason for the idea of "liberated" HSPs was the seemingly odd mixture of traits emerging from study after study of gifted adults: impulsivity, curiosity, the strong need for independence, a high energy level, along with introversion, intuitiveness, emotional sensitivity, and nonconformity.

Giftedness in the workplace, however, is tricky to handle. First, your originality can become a particular problem when you must offer your ideas in a group situation. Many organizations stress group problem solving just because it brings out the ideas in people like you, which are then tempered by others. The difficulty arises when everyone proposes ideas and yours seem so obviously better to you. Yet the others just do not seem to get it. When you go along with the group, you feel untrue to yourself and are unable to commit to the group's results. When you do not, you feel alienated and misunderstood. A good manager or supervisor knows these dynamics and will protect a gifted employee. Otherwise, you may want to offer your giftedness elsewhere.

Second, you can be intensely excited about your work and ideas. In your excitement you may seem to others to take big risks. To you the risks are not great because the outcome is clear. But you're not infallible, and others may take particular pleasure in your failures, even if they're rare. Furthermore, those not understanding this intensity will say you work all the time and probably resent it—you make them look bad. But for you, work is play. *Not* to work would be work. If this is you, you may have to keep your long hours a secret, known only to your supervisor.

Or better, skip the long hours. Try treating even the most positive excitement as a state of overarousal and strive to balance work with recreation. Your work will benefit.

Another result of your intensity is that your restless mind may drive you onward to other projects before you have completed the details of the last, and others may harvest what you planted. Unless you plan around this, which is not usually your style, the result will have to be accepted.

A third aspect of giftedness, emotional sensitivity, can draw you into others' complicated private lives. In the workplace especially this is not a good idea. You want to have some professional boundaries. Especially at work, you need to spend more time with the less sensitive, who can be a great balance to you, and you to them. Develop outside of work the more intense sorts of relationships that offer you the emotional depth you seek.

Also outside of work should be the relationships that offer the safe harbor from the emotional storms created by your sensitivity. Don't look for that among your colleagues, and especially not from your supervisors. You're just too much for them to handle, and they may decide there's "something wrong with you."

A fourth trait of the gifted, intuition, can seem almost magical to others. They don't see what you see—this contrast between the surface and "what's really going on." So as with your unusual ideas, you must decide whether to be honest or go along with things as others see them and feel secretly a bit alienated.

Finally, your giftedness may give you a certain charisma. Others may hope you will guide them rather than their having to guide themselves. It is a flattering temptation, but you can only end up seeming to have stolen their freedom, which in a sense you would have.

From your side, you may find that others seem to have little to offer in return. Initial sharing may be followed by a sense of disappointment. But giving up on others leads to more alienation, whereas in fact you need others.

One solution to all of this is not to insist that your gifts all be expressed at work. Express yourself through private projects and art, schemes for future or parallel self-employment, and through life itself.

In other words, expand your use of your giftedness beyond producing the most noticed ideas at work. Use it to attain greater self-insight and to gain wisdom about human beings in groups and organizations. When that is your goal, sitting back and observing are okay. So is participating as an ordinary person sometimes, not a gifted one, and seeing how that feels.

Finally, stay in good contact with many kinds of other people, at work and elsewhere, accepting that no one person can relate to all of you. Indeed, accepting the loneliness that goes with giftedness may be the most freeing, empowering step of all. But also accept its opposite, that there's no need to feel isolated, for everyone is gifted in some way. And then there's the opposite truth: No one, including yourself, is special in the sense of being exempted from the universals of aging and death.

Seeing That Your Trait Is Properly Valued

I hope by now that you can imagine the many ways in which being an HSP can be an asset in your work, whether you are self-employed or working for another. But I've found that it takes considerable work before HSPs can undo past negative ideas about their trait and truly value it. You cannot possibly convince anyone else of its value if you're not convinced yourself. So please do the following, without fail.

List every asset that might possibly belong to an HSP. Follow the rules of brainstorming and accept all ideas without criticism. Don't worry if non-HSPs have some of the same assets. It's enough if we have them more or also. And use every strategy: logical deduction from the basic trait; thinking about your growing image of the typical HSP; considering the HSPs you know and admire; thinking about yourself; looking through this book. Your list should be *long*. It's very long when HSPs do it as a group—with my pushing them. So keep at it until yours is substantial.

Now do two things: Write a little speech you might use during an interview and also a more formal letter, and in both of them express some of your assets, embedding your trait of sensitivity among them in a way that quietly educates your employer.

Here is part of a possible script (which would be a little informal for a letter):

> And besides my ten years of experience with young children, I have considerable knowledge of graphic arts and practical experience with layout. In all of this, I am aware of the unique contribution of my personality and temperament—I am one of those persons who is extremely

conscientious, thorough, and concerned about doing a good job.

At the same time, I think I have a pretty amazing imagination. I've always been seen as highly creative (along with earning excellent grades in school and having a high IQ). My intuition about my work has always been one of my greatest strengths, including being able to spot possible potential trouble or errors.

Yet I am not one to cause a fuss. I like to keep things calm around me. Indeed, you should know I work best when I'm feeling calm, when things around me are quiet. So most people find me especially comfortable to work with, although I myself am just as happy working alone as with a few others. My independence in that regard, my ability to work well alone and on my own, has always been another one of my strengths. . . .

Training

Training situations can be very overarousing because you tend to perform worse when being observed or when overaroused in any other way—for example, being given too much information at once, having too many people around talking or straining to learn, imagining all the dire consequences of failing to remember something.

If possible, try to train yourself. Take home the instruction manuals or stay after hours and work on your own. Or arrange to be trained one-on-one, preferably by someone who puts you at ease. Ask to be shown a step, then to be left to practice it alone. Next, allow someone else to watch you who is not a supervisor, someone who doesn't make you so nervous.

Being Physically Comfortable on the Job

Because you're more sensitive, you don't need extra discomfort or stress around you. A situation may have been deemed safe but still be stressful for you. Likewise, others may have no problem with fluorescent lights, low levels of machine noise, or chemical odors, but you do. This is a very individual matter, even among HSPs.

If you do have to complain, think realistically about what you're up against. If you still want to go ahead, mention the efforts you've made on your own to solve the situation. Emphasize your productivity and accomplishments but that you can do still better when this problem is resolved (if that's realistic).

Advancing in an Organization

Research on "shy" people claims that they tend to be paid too little and to work below their competence level. I suspect this is true of many HSPs, although it's sometimes our choice. But if you want to be advancing and are not or if layoffs are being considered and you don't want to be among them, you have to pay attention to strategy.

Often HSPs don't like to "play politics." But that in itself can make us subject to suspicion. We're so easily misperceived in all sorts of ways, especially if we spend less time with others in our workplace or do not share our thoughts with them. We can seem aloof, arrogant, odd. If we're also not pushy, we can seem uninterested or weak. Often these are utterly unwarranted projections. But you have to be watchful for these dynamics and plan to defuse the projections.

When it is appropriate, casually (or formally) let others know your good feelings about them and the organization. You may think your positive feelings are obvious, but they may not be if you are low key and the others are not very aware. Consider whether you also need to talk more openly about what you think you contribute, where you would like to see yourself eventually in the organization, and how long you are willing to wait to see it happen.

Meanwhile, be sure that you will not be taken for granted when the next promotions are handed out by writing down once a week all your latest contributions to your organization, plus any achievements elsewhere in your profession or your life. Be very detailed. At least you'll be aware of them and more likely to mention them, but if possible, show a summary of these achievements to your supervisor at your next review.

If you resist doing this task or a month from now find you still haven't done it, think deeply about why. Does it feel like bragging? Then consider the possibility that you do your organization and supervisor a major disservice by not reminding them of your value. Sooner or later you'll feel dissatisfied and want to move on, or you'll be lured away by the competition, or you'll be laid off while someone less competent is kept. Do you wish others would notice your value without your having to remind them? That is a common desire stemming from childhood that is seldom fulfilled in this world.

Or, are you in fact accomplishing very little? Do you care? Maybe you need to keep a record of the accomplishments that do matter to you—trails biked, books read, conversations had with friends. If something besides work takes most of your energy, it may be what you most enjoy. Is there any way to be paid for doing that? And if a responsibility such as children or an aging parent is taking up your time, feel pride in meeting that responsibility. List this as an accomplishment, too, even though it cannot be shared with most employers.

Finally, if you are not advancing or feel "someone is out to get you," it's quite possible that you're just not savvy enough.

Bette Meets Machiavelli

Bette was an HSP who saw me in psychotherapy. One of the issues she often brought to me was her frustration at work. Therapists can never know for certain what's going on in situations we only hear one side of. But it sounded as if Bette was doing a fine job at work but was never promoted.

Then, at one review, she was criticized for the very sorts of behaviors that seemed to us would be valued by most supervisors. Very reluctantly, Bette began to wonder if her supervisor was "out to get her." The supervisor had a distressed personal life, and Bette had been warned by the last supervisor she might "stab her in the back."

Most of the other employees got along all right with the new supervisor, but Bette's intuition told her they were going out of their way to placate their boss because they feared her. Being much older, Bette had just seen her as immature but not a threat. But Bette was also dedicated and conscientious. She often received praise from visitors implying that she was the most competent of those they had met in her department. She thought she had nothing to fear, but she had overlooked her supervisor's envy. But then Bette didn't like to think anything negative of anyone.

Eventually, Bette took the step of asking someone in personnel to let her see her file (an appropriate move in this organization) and found that her supervisor had been putting in notes about her that were simply untrue, while positive information Bette had asked to be included was missing.

Bette finally had to admit she was in a power struggle with her supervisor, but she didn't know what to do. In particular, she said over and over that she didn't want to stoop to thinking like this nemesis.

The important issue to me became helping Bette see why she had been targeted. Indeed, she admitted it wasn't the first time in her work history. I suspected that in this case it was because, untrue as it was, she seemed aloof, superior, and therefore threatening to an insecure younger person. But underlying that was Bette's failure, even refusal, to see the conflict coming.

Here and in other work settings in the past, Bette made herself an easy target by preferring to be "separate from the herd." Like the many HSPs who are introverted, she preferred to go to work, do her job well, and go home without adding to her stimulation by socializing. She often told me, "I don't enjoy gossiping like the others." One effect of this style was that it kept her too uninformed about what was going on at an informal level. She needed to haul out her persona and do some chatting simply to protect herself, to know what was up, to "have some friends at court." A second effect was that, in a sense, she was rejecting the others, or so they felt. At any rate, they felt no urge to come to her aid, and thus the supervisor had known she would be safe to act against Bette.

Another understandable mistake that Bette made, so typical of an HSP, was to be totally unaware of her supervisor's "shadow" or less desirable aspects. In fact, Bette tended to idealize superiors. She expected only kindness and protection from someone in charge. When she didn't receive it, in this case she went to the person over her supervisor for help. But she thought it "only right" to let her supervisor know what she was doing! The supervisor, of course, beat her to it, turning the higher-up against Bette. Another overidealized authority had behaved, predictably, like a mortal.

When I asked Bette to be more savvy, more "political," at first she felt I was asking her to dirty herself. But I knew such purity had to be casting a long shadow, and eventually she encountered in her dreams an angry, fenced-in goat, then a tough little "street fighter," and finally a rather sophisticated businesswoman. In getting to know these dream figures, each added something to Bette that she had in fact possessed but hadn't used and was vehemently repressing as unacceptable. They taught her how to be at least a little suspicious of everyone, especially those she was idealizing (including me).

As she advanced in her self-reflection—much of it obviously requiring considerable courage and intelligence—Bette admitted that she had deep doubts about the motivations of everyone. But she was always trying to suppress these suspicious as one more unsavory aspect of herself. By becoming aware of them and checking them out, she found she could trust some people more, not less, and her own less conflicted intuitions most of all. You will have a chance to meet your own inner power broker at the end of this chapter.

Regrets—Evitable and Inevitable

It is hard to face all the things we're not going to get to do in this lifetime. But that's part of being mortal. How wonderful if we can make even a little progress on the question life has asked us. It is even more wonderful if we find a way to be paid while doing this. And nearly a miracle if we're able to work on that in the company of others, in harmony and mutual appreciation. If these are your blessings, do appreciate them. If you have not achieved them yet, I hope you now have a sense of how you might.

On the other hand, you may be having to come to terms with a vocation that was often blocked by other responsibilities or by your culture's failure to appreciate you. If you can reach a place of peace about this, then you may well be the wisest of us all.

```
┌─────────────────────────────────────────────────────┐
│                                                       │
│        • Working With What You Have Learned •         │
│            Meeting Your Machiavelli                   │
│                                                       │
└─────────────────────────────────────────────────────┘
```

Machiavelli, a Renaissance advisor to Italian princes, wrote with brutal frankness about how to get ahead and stay ahead. His name is associated, perhaps too much, with manipulating, lying, betraying, and all the rest of the conniving that goes on "at court." I do not recommend that you become Machiavellian, but I do assert that the more his qualities repulse you, the more you need to be aware of their lurking in yourself and others. The more you claim to know nothing about such things, the more you will be troubled by secret conniving in yourself or others.

In short, somewhere inside you there is a Machiavelli. Yes, he is a ruthless manipulator; but no prince, especially a kind one, would stay in power long without at least one advisor with as remorseless a point of view as that of the enemies a prince will surely have. The trick is to listen well but keep Machiavelli in his place.

Maybe you already know this part of yourself. But give that aspect flesh. Try to imagine how he or she looks, what he or she says, his or her name. (It probably will not be Machiavelli.) And then have a chat. Let him or her tell you all about the organization where you work. Ask who's doing what to get ahead and who's out to get you. Ask what *you* could do to get ahead. Let that voice speak for a while.

Later, being very careful to keep your values and good character intact, think about what you learned. For example, were you told that someone is using unfair tactics and hurting you and the organization in the process? Is this inner voice being paranoid, or is it something you have known but didn't want to admit? Are there any wise moves you can make to counter these or at least protect yourself?

7

Close Relationships
The Challenge of Sensitive Love

This chapter is a love story. It begins with how HSPs fall in love and into loving friendship. Then it helps with the rewarding work of keeping that love alive, HSP style.

HSP Intimacy—So Many Ways We Do It

Cora is sixty-four, a homemaker and author of children's books. She has been married once, to her "only sexual partner," and informed me firmly that she is "very content with this aspect of my life." Dick, her husband, is "anything but an HSP." But each enjoys what the other brings to the marriage, especially now that the rough spots are worked out. For example, over the years she learned to resist his wanting her to share his pleasure in adventure movies, downhill skiing, and attending Superbowls. He goes with friends.

Mark, in his fifties, is a professor and poet, an expert on T. S. Eliot. He is unmarried and lives in Sweden, where he teaches English literature. Friendships are central to Mark's life. He has become skilled at finding those few souls in the world like himself and cultivating deep relationships with them. I suspect they consider themselves very fortunate.

As for romance, Mark remembers intense crushes even as a child. As an adult, his relationships have been "rare but overwhelming. Two are always there. Painful. There is no end, although the door is closed." But then I recall his tone becoming wry. "But I have a rich fantasy life."

Ann also recalls being intensely in love as a child. "There was always someone; it was a quest, a search." She married at twenty and had three children in seven years. There was never enough money, and as the tensions mounted, so did her husband's abusiveness. After he hit her hard a few times, she knew she had to leave, had to grow up and somehow support herself.

Over the years there were other men in Ann's life, but she never married again. At fifty, she says her quest for the "magical other" has ended at last. Indeed, when I asked her if there were special ways she had organized her life to accommodate her sensitivity, her first response was "I finally got men out of my life, so I'm not tried by *that* anymore." Close friendships with women, however, and close ties to her children and sisters give Ann great happiness.

Kristen, the student we met in chapter 1, was yet another with intense crushes throughout her childhood. "Each year I would pick out one. But as I got older and it became more serious, especially when I was actually with them, I wanted them to leave me alone. Then there was the one I went to Japan for. He was so important to me, but that's ending, thank goodness. Now that I'm twenty, I'm not so into boys. I want to figure out who I am first." Kristen, so worried about her sanity, is definitely sounding very sane.

Lily, thirty, spent a promiscuous youth in rebellion against her strict Chinese mother. But two years before, when Lily's health failed due to her wild life, she finally realized she was miserable. During our interview she even began to wonder whether she had chosen this overstimulating life in order to distance herself from a family she had seen as boring and lacking American vigor. At any rate, when she regained her health, she entered a relationship with a man she saw as even more sensitive than herself. At first, they were merely friends; like her family, he seemed boring. But something gentle and thoughtful grew between them. They moved in with each other, but she didn't rush into marriage.

Lynn is in her twenties and recently married Craig, with whom she shares a common spiritual path and deep, new love. But one issue between them is how much sex they want. In keeping with the spiritual tradition he was part of, which she embraced upon meeting him, Craig was abstaining from sexuality. At the time of our interview, he had changed his mind, and she was the one who wanted to follow this tradition and abstain. The compromise that pleases them both thus far has been lovemaking that is "infrequent" (once or twice a month) but "very special."

These examples illustrate the richly diverse manner in which HSPs fulfill their very human desire to be close to others. Although I have no large-scale statistical data yet to confirm this, it is my impression from my interviews that HSPs vary more than others in the kinds of arrangements they work out in this area, choosing being single more often than the general population, or firmer monogamy, or close relationships with friends or family members rather than romance. True, this marching to a different love song may be due to HSPs' different personal histories and needs. But then necessity is the mother of invention.

With all this diversity, we HSPs still have some common issues to consider regarding our close relationships, all arising from our special ability to perceive the subtle and our greater tendency to become overaroused.

HSPs and Falling in Love

In respect to falling in love, my research suggests that we HSPs do fall in love harder than others. That can be good. For example, research shows that falling in love tends to increase anyone's sense of competence and the sheer breadth of the person's self-concept. When in love, one feels bigger, better. On the other hand, it is good to know some of the reasons we fall in love harder that have little or nothing to do with the other—just in case there are times when we would rather not.

Before we begin, however, write down what happened to

you on one or more occasions when you fell deeply in love. Then you can watch to see if any of what I describe was operating in your case.

I realize that some HSPs never seem to fall in love. (They usually have the avoidant-attachment style I have described earlier.) But saying I will never love is like saying it will never rain in the desert. Anyone who knows the desert will tell you that when it does rain, watch out. So if you think you never fall in love hard, you might just read on, anyway—in case of rain.

When It Is Too Intense

Before turning to the kind of powerful falling in love or friendship that can lead to a wonderful relationship, you might be interested in the rarer but more notorious case of overwhelming, impossible love. It can happen to anyone, but it seems to happen a little more often to HSPs. And since it is often a miserable experience for both parties, some information may be helpful should you stumble into such a situation.

This sort of love is usually unrequited. The failure to be loved back can be the very cause of the intensity. If a real relationship could develop, the absurd idealization would cool as one came to know the beloved better, warts and all. But the intensity can also stop the relationship. Extremely intense love is often rejected by the beloved just because it is so demanding and unrealistic. The one being loved often feels smothered and not really loved at all in the sense that his or her feelings are being considered. Indeed, it can seem as if the lover has no *real* understanding of the loved one, only some impossible vision of perfection. Meanwhile, the lover may abandon everything for the dream of perfect happiness which the other alone can fulfill.

How does such love happen? There is no one answer, but some strong possibilities. Carl Jung held that the habitually introverted (most HSPs) turn their energy inward to protect their treasured inner life from being overwhelmed by the outer world. But Jung pointed out that the more successfully introverted you are, the more pressure builds in the unconscious to compensate for the inward turning. It is as if the house becomes filled with bored (but probably gifted) kids who eventually find their way out the back door. This pent-up energy often lands on one person (or place or thing), which becomes all-important to the poor upended introvert. You have fallen intensely in love, and it really has less to do with the other person and more to do with how long you have delayed reaching out.

Many movies and novels have captured this kind of love. The classic film example might be *The Blue Angel*, about a professor falling in love with a dance-hall girl. The book classic might be Hermann Hesse's *Steppenwolf*, about a highly introverted older man meeting a provocative young dancer and her passionate, sensuous crowd. In both cases, the protagonists are hopelessly drawn into a world of love, sex, drugs, jealousy, and violence—all the stimulation and stuff of the senses which their intuitive, introverted self had once rejected and knew nothing about handling. But women experience it, too, as in some of the novels of Jane Austen or Charlotte Brontë, in which controlled, introverted, bookish women are swept away by love.

No matter how introverted, you are a social being. You cannot escape your need and spontaneous desire to connect with others even if your conflicting urge to protect yourself is very strong. Fortunately, once you have been out there a bit and in love a few times, you will realize that no one is that perfect. As they say, there are always other fish in the sea. The best protection against falling in love too intensely is being more in the world, not less. Once you reach a balance, you may even find that certain people actually help you stay calm and secure. So since you are going to be soaked someday, anyway, you might as well dive in with the rest of us now.

Look back at your own story of falling in love or friendship. Did it follow a long period of isolation?

Human and Divine Love

Another way to fall in love hard is to project one's spiritual yearnings onto another person. Again, mistaking your human beloved for a divine beloved would be corrected if you could live with that person for a while. But when we cannot, the projection can be surprisingly persistent.

The source of such love has to be something pretty big, and I think it is. As Jungians would put it, we each possess an inner helpmate who is meant to lead us to the deepest inner realms. But we may not know that inner helpmate very well, or more often, we mistakenly project him or her onto others in our desperate desire to find that one we need so much. We want that helpmate to be real, and of course, while things can be very real that are entirely inner, that is an idea that can be hard to learn.

Jungian tradition holds that for a man this inner helpmate is usually a feminine soul or anima figure and for a woman it is usually a masculine spiritual guide or animus. So when we fall in love, we are often really falling in love with that inner anima or animus who will take us where we long to go, to paradise. We see the anima or animus in flesh-and-blood people with whom we hope to share an earthly, sensual paradise (usually including a tropical cruise or a weekend of skiing at Vale—advertisers are happy to help us project these archetypes onto the outer world). Don't get me wrong. Flesh and blood and sensuality are all great. They just aren't going to substitute for the inner figure or the inner goal. But you can see what a confusion divine love can make when two mortals set out to love each other in a human way.

But maybe the confusion is okay, for a time, at some point in one's life. As the novelist Charles Williams wrote, "Unless devotion is given to the thing which must prove false in the end, the thing that is true in the end cannot enter."

Overwhelming Love and Insecure Attachment

As we already have discussed, HSPs' relationships to everyone and everything are greatly affected by the nature of their childhood attachments to their first caretakers. Since only about 50 to 60 percent of the population enjoyed a secure attachment in childhood (a shocking statistic, really), those of you HSPs who tend to be very cautious about close relationships (avoidant), or very intense in them (anxious-ambivalent), can still consider yourselves quite normal. But your responses to relationships are powerful because there is so much unfinished business in that department.

Often those with insecure attachment styles try very hard to avoid love in order not to be hurt. Or maybe it just seems like a waste of time and you try not to think about why you see it differently than most of the world. Yet no matter how hard you try, someday you may find yourself trying again to get it right. Someone appears, and it seems safe enough to risk an attachment. Or there is something about the other person that reminds you of some safe person who passed too briefly through your life. Or something inside is getting desperate enough to take another chance. Suddenly you attach, as Ellen did.

Although Ellen had never felt as close to her husband as he would have liked, she had thought she was fairly happily married at the time that she finished her first large sculpture. But after the yearlong project was completed and shipped out, she found herself feeling oddly empty. She rarely shared such feelings with anyone, but one day she slipped into talking about it with an older, stout woman who wore her long gray hair in a bun.

Until that conversation, Ellen had never noticed the woman, who was considered something of an eccentric in Ellen's community. But the older woman happened to have been trained as a counselor and knew how to listen empathically. The next day, Ellen found herself thinking about the woman all the time. She wanted to be with her again. The woman was flattered to have such a glamorous artist as a friend, and the relationship bloomed.

But for Ellen it was more than friendship. It was a strangely desperate need. To her own amazement, it soon became sexualized for both of them, and Ellen's marriage grew turbulent. For the sake of her husband and children, she decided she wanted to break off the relationship, but she could not. It was utterly impossible.

After a year of stormy scenes among the three of them, Ellen began to find intolerable faults in the other woman—mainly, a violent temper. The relationship ended, and Ellen's marriage survived. But she never understood what had happened to her until years later in psychotherapy.

In the course of exploring her early childhood, Ellen learned from her older sister that their busy mother had had little time or inclination for babies. Ellen had been raised by a series of baby-sitters. Ellen could remember one, a Mrs. North, who later was her first Sunday school teacher. Mrs. North had been extraordinarily kind and warm; indeed, little Ellen had thought Mrs. North was God. And Mrs. North had been a stout, homely woman who wore her gray hair in a bun.

Ellen had grown up unconsciously programmed. First, she was programmed to avoid attaching to anyone, since her caretakers had changed so often. But at a deeper level she was programmed to watch for someone like Mrs. North and then to risk everything to be secure once again, as she had been for a few hours each day in infancy with the actual Mrs. North.

We all go out programmed in some way: to please and cling to the first kind person who promises to love and protect us; to find the perfect parent and worship that person totally; to be extremely careful of attaching to anyone; to attach to someone just like the person who did not want us the first time (to see if we can change them this time) or who insisted we never grow up; or just to find another safe harbor like the one we enjoyed as children.

Look back over your love history. Can you make sense of it in terms of your early attachment? Did you bring to it intense needs left over from childhood? To have some of those needs left over is to be supplied with the normal "glue" of adult closeness. But we can ask only so much from a fellow adult. Anyone who really wants an adult with a child's needs (e.g., a need to never have the other out of sight) has something unresolved going on from the past, too. Psychotherapy is about the only place where one can wake up to what was lost, mourn the rest, and learn to control the overwhelming feelings.

But what about normal romantic love, which temporarily makes life so wonderfully nonnormal?

The Two Ingredients for Mutual Love

In studying hundreds of accounts of falling in love (and friendship) written by people of all ages, my husband (a social psychologist with whom I have conducted considerable research on close relationships) and I found two themes to be most common. First, obviously the person falling in love liked certain things about the other very much. But also Cupid's arrow usually pierced their armor only at the moment when they found out that the other person liked them.

These two factors—liking certain things about the other and finding out the other person likes you—give me an image of a world in which people walk around admiring each other, just waiting for someone else to confess their love. This image is important for HSPs to keep in mind because one of the most arousing moments in one's life is either confessing or receiving a declaration of affection. But if we want to be close to someone, we must do it! We must endure all the risks of getting closer and being close, including speaking up. Cyrano de Bergerac learned that lesson, and so did Capt. John Smith.

How Arousal Can Make Anyone Fall In Love

A man meets an attractive woman on a flimsy suspension bridge swaying in the wind high over a mountain gorge. Or he meets the same woman on a sturdy wooden bridge a foot above a rivulet. In which place is the man more likely to be romantically attracted to the woman? According to the results of an experiment done by my husband and a colleague (which is now famous in social psychology), there will be far more falling in love on the suspension bridge. Other research has found that we are more likely to be romantically attracted to someone else if we are aroused in any way, even from running in place or listening to a tape of a comedy monologue.

There are several theories about why arousal of any kind can lead to attraction if someone appropriate is at hand. One reason might be that we always try to attribute arousal to something, and if we can, we would especially like to attribute it to feeling attraction. Or it may be that high but tolerable levels of arousal are associated in our minds with self-expansion and excitement, and these in turn are associated with being attracted to someone. This discovery has interesting implications for HSPs. If we are more easily aroused than others, we will on average be more likely to fall in love (and perhaps harder as well) when we're with someone who's attractive.

Look back at your own love history. Did you go through an arousing experience before or while meeting someone you've loved? For that matter, after going through some ordeal, have you ever felt strongly attached to the people who went through it with you? Or to doctors, therapists, family members, or friends who've helped you deal with a crisis or with pain? Think of all the friendships formed in high school and college, while everyone is experiencing so many new, intensely arousing situations. Now you understand why.

Two Other Reasons HSPs Are More Prone to Love

Another source of falling in love can be doubts about one's own self-worth. For example, one study found that women students whose self-esteem had been lowered (by something they were told during the experiment) were more attracted to a potential male partner than those whose self-esteem had not been compromised. Similarly, people are especially likely to fall in love after a breakup.

As I have emphasized, HSPs are prone to low self-esteem because they are not their culture's ideal. So sometimes they consider themselves lucky if someone wants them at all. But love on this basis can backfire. Later, you may realize that the person you fell in love with was very much your inferior or simply not your type.

Look back at your own love history. Has low self-esteem played a role?

The main solution, of course, is to build up your self-esteem by reframing your life in terms of your sensitivity, doing some inner work on whatever else lowered your confidence, and getting out in the world on your terms and proving to yourself that you're okay. You'll be surprised how many people will love you deeply just *because* of your sensitivity.

Then there is the very human tendency to enter or persist in a close relationship out of sheer fear of being alone, overaroused, or faced with new or frightening situations. I think this is a major reason why research finds that one-third of college students fall in love during their first year away from home. We're all social animals, feeling safer in each other's company.

But you don't want to put up with just anyone out of fear of being alone. The other will sense it eventually and be hurt or take advantage of you. You both deserve better.

Look back over your love history. Did you fall in love out of fear of being alone? I believe that HSPs ought to feel that they can survive at least for a while without a close, romantic relationship. Otherwise, we are not free to wait for a person we really like.

If you cannot live alone yet, it's nothing to be ashamed of. Most likely something damaged your trust in the world, or someone wanted you not to develop that trust. But if it's practical, do try living on your own. Should it seem too difficult, work it through with a therapist to support and coach you—someone who will not abuse or abandon you and who has no interest in the outcome except seeing you self-sufficient.

Nor do you have to be *totally* alone. There are some great other comforts available, like good friends, loyal family members, the roommate who happens to be home and ready to go to a movie, big-hearted dogs, and cuddly cats.

Deepening a Friendship

HSPs in particular should never underestimate the advantages of deep friendships. They do not have to be so intense, complicated, or exclusive as romantic relationships. Some conflicts can be left to work themselves out. Annoying traits can be ignored a little longer, maybe for the entire life of the relationship. And in friendship you can check out what is possible with another person without such lasting harm being done if you're rejected or decide to reject the other. Occasionally, a romantic relationship even arises from what started as a friendship.

To deepen a friendship (or family relationship), use a little of what you now know about the healthy reasons people fall in love. Tell the other person you like them. And don't hesitate to share an intense experience—go through an ordeal together, work on a project, be a team. It's hard to get close if all you do is sometimes go to lunch together. In the process of your shared experience, you'll also share self-disclosures. When these are mutual and appropriate, they're the fastest route to closeness.

Finding the Right Other

Actually, often it's the non-HSP who finds us. At one time most of my friends were extraverted, not-so-sensitive (but certainly nice and empathic) people who seemed a bit proud to have discovered me, the reclusive writer. These were good friendships for me, bringing me perspectives and opportunities I would not have encountered on my own. For many reasons, however, it's always good for HSPs to be close to some other HSPs, too.

One excellent tactic for finding other HSPs is to ask your extraverted friends to introduce you to others they know who are like you. Otherwise, you can find an HSP by thinking like one. No happy hours, gyms, and cocktail parties. At the risk of fostering stereotypes, HSPs might be a little more likely to show up—just as examples—at adult education courses, Audubon or Sierra Club outings, Unitarian or Quaker churches, study groups for Catholics or Jews wanting to know about the deeper or more esoteric aspects of their religions, art classes, lectures on Jungian psychology, poetry readings, Mensa gatherings, symphonies, opera and ballet performances, the lectures before those performances, and spiritual retreats of all sorts. That list should get you started.

Once you have found another HSP, you can fall into conversation easily by saying something about the noise or stimulation where you are. Then you can agree to get away, take a walk, find some quiet together, and you're on your way.

HSPs at the Dance

I have said and will say again that HSPs need close relationships and can be very skilled in them. Still, we have to watch for that side of us that wants to be introverted, to protect ourselves. Often we can find ourselves in the following sort of dance:

First we want to be close, so we give out all the signs that invite closeness. Then someone responds. They want to see more of us, get to know us, maybe touch us. Then we back off. The other person is patient for a while, then backs off, too. We feel alone and put out the signs again. That person or another one tries again. We are so glad—for a while. Then we feel overwhelmed.

Step forward, step back, step forward, step back, until you both are tired of the dance.

Getting the right balance between distance and closeness can seem impossible. If you try to please others, you'll lose track of your own needs. If you only try to please yourself, you'll often fail to express very much love and will not make the compromises that relationships require.

Having a relationship with someone like yourself is one solution; however, you can both end up so out of touch that the two of you will dance on opposite sides of the room. On the other hand, a relationship with someone wanting to be more involved and stimulated can turn the dance into an ordeal. I don't know the answer for you. But I know HSPs must stay at the dance and neither give up nor wish it would end. At its best, it is a flow which balances the needs of each and acknowledges that feelings fluctuate. You simply become more graceful with time, you step on fewer toes. So let's look closer at your closest relationships.

Close Relationships Between Two HSPs

Being close to another HSP should have great advantages. Each feels so understood, at last. There ought to be fewer conflicts about how much is too much, about spending time alone. You probably enjoy similar pastimes.

The disadvantages could be that you are more likely to have difficulty doing the same sorts of tasks, whether asking for directions from strangers or spending a day shopping. So these things tend not to get done. Also, if you both tend to keep your distance from others, there will be no one to force the two of you to be more intimate, to face your insecurity. A distant relationship might feel okay to both of you, but have an arid quality that would be absent in a relationship with a person who asked for greater closeness. But this is really up to both of you. Popular psychology notwithstanding, if you are both happy, there is no law, natural or human, that says you have to be intimate and intensely sharing in order to be content.

Finally, it is my impression that, in general, whenever two people in a relationship have similar personalities, their understanding of each other is strong and their conflicts are minimal. That can be boring. But it can also create a safe, quiet harbor from which you each can journey, either out into the world or inwardly. Returning to each other, you can share the excitement vicariously of each other's experiences.

When the Other Is Not As Highly Sensitive

Any difference in a pair spending lots of time together will tend to grow. If you are a little better at map reading or bank statements, you will do it all the time for both of you and become the expert. The trouble is, when left alone with a map or a bank wanting to know what is going on with your account, the one who "can't" really feels foolish and helpless. (Although on occasion one is surprised to find that, thanks to watching the other, he or she knows far more than both thought.)

Everyone has to decide for themselves the areas in which it is good enough to be dumb but paired with an expert, and those in which it is not okay at all to be a dummy. Self-respect is an issue, and in heterosexual couples I think gender stereotypes also tend to take hold. Maybe you feel uncomfortable doing things that someone of your gender does not usually do. Or maybe, like myself and my husband, you feel uncomfortable letting those stereotypes stand. (I like knowing how to change a tire, he likes knowing how to change a diaper.)

This specialization is most problematic and tempting to ignore when it happens around psychological "work." One member feels the emotions for both; the other stays cool. Or one feels only good feelings, gaining no resilience in dealing with grief, fear, and so forth. The other gets stuck with all the anxiety and depression.

When it comes to your trait, whoever is even a little less sensitive becomes the expert in doing anything that might overarouse the more sensitive one. (Or if you are both sensitive, you may specialize in different areas.) There are advantages for both parties. There is more calm, and one person feels helpful, the other, helped. Indeed, the less sensitive person may come to feel indispensable and find this all too reassuring.

Meanwhile, the more sensitive one does all the attending to the subtle for both. Some of this may seem less crucial—to have creative new ideas, know why you are living, deepen communications, appreciate beauty. But if there is a strong bond between the two, it is probably because the less sensitive person truly needs and values what, you, the more sensitive one contributes. Without it, all the efficient doing of things would be for nothing and probably be much less effective as well. Sometimes, the more sensitive person may even sense all of this and feel indispensable and all too superior.

In a relationship that has lasted for many years, both partners may become quite content with their particular distribution of tasks. However, in the second half of life especially, one or both may become dissatisfied. The desire to be whole, to experience the half of life one did not specialize in, can become more compelling than the desire to be efficient or avoid failure. Moreover, if this specialization has become extreme, as it can in a long marriage, each person may feel so dependent on the other that they may lose any sense of choice about being in the relationship. In the case of sensitivity, one of you may feel unable to survive in the outer world; the other may feel unable to find the way inward. At that point, the glue is no longer love but a lack of any alternative.

The solution is obvious but not easy. Both must agree that the situation must change, even if for a time things are not done as efficiently as before. The more sensitive one must try new things, take charge more, go it alone sometimes. The less sensitive one must experience life without the other's "spiritual" input and make contact with the subtle as it comes up in his or her own awareness.

Each can be a coach for the other if each can keep from stepping in and taking over. Otherwise, the most useful role is to stay a supporter in the stands. Or maybe the role of someone who forgets about the other entirely for a time so that the rank amateur can struggle along without being observed and ashamed of his or her puny efforts. The amateur knows where to turn for expert and loving help if it is needed. That is still a wonderful offering. Maybe in this situation it is the greatest gift of all.

Differences in Optimal Arousal Level

We have just considered a situation in which you and your less sensitive partner or friend make things almost too comfortable for you, the "sensitive one." But there are also going to be many times when the other does not appreciate that you are over-stimulated. Times when the two of you have been doing the very same things, after all, and he or she is still feeling just fine. What's the matter with you?

How do you respond to a well-intentioned request that you "just try it" and not "spoil the fun"? This is a dilemma from my own past—first as a child in my family, then later with my husband. If I said I could not participate, either the others would not go because of me and I would feel guilty, or they would go without me and I would feel I had missed out. What a choice! Not understanding my trait, my solution usually was to go along with what was planned. Sometimes it worked out, sometimes it was agony, and sometimes I ended up sick. No wonder many HSPs lose touch with their "authentic self."

During a year we spent in Europe when our son was an infant, we traveled a few weeks of summer with friends. Our first day out, we drove from Paris to the Mediterranean coast, then east along the Riviera into Italy. We had not foreseen that we would be joining European vacationers, all of us winding through town after town, bumper to bumper, horns honking, mopeds sputtering. Meanwhile, the five of us were trying to decide on a town and a hotel that would turn our Riviera fantasy into reality in spite of our having no reservations and not much money. My infant son, happy for hours using me as a trampoline, was eventually tired and began crying and fussing, then shrieking. It was not much fun by sundown.

Once in our hotel room, I yearned for rest and to have my

son bedded down. At the time, I did not understand any of this as a special trait; I just knew what the two of us needed. Now.

My husband and our friends, however, were ready to do the casinos at Monte Carlo. Like many HSPs, I don't enjoy gambling. Still, it sounded glamorous. But, there was no way I could stand going. Still, if a baby-sitter could be arranged—I just hated staying home.

I did stay behind finally. My son slept well; I lay awake feeling sad, lonely, envious of the others, and on edge being alone in a strange place. Of course, when the others returned, in a gay mood, they regaled me with funny stories and "you-should-have-been-theres." I had not gone and had not slept, either, and then was not sleeping because I was upset that I had not slept!

How I wish I had known then what I know now. Over-arousal is easily displaced onto worries, regrets—anything that is handy—and going to bed does not mean you will sleep; you may be far too stirred up. But it is still the best place to be. And there is usually another chance, even to see Monte Carlo. Most of all, it can feel wonderful to stay home once you accept that home is truly where you sometimes belong.

In these situations your friend or partner is in a real bind. He or she wants you to come, and since sometimes in the past it has worked out, pushing you is tempting. And besides missing having you along if he or she goes without you, the other may feel deeply guilty about leaving you alone.

I think the HSP has to take charge in these situations in order not to have anyone else to blame later. After all, you are the one who knows best how you are feeling and what you can enjoy. If you are hesitating to do something out of fear of over-stimulation—not out of your current state of fatigue—you have to weigh that against the fun you might have. (And add a little weight in favor of going if you have an extra fear of the unfamiliar left over from childhood.) You have to decide for yourself and act. If your action turns out to have been a mistake, you are the one who made it. At least you tried. If you know you are overstimulated and need to stay home, do it gracefully and minimize the regrets you express. Urge others to have fun without you.

Daily Time Alone

Another frequent problem in a close relationship with a less sensitive partner or friend is your greater need for solitude, just to think and digest the day. The other may feel rejected or simply still want your company. Make clear why you need the break. State when you will be available again and keep that promise. Or perhaps you can still be together, but resting in silence.

If you meet with resistance about your need for solitude (or any of your special needs), you will need to discuss the issue more deeply. You have a right to your different experience and needs. But realize that they are not those of your partner or friend and not like most of the people he or she knows. So try to listen and see what the other is feeling. Maybe he or she wants to deny that such a major difference could exist between you. Or perhaps there is a fear that something is the matter with you, a flaw or an illness. The other may have a sense of loss because of adventures, real or imagined, that this trait seems to be making impossible for both of you. There may be anger or a feeling that you must be making it all up.

It helps to remind the other, modestly and with tact, of all the good things he or she is getting because of your trait. And you must watch that you do not use your sensitivity as an excuse to always get your way. You *can* tolerate high levels of stimulation, *especially* when you are with someone who relaxes you and makes you feel safe. Sometimes making an honest effort to go along with your friend or partner will be appreciated. It may work out well. When it does not, you will have demonstrated your limits—preferably without saying, "I told you so." It will become clear that you are usually happier, healthier, and less resentful when you each recognize and respect the other's optimal level of arousal. You will each encourage the other to do what is necessary—go out and have fun, stay in and rest—in order to remain in that comfortable range.

Other issues, of course, can come to the surface when you assert yourself about your needs. If the relationship is already on shaky ground, announcing your trait as a factor that your friend or partner must live with could produce a major earthquake. But if the fault line was there all along, do not blame your trait or your defense of it no matter how much it becomes a point of contention.

The Fear of Honest Communication

Overall, sensitivity can greatly enhance intimate communication. You pick up on so much more of the subtle cues, the nuances, the paradoxes and ambivalences, the unconscious processes. You understand that this sort of communication requires patience. You are loyal, conscientious, and appreciative enough of the value of the relationship to be willing to give it the time.

The main problem is, as always, overarousal. In that state we can be extremely insensitive to everything around us, including those we love. We can blame our trait—"I was just too tired, too overwhelmed." But it is still our duty to do whatever we can to communicate in a helpful way or let the other know, ahead of time if possible, when we are unable to hold up our end.

HSPs probably make their greatest communication errors by avoiding the overarousal caused by unpleasantries. I think most people, but HSPs especially, dread anger, confrontation, tears, anxiety, "scenes," facing change (it always means the loss of something), being asked to change, being judged or shamed by our mistakes, or judging or shaming anyone else.

You probably know rationally—from reading, experience, and perhaps relationship counseling—that one has to have all of the above if a relationship is going to stay fresh and alive. But for some reason that knowledge does not help when it comes time to plunge in and blurt out your feelings.

Furthermore, your intuition is leaping ahead. In a very real, arousing, semiconscious imaginary world, you are already experiencing various ways the conversation might go, and most of them are distressing.

There are two ways to tackle your fears. First, you can become conscious of what you are imagining and imagine other possibilities, too—for example, how it will be after the conflict is cleared up or how it will be if you do *not* work on the problem. Second, you can discuss with your friend or partner what you are imagining that is keeping you from being more open. Saying something like this is inevitably manipulative: "I would like to talk to you about such and such but cannot if you react by saying such and such." But it may also take you to deeper issues about how you communicate.

The Need for Time-outs During Conflicts

A couple in which one or both are HSPs need to work out some extra ground rules for their most arousing communications, which are usually their arguments. I presume that you already ban name-calling, the muddling of the present conflict with past issues, and the abuse of confidences shared when you were both feeling safe and close. But the two of you might agree on other rules just to handle overarousal. One is taking time out.

In general, one should not walk out in the middle of an argument (or bring up the issue of "ending it for good"). But when someone has a strong desire to get away, that person is feeling desperate and cornered—words are not working. Sometimes this is due to guilt because of having seen something about one's self that was very unpleasant. This is the time for the other to back off and show some sympathy, not drive the point home and shame the partner more. Sometimes the cornered one still feels in the right but outgunned. The words are too fast, too sharp, there is no comeback that will work. Fury rises, and leaving is the only safe way to express it.

In any case, as an HSP you may find yourself sometimes so overaroused just from arguing that your fight is rapidly becoming one of the worst moments in your life. Since your relationship is bound to become bitter and distant without the occasional expression of legitimate gripes, you want both parties to look back on quarrels as worthwhile even if painful at the time. That means being civilized. So take a time-out. Offer an escape hatch, even if for only five minutes, an hour, a night to sleep on it. No one is walking out, just postponing.

Waiting to finish an argument can be hard on both of you, so both must agree to the pause. Discuss it ahead of time as a truly helpful ground rule, not a cop-out. Actually, you may find it so helpful that you will readily agree to it in the future. Things always look different after a time-out.

The Power of Positive Metacommunications and Reflective Listening

Metacommunications mean talking about how you talk or just about how you feel in general, apart from the moment. Negative metacommunications sound like this: "I just hope you are aware that even though I am discussing this with you, I plan to do whatever I want." Or, "Have you noticed that every time we argue you become irrational?" Such statements escalate arguments to a new level. Avoid them, potent weapons as they are.

Positive metacommunications, however, do the opposite, putting a safe ceiling on how much damage is being done. They sound like this: "I know we are arguing pretty hot and heavy right now, but I just want you to know that I want this to work out. I care about you, and I appreciate your struggling through this with me."

Positive metacommunications are important in all tense moments between people. They lower arousal and anxiety by reminding those involved that they do, or could, care for each other and that things will probably work out. Couples in which either or both are HSPs should be especially sure to include them in their close-relationships toolbox.

I also suggest you try "reflective listening." This valuable tool has been around since the sixties, and you probably know it well. I've included a reminder of it here because it has saved my marriage twice, and that's no exaggeration. How could I leave it out? This is the CPR of love and friendship.

Reflective listening boils down to hearing the other person, especially his or her feelings. To be sure you heard, you say the *feelings* back. That's it. But it's harder than it sounds. First of all, you'll say it sounds stilted or "like a therapist." It does when done exclusively. But that reaction also may be due to a discomfort with feelings, at least partly taught by your culture. Believe me, it seems far less phony to the person receiving the attention. And just as good basketball players must sometimes do nothing but shoot baskets or dribble, you need to practice listening exclusively now and then so that it's there as a "move" when you need it. So try exclusive, pure reflective listening at least once, preferably with someone you're close to.

Still unsure? Another reason for sticking to feelings is that out in the world they are rarely heard. We want them to be honored, at least in our close relationships. And feelings are deeper than ideas and facts in that they often color, control, and confuse the ideas and facts. Once the feelings are clear, the ideas and facts are clearer, too.

When doing reflective listening during a conflict in your relationship, you'll be forced to hear when you're being unfair, when it's time to outgrow certain needs and give up certain habits, and to hear the negative impact you're having without defending yourself and shutting out the bad news and without getting overaroused and breaking down so that the other has to take care of you. This leads us to a deep topic.

Close Relationships As a Path to Individuation

In chapter 6 I described what Jungian psychologists call the individuation process, the process of following one's path in life, learning to listen to one's inner voices. Another aspect of that process is listening specifically to those voices or parts of ourselves which we have shunned, despised, ignored, or denied. These "shadow" parts, as Jungians call them, are always needed in order to become a strong, whole person, even if we live half our lives as though knowing about them would kill us.

For example, someone may be so convinced he is always strong that he can never admit to any weakness. History and fiction are filled with lessons about this dangerous blind spot, which eventually brings the person down. We have all seen the opposite, too—people convinced they are always weak, innocent victims, forfeiting their personal power but gaining the opportunity to think of themselves as all good and of others as bad. Some people deny the part that loves; others, the part that hates. And so on.

The best way to handle shadow aspects is to know about

REFLECTIVE LISTENING

When done as an exercise, set a time limit (ten minutes minimum, forty-five minutes maximum). Then reverse roles, giving the other equal time, but do not reverse right away. Wait an hour or even a day. If the subject was some conflict or anger between the two of you, also wait before discussing at all what was said. You can take some notes on what you want to say if you want to. But your best bet in this case is to express your reactions during your turn at reflective listening.

THE DOS:

1. Bear yourself physically as one who is really listening. Sit up, arms and legs uncrossed. Lean forward, perhaps. Look at the other person. Do not check your watch or clock.

2. In words or tone, reflect back the actual feelings that were expressed. The factual contents are secondary and will come out as you talk—be patient. If you suspect that other feelings are present, wait until they show themselves in words or are utterly obvious from the tone of voice.

To start with a somewhat silly example to demonstrate the idea of emphasizing the reflection of feelings, your partner might say, "I don't like the coat you're wearing." In this exercise, aimed at emphasizing the feeling, you would say, "You *really dislike* this coat." You don't say, "You really dislike *this* coat," which emphasizes the coat as though you're asking what's wrong with it. And you don't say, "You really dislike *me* wearing this coat," which focuses on yourself (usually defensively).

But silly examples can lead to much more. Your partner responds to your reflection of these feelings by saying, "Yes, that coat always makes me think of last winter." Here there aren't many feelings—yet. So you wait.

Your partner says, "I hated living in that house." You emphasize the feelings again: "It was pretty bad there for you." Not "why?" Not, "I tried to get us out of there as soon as I could."

And soon you may be hearing things about last winter you never knew about before. "Yes, I realize now that I never was so alone, even with you in the same rooms with me." Things that need to be discussed. That's where the reflection of the other's feelings can lead, as opposed to focusing on facts or your own feelings.

THE DON'TS:

1. Don't ask questions.

2. Don't give advice.

3. Don't bring up your own similar experiences.

4. Don't analyze or interpret.

5. Don't do anything else that is distracting or not reflecting the person's feeling experience.

6. Don't lapse into a very long silence, letting the other do a monologue. Your silence is the "listening" half of reflective listening. When timed right, silence gives the other the space to go deeper. But also keep reflecting what has been said. Use your intuition in the timing of these two.

7. And no matter what the other says, don't defend yourself or give your view of the matter. If you think it's necessary, you can emphasize afterward that your listening did not mean you agreed. While the assumptions behind feelings can be wrong (and we can do something wrong because of what we feel), feelings in themselves are not right or wrong and usually lead to less trouble, not more, if respectfully heard.

them and form an alliance with them. Up to now I have been upbeat about HSPs, speaking of our conscientiousness, loyalty, intuition, and insight. But I would do you a disservice if I did not also say that HSPs have as much or more reason to reject and deny parts of themselves. Some HSPs deny their strength, power, and capacity at times to be tough and insensitive. Some deny their irresponsible, unloving parts. Some deny their need for others or their need to be alone or their anger—or all of the above.

Learning about these rejected parts is difficult because usually we rejected them for good reasons. And while your casual friends may know quite a bit about your shadow aspects, they will probably hesitate to speak of them. But in a very close relationship, especially if you live together or must count on each other for the basics in life, you will not be able to avoid seeing and discussing each other's shadow—sometimes heatedly. Indeed, one could say that a close relationship does not really begin until you do know about these aspects of each other and decide how you will live with or change them.

It is painful and shameful to be shown your worst side. That is why it can only happen when you are forced to by the one you care most for and when you know you are not going to be abandoned for speaking of or possessing these "horrible," secret parts. Thus, a close relationship is the best way to take possession of them, to gain the positive energy that was lost along with the negative and individuate along the path to wisdom and wholeness.

Self-Expansion in Close Relationships

We humans seem to have a strong need to grow, to expand—not just to have more territory, possessions, or power but to expand in knowledge, consciousness, and identity. One way we do this is to include others in our selves. One stops being "I" and becomes something bigger: "we."

When we first fall in love, the self-expansion due to including another in our lives is rapid. Research on marriage, however, shows that after a few years the relationship becomes much less satisfying, but good communication slows that decline and, with the individuation process just described, the decline can be even further slowed, or reversed. My husband and I did research that uncovered another way of increasing satisfaction. In several studies of married and dating couples, we found that the pairs felt more satisfied with their relationships if they did things together that they defined as "exciting" (not just "pleasant"). This seems logical; if you cannot expand anymore by incorporating new things about the other into yourself, you can still create an association between the relationship and self-expansion by doing new things together.

To an HSP especially, it may seem that life is too stimulating already and when you come home you want quiet. But be careful not to make your relationship so soothing that you do not do anything new together. Perhaps to do that, your hours apart have to be less stressful. Or you have to search for what expands you without overarousing you—a concert of quiet but unusually beautiful music, a discussion of last night's dreams, a new book of poetry to share by the fire. You don't have to ride a roller coaster together.

If the relationship has been a source of comfort, it also deserves your seeing that it continue to be a source of satisfying self-expansion.

HSPs and Sexuality

This is a topic deserving good research and an entire book. Our culture feeds us all so much information about what is ideal, what is abnormal. But that comes from the 80 percent who are not HSPs. What is ideal and normal for us? I cannot say for certain, but it makes sense that if we are more sensitive to stimulation, we might be more sensitive to sexual stimulation. This might make our sexual lives more satisfying. It could also cause us to need much less variety. And those times when we are overaroused from general stimulation could obviously interfere with our sexual functioning and pleasure. You know enough now about this trait, in theory and practice, to think through how your sexuality is affected by it. If this area of your life has been confusing or distressing, you might also want to do the reframing exercise with some of your sexual experiences or feelings.

HSPs and Children

Children seem to thrive when their caretakers are sensitive. And I have met many highly sensitive caretakers who were at their happiest tending their children or the children of others. I have also met some who have not had children or who limited their family to one child entirely because of their sensitivity. Not surprisingly, this depended in part on their past experiences with children—was it pleasant, or was it too much?

When thinking about whether you want to raise children, it is good to remember that your children and future family will be more suited to you than those of others. They will have your genes and your influence. When families are loud, boisterous, or filled with dissension, it is often because the members find that comfortable or at least okay. Your family life can be different.

On the other hand, no one can deny that children do greatly increase stimulation in life. To a conscientious HSP, they are a great responsibility as well as a joy. You have to be in the world with them, at play school, elementary school, junior high, high school. You have to meet other families, doctors, dentists, orthodontists, piano teachers. It goes on and on. They bring the whole wide world to you—issues of sex, drugs, driving a car, getting an education, a job, a partner. It is a lot to handle (and one cannot assume one will have a partner during the whole process). You will have to give up other things to do it—that is a certainty.

It's all right not to have children. We cannot have everything in this world. Sometimes it's smart to see our limits. On this subject, in fact, I often say that it's *wonderful* not to have children. And *wonderful* to have them. Each is its own kind of wonderful.

Your Sensitivity Enriches Your Relationships

Whether you are an extraverted or introverted HSP, your greatest social fulfillment tends to come in close relationships. This is the area of life where almost everyone learns most profoundly while gaining great satisfaction, and it is where you can shine. You can help others and help yourself by applying your sensitivity to these relationships.

· • **Working With What You Have Learned** •

*The Three of Us: You, Me, and My (or Our)
Trait of Sensitivity*

The following is meant to be done with another person with whom you are in a close relationship. If you have no one with whom you can do it, imagine doing it with someone with whom you had a relationship in the past or hope to have in the future. You will still learn a great deal.

If the other person does exist and has not read this book, have him or her read the first chapter and this one, at least making note of whatever seemed unusually relevant to your relationship. Reading some parts out loud together might be valuable, too. Then set aside time to discuss the following questions. (If you both are HSPs, do the set for one of you, then again for the other.)

1. *What aspects of you does the other value that are caused by your being an HSP?*

2. *What aspects of you, caused by your sensitivity, would the other like to change?* Keep in mind that the issue is not that the aspects are "bad," just difficult in particular situations or in relation to traits or habits the other possesses.

3. *What are some of the conflicts the two of you have had that are caused by your being an HSP?*

4. *Discuss any instances when the other wished you had taken into account your sensitivity and protected yourself more.*

5. *Discuss any instances when you have used your sensitivity as an excuse not to do something or as a weapon in an argument.* If this discussion becomes heated, use what you learned in "reflective listening" to contain it.

6. *Was there anyone else who was highly sensitive in either of your families? In what ways might that relationship be affecting this one?* For example, imagine a highly sensitive woman married to a man whose mother was highly sensitive. The husband would have deep-seated attitudes toward sensitivity. Be-

coming alert to them could improve relationships among all three—him, his wife, and his mother.

7. *Discuss what you each gain by specializing—one of you being more sensitive, the other less*. Besides the efficiency and specific benefits, do you each enjoy being needed for your own talents? Do you feel indispensable to the other? Do you feel good about yourself when you are doing something the other cannot?

8. *Discuss what you each lose by this specialization*. What do you wish you could do for yourself that the other now does for you? Do you get tired of the other depending on you when you're engaging in your specialty? Do you have less respect for your partner because you do such things better? Does it lower the other's self-esteem?

Healing the Deeper Wounds
A Different Process for HSPs

Remembering a Sensitive Friend From the Past

I knew a boy named Drake in high school. At that time he was the class nerd. Today I would say he was an HSP.

Drake had considerably more to deal with, however. He had been born with a congenital heart defect, epilepsy, a host of allergies, and fair skin that could not tolerate the sun. Unable to play sports or even be out-of-doors, he was completely excluded from our culture's normal boyhood. Naturally, he became bookish and by adolescence was quite passionate about ideas. He also became passionate about girls, as do most boys at that age.

The girls, of course, wanted nothing to do with him. I suppose we did not dare welcome his attentions; his need for acceptance made him too intense. And it would have been social death for any of us. But he loved one after another, anyway, in a shy and hungry way that made him a joke. The highlight of the year for some of his classmates was getting their hands on some of Drake's rejected love poems and reading them out loud all over the school.

Fortunately, Drake was in the program for gifted students, and among us he was more accepted. We admired his essays, his comments in class. So we were proud of him when he received a full scholarship to a top university.

He must have been even more afraid than the rest of us about going away to school. It meant living day and night with others his own age, the very ones who had made his life impossible in the past. Of course, he could never turn down the honor. But how would it be for him? And how would it feel to leave his sheltering home and medical support?

The answer came after the first Christmas vacation. On the first night back in his dorm room, Drake hung himself.

HSPs and the Healing of Psychological Wounds

I do not mean to startle you with such a story—again, Drake had many difficulties. HSPs' lives rarely have such bad endings. But if this chapter is going to be helpful, it needs to serve as a warning as well as a comfort. My research results make it clear that HSPs who faced extreme difficulties in childhood and adolescence are going to be at a much greater risk for anxiety, depression, and suicide until they acknowledge their past as well as their trait and begin to heal their own wounds. HSPs with serious current problems also need to give themselves special consideration. Non-HSPs simply do not take in as many of the subtle, disturbing aspects of these situations. Your trait in itself is not at fault; but like a finely tuned instrument or machine, or a high-spirited, finely bred animal, you do need special handling. And many of you received mediocre or even damaging care as a child.

In this chapter I'll discuss the various ways of dealing with past and present difficulties, mainly through psychotherapy in the broadest sense. I'll also discuss the pros and cons of psychotherapy for HSPs without major problems, the different approaches, how to choose a therapist, and the like. But I'll begin with the issue of childhood wounds.

How Much Emphasis Should We Place on Our Childhoods?

I do not believe that our psychological life can all be reduced to what happened to us while growing up. There is the present—the people who influence us, our physical health, our environment—and there is also something within us calling us forward. As I said in chapter 6 about vocation, I do believe we each have at least a part of a question to answer for our generation, a task to advance a little bit for our times. And while a difficult past may seem at first to hamper our living our life's purpose, sometimes it serves the purpose, too. Or it *is* the purpose—to fully experience and understand a certain kind of human problem.

I also want to emphasize a common mistake of many psychotherapists, those who do not yet understand about HSPs. Naturally, these therapists look for something in an HSP's childhood to explain "symptoms" that may be in the normal range for us. They may think the HSP is withdrawing "too much," reporting feelings of dissociation "for no reason," having "excessive" or "neurotic" anxiety, and "unusual" problems at work, in close relationships, or with sexuality. Having an explanation is always a relief for both therapist and client even if it is that someone did something bad to us that we have since forgotten or underestimated.

I find that people whose real difficulties begin with their trait (perhaps misunderstood or mismanaged) are greatly relieved and improved when they learn the basic facts about sensitivity. There still may be significant work to do in therapy, such as reframing experiences and learning how to live with their trait, but the focus naturally shifts.

I also think people don't know what they're talking about when they say, "Oh, come on! Childhood is hard for everybody. No family is perfect. Everybody has some skeletons in their closet. It's just infantile the way people go on and on with years of therapy. Look at their brothers and sisters—same problems—and they aren't making a big deal. *They're* getting on with their lives."

All childhoods are not equal. Some are truly horrible. And they can differ within the same family. Statistical analyses of the influence of family environment on different children in the same family show *no* overlap. Your brothers or sisters lived a totally different childhood. You had different positions in the family, different early experiences, even in a sense different parents, given how adults change with circumstances and age. Finally, you were highly sensitive.

Those born highly sensitive are more affected by everything. Furthermore, whoever is the most sensitive in the family often becomes the focus. In a disturbed family especially, he or she becomes the family's seer, for example, or harmonizer, prodigy, target, martyr, patient, parent, or the weak one whose protection becomes someone else's life purpose. Meanwhile, the sensitive child's extra need, to learn to feel secure in the world, is overlooked.

In sum, believe it if it seems to you that the "same" childhood or an "okay" childhood has been harder for you than for others in your family or for others with a similar past. And if you think you need therapy to heal childhood wounds, *get it*. Each childhood is its own story, deserving to be heard.

How Dan Survived

At first, Dan's answers to my questions were typical, if extreme, for an HSP. He considered himself highly introverted and had always needed a lot of time alone. He disliked violence in any form. He told me that he managed the accounting office of a large nonprofit agency, where he thought he was appreciated for being kind and "diplomatic." He found most other social situations too draining. But then the interview returned to his dislike of violence.

Dan recalled frequent brawls with his brother, who would hold him down and pound and kick him. (Sibling abuse remains one of the least studied forms of family violence.) Meanwhile, I was wondering what else was wrong, why this bullying had been allowed in his family. I asked if his mother had considered him a sensitive child.

"I don't know. She wasn't very attentive."

A red flag. As if reading my thoughts, he said, "My mother and father were not demonstrative."

I nodded.

"In fact, they were bizarre. I remember nothing positive about them. Cuddling, that stuff." Then the stoicism melted. The story unfolded of his mother's mental illness, never treated. "Chronic depression. Schizophrenia. People in the TV talking to her." Binge alcoholism—sober Monday through Friday, "drunk and gone" from Friday night to Sunday morning. "My father was an alcoholic, too. He'd hit her. Beat her. It would always get out of control."

When drunk, his mother would always tell him the same story—of her own mother being a cold and withdrawn invalid, of her only caretakers being a succession of maids and nurses, of her father's illnesses and of being forced to stay alone with him, day after day, as he was slowly dying. (So often this is the story—lack of nurturing, generation after generation.)

"She would sob and sob when she would tell it. She was a good woman. *She* was the sensitive one. Far more than me." And in the same breath: "But so vicious. She could always find my Achilles heel. She had that incredible knack." (HSPs are not all saints.)

Dan was struggling with the terrible ambivalence that develops when a child's only protector is also dangerous.

He described hiding as a child—in closets, under the bathroom sink, in the family car, in a certain window seat. But, as in most such stories, there was one person who made the soul-saving difference. Dan had a paternal grandmother, a rigid woman who was "fanatical about cleanliness." But after her husband died, she made a companion of little Dan.

"One of my earliest memories is of sitting with three women, in their sixties, playing canasta, and I'm six and can barely hold the cards. But they needed a fourth, and when I was playing canasta, I was an adult and important and could say things to them I could say to no one else."

This grandmother provided the crucial stability required for a highly sensitive child to develop strategies for survival.

Dan also had wonderful resilience. "My mother used to sit and lecture me like this: 'Why do you try so hard? You'll never make anything of yourself. You haven't a chance.' And I just made up my mind to defy her."

Being highly sensitive does not at all rule out being, in your own way, a tenacious survivor. And Dan needed that as he told me the rest of the story.

At fourteen Dan took a job. There was a man he worked

with whom Dan looked up to because he was well-read and talked to Dan as an adult. "I trusted him, and I ended up being molested by him."

(Again, it is not only the single instance of abuse that is a concern but the lifelong situation that made it more likely. Given Dan's childhood, his hunger for closeness must have led to his overlooking subtle signs of danger. Plus he would have been slow to protect himself, given that he had no role models—no one else had looked out for him.)

Dan shrugged. "So, from that I learned, 'If you can make it through this, they can throw just about anything they've got at you and it isn't going to make a hell of a lot of difference. If you can get through this.'"

Dan married his childhood sweetheart, who had had a family as disrupted and chaotic as his own. They had made up their minds to make it work, and they had, for twenty years. Part of their success was due to firmly establishing limits with his family and hers. "I know how to take care of myself now."

Some of that lesson came from three months of psychotherapy the year before, when he had fallen into a deep depression. He had also read many books on the psychology of codependency and on adult children of alcoholics. Their groups, however, he did not attend. Like many HSPs, he would rather not reveal his life to a roomful of strangers.

"Permission to do what *I* need to do—that has been most important. To acknowledge my sensitivity and respect it. To project positive, solution-oriented calm at work. But to watch for looking too much on the outside like someone or something I don't feel inside."

Because inside "there is a black hole. Sometimes I can't think of a single reason to go on living. I just don't care if I live or die."

Then, in the same even tone, he told me he had a friend, a psychiatrist, who was helpful, and two other friends who are counselors. And that he knew there was a richness resulting from his sensitivity in combination with his life experience.

"I am deeply moved by things. I'd hate to miss the intense joy of that." He smiled bravely. "Although there's a lot of loneliness. It has taken longer to appreciate the grief in life. But life is about both. I search for a spiritual answer."

And so Dan survives.

What About Your Own Past?

At the end of this chapter you will have a chance to assess your own childhood and think about what was there. I want to repeat my research finding discussed in chapter 4: HSPs are more affected by a troubled childhood in that they are more depressed and anxious as adults. Also keep in mind that the earlier the problem occurred or began and the more that it was rooted in the behavior of your primary caretaker, usually your mother, the more deeply rooted and long-lasting the effects. You must have great patience with yourself throughout your life. You will heal, but in your own way and with some qualities you could not have gained had there been no problems. For example, you will be more conscious, more complex, and more understanding of others.

Let's not forget the advantages of being sensitive in childhood, even in a dysfunctional family. You were more likely to withdraw and think it over rather than being totally enmeshed. Like Dan with his grandmother, you may have known intuitively where to turn for help. You may have developed vast inner and spiritual resources as a compensation.

My oldest interviewee had even come to believe that difficult childhoods are chosen by souls destined for a spiritual life. It keeps them working on their inner life while others are settling down into a more ordinary existence. Or as one friend of mine put it, "In the first twenty years we are given our curriculum. In the next twenty we study it." For some of us that curriculum is the equivalent of graduate study at Oxford!

As adults, HSPs tend to have just the right personalities for inner work and healing. Generally speaking, your keen intuition helps you uncover the most important hidden factors. You have greater access to your own unconscious and so a greater sense of others' and how you were affected. You can develop a good sense of the process itself—when to push, when to back off.

You have curiosity about inner life. Above all, you have integrity. You remain committed to the process of individuation no matter how difficult it is to face certain moments, certain wounds, certain facts.

Assuming that you are one of the many HSPs with a difficult childhood or a difficult present, let's explore your options.

The Four Approaches

One can "cut up the pie" of healing methods with many divisions—long or short, self-help or professional help, individual or group therapy, treating yourself or treating your whole family together. But we can cover it well by serving up four big slices: cognitive-behavioral, interpersonal, physical, and spiritual.

There are therapists who use all four, and perhaps they are the best. But do ask which is their private favorite, mentioning these four explicitly. It is a great shame to spend time in therapy with someone whose basic philosophy is not what you would have preferred.

Cognitive-Behavioral

Short-term "cognitive-behavioral" therapy, aimed at relieving specific symptoms, is the most accessible through insurance and managed-care plans. This approach is "cognitive" because it works on how you think, and it is "behavioral" because it works on how you behave. It tends to ignore feelings and unconscious motive. Everything is meant to be practical, rational, and clear.

You'll be asked what you want to work on. If your complaint is that you're generally anxious, you'll be taught the latest techniques of relaxation or biofeedback. If you fear specific things, you'll be very gradually exposed to them until the fear is gone. If you're depressed, you'll be taught to examine your irrational beliefs that everything is hopeless, no one cares about you, you should not make mistakes, and so forth. If you persist in those beliefs while depressed, you'll be taught ways to stop those thoughts.

If you're not engaging in specific tasks that might help you psychologically, like getting dressed and going out each day or making friends, you'll be helped to set goals around those specifics. You'll learn whatever skills you need to meet your goals and how to reward yourself when you do.

If you're struggling with stress from work, a divorce, or family problems, you'll be helped to reframe them in ways that include more of the facts, more insights that will help you cope.

These methods may not seem very deep or glamorous, but they often work and are always worth trying. The skills will be useful even if they do not fix everything. And the increase in self-confidence from solving one difficulty often improves life generally.

Besides learning these techniques in psychotherapy, you can find all of the techniques in books. But it usually helps to have a caring coach to take you through the steps. You and a friend might be able to do that for each other. But the professionals have considerably more experience. In particular, they should know when to drop an approach and try another.

Interpersonal

Interpersonally oriented psychotherapy is what most people think of as "therapy." Examples are Freudian, Jungian, object relations, Gestalt, Rogerian or client-centered, transactional analysis, existential, and most eclectic therapies. They all involve talk and making use of the relationship between you and another person or persons—often a therapist but sometimes a group or peer counselor.

There are probably hundreds of theories and techniques here, so I have to speak in general terms. Besides, most therapists use a blend to fit the client's needs. Still, there are different emphases. Some make the relationship a safe place to explore anything and everything. Some see it as a place specifically to give you a new experience of early attachment, a new mental picture of what to expect in future close relationships. Some say it is a place to mourn the past and let go of it, find meaning in it; others, a place to observe and try new behaviors; still others, a place to explore your unconscious until you're in better harmony with it.

You and your therapist work together on your feelings about

the therapist, other relationships, your personal history, your dreams (maybe), and anything else that comes up. Not only will you learn from what is discussed; you'll learn how to do this kind of inner work on your own.

Disadvantages? One can talk and talk and get nowhere if the therapist is not skilled or your real problem lies elsewhere. The therapist has to understand his or her own issues to a great degree. It can take years to work through your prior relationships, the one with the therapist, plus your existing ones. But sometimes great progress is made in just a few months, as happened with Dan.

Physical

Physical approaches include exercise, improving nutrition or being careful about food allergies, acupressure, herbal supplements, massage, tai chi, yoga, Rolfing, bioenergetics, dance therapy, and of course all the medications, especially antidepressants and antianxiety drugs. Indeed, today physical approaches mainly mean medications prescribed by a psychiatrist, which chapter 9 will discuss.

Anything done to the body will change the mind. We expect this to be the case with drugs specifically designed for that purpose. But we forget that our brain and therefore our thoughts can also be changed by sleep, exercise, nutrition, environment, and the state of our sexual hormones, to name a few factors we can often control ourselves. It is equally true that anything done to the mind will also change the body—meditating, telling our troubles to a friend, or even just writing them down. Each "talking therapy" session must change the brain. Thus, it should not be surprising that the three forms of therapy discussed so far—cognitive-behavioral, interpersonal, and physical—have been found to be equally good for curing depression. So you do have a choice.

Spiritual

Spiritual approaches include all the things people do to explore the nonmaterial aspect of themselves and their world. Spiritual approaches comfort us, telling us there really is more to life than what we see. They heal or make more bearable the wounds received in this world. They tell us we are not trapped in this situation, that there is more. Maybe there is even some order or plan behind it all, a purpose.

Additionally, when we open to a spiritual approach, we often begin to have experiences that convince us that there truly is something more here to know. Then we want a spiritual approach to therapy; anything else would seem to leave out an important aspect of life.

Some therapists are mainly spiritually oriented. Be sure to ask before you begin and think about whether you feel compatible with the person's particular spiritual path. Or you can seek out clergy members, spiritual directors, or others directly associated with a religion or spiritual practice. In this case, explore carefully whether they have suitable psychological training to do the work you agree to do together.

HSPs and the Behavioral-Cognitive Approach

As for how these four approaches suit HSPs, what matters, of course, is how they suit you. But here are a few thoughts. At some points probably all HSPs should be exposed to the behavioral-cognitive methods. As discussed in chapter 2, HSPs benefit from fully developing the brain systems that give us control over where we place our attention and how we handle conflicts between the activation and pause-to-check systems. As with muscles, these attention systems are probably inherently stronger in some. But all of us can develop them, and the cognitive-behavioral approach is the best gym in town.

This is a very rational approach, however, and generally developed by non-HSPs who I think sometimes secretly believe that sensitive people are just being silly and irrational. This attitude on the part of a therapist or book author can lower your self-esteem and raise arousal, especially if you fail to reach the level or goal they set for you. It will be implied that this goal is "normal," but it may really be the goal of being like them or like the majority of people, ignoring differences in temperament. A good cognitive-behavioral therapist, however, will be attuned to individual differences as well as the importance of self-esteem and self-confidence in all psychological work.

Also, HSPs often prefer an approach that is "deeper" or more intuitive rather than focused on surface symptoms. But this sort of bias in some of us against the practical and down-to-earth could be a good reason in itself to explore this approach.

HSPs and the Interpersonal Approach

Interpersonal psychotherapy has broad appeal to HSPs, and we can learn a great deal from it. We discover our intuitive abilities, our depths. We become skilled in very close relationships. With some interpersonal methods, our unconscious becomes our ally instead of a source of symptoms.

The disadvantages are that HSPs can stay too long in interpersonal therapy just because we are so good at working through those details. A good therapist, however, will insist that you do your inner work on your own when you appear ready. HSPs can also use this kind of therapy to avoid being out in the world, although a good therapist will not allow that, either.

Finally, there is usually a strong attraction to the therapist with whom we make all these explorations—what is called a positive or idealizing transference. For HSPs this is often especially strong, which can make therapy expensive to stay in and almost impossible to leave.

More About Transference

Actually, a strong, positive transference or attachment to the therapist can happen with any of these approaches, so it deserves further comment.

Transferences are not always positive. They are thought to be the transfer of repressed feelings you once had toward important others in your life, so anger, fear, and all the rest are possible. But positive feelings usually predominate, increased by gratitude toward the therapist, the hope for help, and the displacement of all sorts of other feelings onto this target.

A strong positive transference has many benefits. By wanting to be like the therapist or liked by him or her, you will change in ways you otherwise never would have attempted.

By facing the fact that the therapist cannot be your mother, lover, or lifelong friend, you face a bitter reality and learn to handle it. By realizing the nature of the feelings—this person seems perfect, it would be heaven to be with him or her—you can think about where such strong feelings might be more appropriately directed. Finally, it can be nice to enjoy the help and company of someone you like so much.

Still, the transference can be the equivalent of an intense love affair with a person who cannot reciprocate. (And if your therapist does, it is unethical behavior. You are seeing the wrong therapist and need *more* professional help to get you out of the situation, as you probably cannot on your own.) As such, it can be an unexpected, unwanted, rough experience. A strong transference affects your self-esteem in that you may feel utterly dependent and ashamed. It affects others you're close to who feel your deep attachment to this new person. If the transference prolongs your therapy, it will affect your budget. It has to be considered, and the time to do so is before getting into therapy.

There are many reasons why transference could be stronger for HSPs. First, it is stronger when the unconscious wants big changes made but the ego cannot or will not make them. HSPs frequently need to make such vast changes in order to be more out in the world, or less, or in order to be "liberated" from their oversocialization or acceptance of cultural biases against them, or simply to come to better terms with this aspect of their personality. Second, psychotherapy contains all the elements described in chapter 7 that cause people to fall in love and HSPs to fall in love harder. The therapist whom you choose will obviously seem desirable to you, wise and capable. You will experience her or him as liking you. And you are going to share everything you feared no one would listen to or accept—everything you feared even thinking about. This makes the situation very arousing.

I'm not at all suggesting that you should avoid therapy because you might develop a strong transference. Indeed, it may be a sign that therapy is needed. And in the hands of a competent therapist, the transference will be the greatest force for change. But be forewarned about attaching prematurely, to the first therapist you meet, or long past the point where you have received all the benefits you could from this particular other person.

HSPs and the Physical Approach

HSPs can especially benefit from physical approaches when we need to stop a psychological situation that is threatening to spiral out of control physically and mentally. Maybe you are losing sleep, feeling tired and depressed or terribly anxious or both. The causes of such downward spiraling can vary greatly. I have seen a physical solution, usually medication, work on depressions caused by a virus, a failure at work, the death of a close friend, and getting into painful issues in psychotherapy. In all cases it made sense to stop the spiral physically because there was no way the person could think differently until the body was calmer.

The most usual method is medication. But I have also seen an HSP halt the same spiral by taking a vacation to a new place in the warm tropics, forgetting problems for a while. Upon returning, the person took up the old issues with a fresh perspective and physiology. In another case, instead of taking a trip, this person had to come home from a vacation to stop a spiral of anxiety. What was needed was less stimulation. Your intuition can be a fine guide for knowing exactly what you need to do physically to change your mental chemistry.

A third case responded to careful nutritional guidance. All humans vary greatly in their nutritional needs and the foods they need to avoid, and HSPs seem to vary even more so. Especially if we become chronically aroused, we will need extra nutrients right when we are probably paying least attention to such things. We may even lose our appetites or have poor digestion so that we are receiving very little of what we need from what we do eat. Good nutritional advice is very important for HSPs.

On one point we seem to vary less, and that is how quickly we crash when hungry. So keep eating small, regular meals no matter how busy or distracted you become. If you are an HSP with an eating disorder, you are certain to be headed for serious trouble until you solve it, and there are many resources out there for doing just that.

I also want to mention the powerful influence of fluctuations in levels of reproductive hormones, which I suspect, again, affect HSPs more. The same is true of thyroid hormone production. All of these systems are linked together, affecting cortisol and brain neurotransmitters dramatically. One hint that hormones are the problem is the kind of inexplicable mood swing in which you are feeling okay one hour, and the next, everything seems hopeless, worthless. Or similar huge variations in energy or mental clarity.

With all physical approaches, from medications to massage, remember that you're very sensitive! In the care of medications, ask to be started at the lowest dosage. Choose your body worker carefully and talk about your sensitivity with the person beforehand. Your mentioning it usually calls up for the person a set of experiences with other people like you, and she or he will know just what to do. (If that does not happen, you probably cannot work with the person.)

Be aware that there can be strong transferences to body workers, just as to psychotherapists. This is especially true if they work on your psychological issues, too. This combination, in fact, can be so intense that I think it is often unwise, at least for HSPs. The longing to be held, comforted, understood, can be explored and to some extent gratified either through words or touch. But both from the same person is too much like what you may long for and be just too confusing or upsetting.

If your therapist does work both with your thoughts and your body, be especially careful to inspect the person's credentials and references. They should have years of training in interpersonal psychology, not just body work.

HSPs and Spiritual Approaches

Spiritual approaches often appeal most to HSPs. Spiritual resources were used by almost every HSP I interviewed who had needed to do some kind of healing inner work. One reason HSPs are drawn to the spiritual is that we are so inclined to look inward. Another is that we sense that we could master distressing situations if we could calm our arousal by seeing things differently—transcend, love, trust. Most spiritual practices have the goal of achieving exactly that sort of perspective. And many of us have had spiritual experiences that have indeed been reassuring.

Still, there are disadvantages or at least dangers to a spiritual approach, especially when it is followed exclusively. First, we may be avoiding other lessons, like learning to get along with people or understanding our bodies, thoughts, and feelings. Second, there can be positive transferences to spiritual leaders or movements, too, and often these leaders and movements are unskilled in helping you grow beyond that sort of overidealization. They may even foster it, since these feelings make you ready to do whatever they suggest, and they're certain that that is good for you. I'm not speaking just of "cults." One can feel the same sort of overidealization for a nice minister of a mainstream church and have it mishandled much the same.

Third, most spiritual paths speak of the necessity of sacrificing the self, the ego, one's personal desires. Sometimes one is to abandon one's self to God, sometimes to the leader (often easier but far more questionable). I think there comes a time in life when some kind of sacrifice of the ego's perspective is exactly right. There is some truth in the Eastern view that the ego's desires are the source of suffering and that focusing backward, on our personal problems, distracts us from the present, our true responsibility, and keeps us from preparing for what lies ahead, beyond the personal.

However, I have seen many HSPs abandon their ego too soon. It is an easy sacrifice if you think your ego is not worth much. And if you know someone who has truly managed to abandon the ego, such a person so glows with spirituality that you cannot help but want to do the same. But a charismatic glow is no guarantee. It may simply reflect a quiet, stress-free, well-disciplined life—rare enough in these times. The glowing saintlike soul may still be a mess psychologically, socially, and sometimes even morally. It can be as though bright lights are on upstairs but the lower floors are dark and unkempt.

Real redemption or enlightenment, as much as it can be

achieved in this world, comes through hard work that does not skirt tough personal issues. For HSPs, the toughest task of all may have nothing to do with renouncing the world but involve going out and being immersed in it.

Is Psychotherapy Useful for HSPs Without Specific Adult or Childhood Problems?

If you have no serious traumas or early wounds to heal, you may decide that with the knowledge this book provides you will not need any other help with your life, at least for now.

Psychotherapy, however, is not necessarily about fixing problems or alleviating symptoms. It can also be about gaining insight, wisdom, and developing a partnership with your unconscious. Of course, you can learn greatly about doing inner work from other places—books, seminars, conversations. Many good therapists, for example, are writing books and giving courses. But having an especially keen mind, intuition, and inner life, HSPs tend to gain much from psychotherapy. It both validates these qualities and further hones them. As these treasured parts develop, psychotherapy becomes a sacred space. There is nothing quite like it.

Especially for HSPs—Jungian Analysis and Jungian-Oriented Psychotherapy

The form of psychotherapy I recommend most to HSPs is Jungian-oriented therapy, or Jungian analysis, following the methods and aims of Carl Jung. (If there are childhood traumas to work with, however, one must be certain the Jungian also has training in these areas.)

Jung's approach emphasized the unconscious, as do all "depth psychologies," such as Freudian psychoanalysis or object-relations approaches, all of which would fall into the category of "interpersonal." But the Jungian approach adds the spiritual dimension by understanding that the unconscious is trying to take us somewhere, to expand our awareness beyond our narrow ego's consciousness. The messages are coming to us all the time, as dreams, symptoms, and behaviors that our ego considers to be problems. We need only to pay attention.

The purpose of Jungian therapy or analysis is, first, to provide a container in which frightening or rejected material can be examined safely. The therapist is like an experienced guide in the wilderness. Second, it teaches the client to be at home in that wilderness, too. Jungians do not seek cures but a lifelong engagement in the process of individuation through communication with the inner realms.

Because HSPs have such close contact with the unconscious, such vivid dreams, and such an intense pull toward the imaginal and spiritual, we cannot flourish until we are experts on this facet of ourselves. In a sense, Jungian depth work is the training ground for today's royal-advisor class.

You are in "Jungian analysis" when you see a Jungian analyst, someone trained by one of the Jungian training institutes. Usually, analysts are already competent therapists and can use any approach that seems beneficial, but they obviously prefer Jung's. Jungian analysts hope to work with you for several years, perhaps two times a week. Analysts usually charge more because of their extra training. You can also see a nonanalyst, a Jungian-oriented psychotherapist. But you will want to ask what kind of training is behind the "Jungian." Some have the benefit of extensive reading, course work, internships, or a long personal analysis. The personal analysis is especially important.

Some Jungian training institutes offer lower fees if you are interested in seeing someone still learning—an "analyst candidate" or "psychotherapy intern." These people will be skilled and enthusiastic, so you may be getting a bargain. The only problem is that finding a good match with your personality, considered essential in Jungian work, may be harder to achieve.

Also, beware of Jungians with outdated sexist or homophobic attitudes. Most Jungians have attitudes in tune with their culture rather than Jung's Victorian Switzerland. They are encouraged to think independently. Jung himself once said, "Thank God I am Jung and not a Jungian." But a few follow Jung's quite narrow ideas about gender and sexual preference.

Some Final Observations About HSPs
and Psychotherapy

First, do not be a people pleaser and put up with a therapist who makes himself or herself the center of the process. The therapist should be a container large enough that you're not constantly bumping into the container's ego. Second, don't be too charmed by the intense personal attention (available from most good therapists) during the first few sessions. Take your time to commit yourself.

Once the process has begun, appreciate that it is hard work and not always pleasant. A strong transference is only one example of the kinds of inexplicable forces that are loosed by telling your unconscious it is now free to express itself a bit.

Sometimes psychotherapy just gets too intense, too over-arousing—more like a boiling cauldron than a safe container. If it does, you and your therapist need to discuss how to control that. Maybe you need a break, some sessions that are more calm, supportive, and superficial. A break may actually speed up your progress, even if it appears to be slowing it down.

Psychotherapy in its broadest sense is a collection of paths toward wisdom and wholeness. If you are an HSP with a troubled childhood, it is almost essential that you take that path. Depth work especially can also be a kind of playground for the HSP. Whereas others feel lost, we are as at home there as anyone dares to claim to be. This big, beautiful wilderness lets us travel through all kinds of terrain. We camp happily for a while with anything useful—books, courses, and relationships. We become companions with experts and amateurs discovered along the way. It's a good land.

Don't let society's attitudes keep you away either when it makes your path the latest hot fad or a source of jokes. There is something here for HSPs that sometimes others cannot fully appreciate.

• **Working With What You Have Learned** •

Assessing the Wounds of Childhood

If you know that your childhood was reasonably happy and un-eventful, you can skip this assessment, or you can use it to appreciate your good fortune and increase your compassion for others. Skip it, too, if you have worked through your childhood issues to your present satisfaction.

For the rest of you, this task can be upsetting, so skip it if it doesn't seem like the time in your life for such history searching. Even if your intuition says go ahead, be prepared for some aftershocks. As always, consider therapy if you feel more distress than you can handle.

For those who proceed, go down the list and check what applies to you. In addition, put a star by anything that happened in the first five years, a second star if it happened before you were two. If the situation continued for a long time (define *long* however seems right to you), circle your check or stars. Do the same if the event still seems to rule your whole life.

These little checks, stars, and circles will give you some idea of where the biggest issues lie, without trying to attach numbers.

— Your parents were unhappy about the signs of your sensitivity and/or were unusually poor at dealing with it.
— You were clearly an unwanted child.
— You were cared for by multiple caretakers who were not your parents or other loving people close to your family.
— You were intrusively overprotected.
— You were forced to do things you feared, overriding your own sense of what was okay for you.
— Your parents thought something was basically wrong with you physically or mentally.
— You were dominated by a parent, sister, brother, neighbor, schoolmate, etc.
— You were sexually abused.
— You were physically abused.

— You were verbally abused—taunted, teased, shouted at, criticized constantly—or the self-image mirrored back to you by close others was extremely negative in any way.

— You were physically not well cared for. (You didn't get enough to eat, etc.)

— You were given little attention, or the attention you received was entirely due to your exceptional achievements.

— You had a parent or close other who was an alcoholic, a drug addict, or mentally ill.

— You had a parent who was physically ill or disabled much of the time and unavailable.

— You had to take care of one or both parents, physically or emotionally.

— You had a parent whom a mental health professional would recognize as being narcissistic, sadistic, or in some other way extremely difficult to live with.

— At school or in your neighborhood you were the victim—a target of abuse, teasing, etc.

— You had other childhood traumas besides abuse (e.g., major or chronic illness, injury, handicap, poverty, a natural disaster, your parents were under unusual stress due to unemployment, etc.).

— Your social environment limited your opportunities and/or treated you as inferior due to your being poor, a minority, etc.

— There were major changes in your life over which you had no control (moves, deaths, divorce, abandonment, etc.).

— You felt a strong sense of guilt over something you felt you were at fault for and could not discuss with anyone.

— You wanted to die.

— You lost your father (through death, divorce, etc.), were not close to him, and/or he was not involved in your upbringing.

— You lost your mother (through death, divorce, etc.), were not close to her, and/or she was not involved in raising you.

— Either of the above two were cases of clear and voluntary abandonment or a rejection of you personally, or you believed you lost your parent through some fault or behavior of your own.

— A brother, sister, or other close family member died or was otherwise lost to you.
— Your parents fought continually and/or were divorced and fought over you.
— As a teenager you were especially troubled or suicidal, or you abused drugs or alcohol.
— As a teenager you were in constant trouble with authorities.

Now that you are done, look at the pattern of checks, stars, and circles. If there aren't many, celebrate and express your gratitude where it is due. The presence of quite a few has probably brought up fresh pain or fear of being deeply flawed or damaged. Let the full picture of your history come to the fore. Then bring into focus your own best traits, talents, and accomplishments, plus all the helpful people and events that offset the negative. Then spend a few moments (maybe take a walk) to honor the child who endured and contributed so much. And consider what he or she needs next.

9

Medics, Medications, and HSPs
Being a Pioneer on the Frontiers of Medicine

(REVISED 2020)

This chapter addresses two related topics. First we will consider how your trait affects your response to medical care in general. Then we will get into specifics about pain, overstimulation, and the medications sometimes associated with the trait in the minds of health care professionals, which you may be taking or be offered because of your trait.

Ways Your Trait May Affect Your Medical Care

- You may be more sensitive to bodily signs and symptoms.
- If you do not lead a life suited to your trait, you can develop more stress-related and/or "psychosomatic" illnesses.
- You are probably more sensitive to medications.
- You are probably more sensitive to pain.
- You will be more aroused, usually overaroused, by medical environments, procedures, examinations, and treatments.
- In particular in "health care" environments your deep intuition probably cannot ignore the shadowy presence of suffering and death, the human condition.

- Given all of the above, and the fact that most mainstream medical professionals are not HSPs, your relationships with them is usually more problematic.

The good news is that you can notice problems before they are major and be wonderfully aware of what helps. As mentioned in Chapter Four, highly sensitive children not living under stress have unusually good health. A long-term study of adults who had been conscientious in childhood, true of most HSPS, were unusually healthy as adults. This was not true of shy adults. This suggests that HSPs are capable of excellent health, but they need to work out their social life and ease their social discomforts so that they have the stress-free, supportive life they need.

But let's discuss the problems implied by the above list, because those concern you more. Being unusually aware of subtle physical signs means that you are bound to have many false alarms. This should be no problem—you go to a doctor and ask. If you are still uncertain, you get a second opinion.

Sometimes it is not that simple though, is it? Doctors can be busy, insensitive people these days. Typically, you the HSP comes in a little nervous and overaroused. You are aware of something small, but it concerns you or you would not have come in. You know it is probably going to turn out to be nothing and the doctor will see you as overly fussy. You know that both your sensitivity to the subtle and your overarousal due to anticipated social discomfort are standing out all over you. You may even cry. I usually do in these situations.

Meanwhile, your health care professional may share the culture's bias in mistaking your trait for shyness, introversion, or just being neurotic,. Further, for some male doctors especially, sensitivity is a dreaded weakness which they had to repress in order to survive medical school. So they project this "overly sensitive" part of themselves (and all the weakness they associate with it) onto patients with any sign of it at all.

In short, there are many reasons a health care professional may begin with the assumption that with you in particular this faint symptom is "all in your head" and possibly hints at that eventually. (Of course the mind and body are so linked, it could have begun with a psychological stressor. But most medical professionals find psychology too much to deal with.)

So you leave, not wanting to seem neurotic by protesting, but wonder if you were heard, if you were well examined, if everything is really all right. You feel embarrassed and do not want to be any trouble. But you go away still worrying, which leaves you wondering if you really are neurotic. And you may decide next time to ignore your symptoms until they are so obvious anybody could see them.

Educating Your Health Care Professionals

The solution is to find or educate health care professionals who fully appreciate your trait. That means the person takes seriously your ability to pick up on subtle aspects of your health and reactions to a treatment. A real professional should be delighted by this excellent alarm system. At the same time, knowing your sensitivity, he or she can be the calm expert and reassure you when there is probably nothing wrong after all. But this reassurance should be respectful, not on the basis of an assumption that something is wrong with you psychologically.

Many who work in alternative medicine, body work, nutrition counseling, and so on are fully onboard with high sensitivity because so many HSPs are seeing them. It helps so much to explain it to those who do not know about it yet. HSPs like them because they listen and because they often help us. But sometimes we need those other doctors and nurses, trained in traditional medical schools. They usually feel they learned everything they really need to know while in school and from their clinical experiences. They don't have time to read journals, and they don't have a term yet for this trait, even though they may know about it in various ways. We need to turn them into sophisticated care givers, fully aware of varying temperaments, and knowledgeable about how to handle HSPs with gentle, attentive respect. In the long run, what's good for HSPs is usually good for everyone. (I was recently visiting someone in a hospital where they now enforce quiet hours midnight to 5 a.m. I am sure this was the result of the complaints of HSPs, but it turned out to be good for all patients.)

How do you create such wonders? You can bring this book as a gift. Make a note of the web address, www.hsperson.com, and mention to the health care professional that all the research is explained there (over one hundred studies now). You want to demonstrate that although new, this is real science. For some, a better alternative than the book will be to bring a copy of the movie *Sensitive: The Untold Story*. Assure them that it is entertaining and at the same time will teach them about the 20 percent or more of their patients who are highly sensitive.

Be careful not to imply that you see them as ignorant of this subject, which is cool enough even to have a movie about it. Rather, suggest that as excellent practitioners, they already know about it to some extent. "I'm sure you've noticed people like me, who are sensitive to pain and to medications, and who can be a bit overstimulated just by being in the office and having to explain their problems—but are very good about following orders!" If they have watched the movie, you can do this through a quick review of DOES. "I know I ask a lot of questions—that's my depth of processing. And you know about O, my being easily overstimulated, including by my reactions to pain and medications. E is for my tears sometimes, but also my empathy for all of you. And S is for my noticing the subtle stimuli—I do notice more symptoms, but also when I am getting better."

Be sure they know it is innate—not some neurotic personality problem. "You know, it's a temperament we're born with. All kids have temperaments, outgoing, active, whatever. And some are more sensitive than others, like I was, and we all grow up keeping our temperaments." As I say in the box "Practicing Dealing in a New Way with Medical Professionals," prepare a script and practice it, if that will help. Or have a few notes with you— patients often bring in notes about things they want to ask, so it will not seem out of the ordinary.

If they are obviously not interested or do not tell you later that they watched the movie or looked at the book, stop seeing them. You are the consumer. Indeed, if they make you feel bad in other ways (their "vibes"), consider not seeing them. I recall an HSP writing for one of my early newsletters about her recovery process, which took years after a serious auto accident, and how she learned not to let negative people touch her, as they only set back her healing. If you are in a medical plan or seeing a specialist whom you must stay with, do not give up on them. Sometimes professionals seem not to listen to new information but then go check it out on their own.

Sensitivity to Medications

As for your sensitivity to medications, this is quite real. We have done two research studies on this. Basically, this just seems to be part of your trait, like your tending to be sensitive to caffeine or hunger. It could be increased, of course, by overarousal and hypervigilance due to being worried about the side effects (and most drugs have them so you are not being neurotic there). Or you could be overaroused about something else at the time you took the first dose. So you may want to wait and see how you do with the medication after you settle down.

When you are sure you are having a bad reaction to a medication, believe it. There are enormously wide variations in sensitivity to drugs. Expect your medical professionals to work with you on this in a respectful way. If they do not, again, you are the customer—you go elsewhere.

Sensitivity to Pain

About your sensitivity to pain, this too varies greatly among people generally. For example, some women feel almost no pain in childbirth, and research on them has found that such women rarely feel pain ever in their lives. The reverse is no doubt also true—that some feel a great deal of pain during their life.

Some HSPs have told me they are not particularly sensitive to pain, but upon questioning, I often find they have become good at managing it in various ways. The best nonpharmacological treatment of pain appears to be distraction and hypnosis. However, not everyone is fully hypnotizable and you may not have anyone around to hypnotize you. Self-hypnosis is an option that is often successful, for example with dental pain. There are many methods offered for learning self-hypnosis. These often involve audio instruction, at least to begin with, but you can also learn to do it from written instructions.

Distraction is an especially easy way to control pain. I am sure you have noticed already how well it works. For example, whenever I am undergoing some procedure that might distress me, up until it is about to begin the nurse or doctor may have been rather quiet or formal, but suddenly begin a conversation with me. I am happy to oblige, on any subject. It works so well to distract me, especially if they ask me questions I like to answer. Try it in other situations. If you are having blood drawn, strike up a conversation with the person doing it (and look away).

Any other sensation in the body can also work as a distraction—putting attention on your hand when your foot hurts and vice versa. Or you can look out the window and "deep process" the leaves on the trees or clouds in the sky (although something more fascinating might work best). If you are suffering with pain for hours or days, you will have to work harder at it, and distractions will not work all the time. But do get into conversations. Maybe catch up with people you have not talked to for a while. Maybe don't even mention being in pain. If you are up to it, work at something that will distract you mentally. Watch comedy, mystery, or action films that will not upset you but will keep you occupied. Virtual reality and video games can be highly effective. Even crossword puzzles.

Our state of mind affects pain perception some, so it always helps if you can be a kind, loving, understanding, calm parent to your infant/body when it is in pain. It is also essential that you communicate about your extra sensitivity to pain to those who can help. If they are well informed on the topic, they will take your reaction as a normal variation in human physiology and treat it appropriately. (But remember you also may be more sensitive to pain-relieving medications.)

Overarousal in General in Medical Situations

Let's consider both overarousal about your medical situation (along with meeting medical professionals) and the overarousal during treatments or procedures. You might turn back to what I said about overarousal in chapter 1. When you are outside of your optimal level of arousal, you not only feel bad but perform less well. For example, your ability to communicate your thoughts and to remember what was said will decrease, often making you even more overaroused, then probably afraid you are being seen as neurotic, not very smart, or whatever.

It helps if you do not confuse overstimulation with fear at the outset; this can add to the distress in a medical situation. Perhaps you think you are more afraid than you really are about the meaning of your symptoms, meeting a new person, a repeat of a past bad medical experience, or how you will be judged. These may be real fears, but try to accept them rather than judge them. I know it sounds strange, but worrying about your fear will only increase your fear, and remember it could just be you are feeling over-aroused. Overstimulated. This will be especially true if this is a new office and new people you will meet.

What to do? You can come with a list of questions and take notes. You can bring someone with you to listen and ask the questions you do not think of. (That way, too, there is another memory to check afterward.) And you can explain your tendency to be overaroused, as I discussed above. They will understand especially well if they have watched the movie and know about DOES. (You could even go to the waiting room on another day to at least make that more familiar. Familiarity really will reduce the over-stimulation you feel during the subsequent visit.)

Let the professionals calm you down with some chitchat or whatever method they prefer. You can ask them to help you compensate for your arousal by asking the person to repeat instructions and to be available for follow-up calls to answer the questions you did not think of.

When they tell you about symptoms or "what might happen," ask to be told what's normal, as you may notice little changes others miss. This way you will not be worried about those changes if they happen (or have to call at night or on the weekend). Some-times it is normal to feel pain, but doctors or nurses want to avoid suggesting that. But even though you may seem to be suggestible (or are), you are probably better off knowing than being sur-prised.

As for overarousal due to treatments and procedures, appre-ciate that you are being faced with new, intense sensations, often threatening invasions of your body. The solutions are, first, once again, explain to whoever is doing the procedure that you are highly sensitive. Express this in a way that is both self-respectful and respectful of them. Hopefully, your self-disclosure will be ap-preciated. The person doing the procedure can take extra mea-sures to make it easier for you, which also means easier for them.

You should be aware of what works best for you in reducing arousal. Some of us do better with everything explained as the person goes along; some prefer silence. Some prefer a friend with them; some want to be alone. Some do fine with extra medication; some find the loss of control while medicated even more distressing. Further, you can probably do a lot for yourself. You can become familiar ahead of time with as much about the situation as possible. You can calm, center, and soothe yourself in all the ways you know how. And you can comfort yourself afterward with loving understanding and acceptance of any intense reaction you had.

If you or your infant body need to stop because "this is not for me," say so or at least insist on a pause to talk about it. If you need anything, say so, whether it's a need to pause, to have the music turned down or off, to have the person stop talking, or whatever. I know it can be difficult—especially if you are the type who always tries to be good or polite, hiding your needs—but do it.

Anytime you set a boundary or express a nonnegotiable need, here's a thought: You do not *have* to give a reason. None at all unless it will help you. As one HSP taught me, "It just doesn't work for me" can be the very best response because it prevents the other person arguing back, wanting to offer a solution to get around your "no." A corollary to that is, if someone says, "You are just too sensitive," respond with "What specifically about my sensitivity is not working for you?" (And eventually getting in "I rather like my sensitivity.") The specifics can be very enlightening and often resolvable.

Obviously the bottom line is that you are often more aroused than the average patient. Even assuming your health professional is smart enough not to treat your arousal as a nuisance or a sign of disturbance, it still makes things more difficult.

Keep in mind, too, that, as explained in chapter 7, it is common to feel an attachment to anyone you have been with during an arousing experience, especially if it was a truly painful or emotionally significant ordeal. In the medical realm you hear it when people are describing their surgeon or when women talk about the person who delivered their child. This is perfectly normal. The solution is simply to know why it happens and compensate for it appropriately.

Overarousal is hard. There's just no getting around it. And in medical situations, with pain and aging and death all right in your face, it gets harder. Still, living life aware of death makes sense to me, provided it increases your appreciation of the moment. When the awareness is too much, you can always enjoy that handy universal defense called denial. And let your friends or family gather around you to help. They have or will face these things someday too. This is not time to feel you are a burden. We are all in it together.

Speaking of friends and family, I have spent time in the hospital at the bedsides of some of mine right after surgery but when they are already beginning to recover; in the hospital when the prognosis was poor; in nursing homes after a stroke or because of dementia; and as they were dying, sometimes very lucid, sometimes not. I think HSPs can be at our best in these situations. In one unpublished study we asked, "Would you be willing to sit at the bedside of a dying stranger and comfort them?" HSPs answered yes more often.

All of DOES can come into play, but that includes overstimulation. You may not realize until you leave the situation how much you were experiencing at a subtle or unconscious level. Chapter 3 deals with general health and lifestyle and most of it is devoted to the problem of overstimulation.

Meditation as Medical Treatment

In chapter 3 I recommended Transcendental Meditation (TM). I will say it again because there is fresh medical research about it, besides what I mentioned about its lowering cortisol, the "stress" hormone generated by overarousal. I also bring TM up again because it is another anniversary—I have been doing it twice daily (rarely missing a session) for fifty years. In a sense, fifty years of practice is a kind of research that demonstrates how much I like the way it relaxes me. I always look forward to it. And I have definitely become a better person overall because of all that rest!

I have also now thoroughly researched other kinds of meditation. To summarize just a little of the new research, It is clear that there are three main types of meditation, each with different effects on the brain. That's right, meditation is not just meditation. There are major differences. Each has its purpose and merits. Focused meditation, such as Zen, as the name implies, helps you learn to focus your attention. In mindfulness mediation, you are gently attuned to your breath, your body, your thoughts, or whatever you are instructed to center on, returning to it when you have gone off of it, so it helps you be more "mindful" or aware of your body and thoughts.

The automatic self-transcending approach, TM and Christian Centering Prayer (basically the same method as TM), aim to allow the mind to go to its quietest possible level of activity. Of course there are thoughts, but these are seen as part of meditation and not resisted. Sleep is also allowed. The basic idea is that you transcend effortlessly—you do not *try* to do it. The brain wants to slow down for a while and reorganize, if allowed to (and for a "deep processor" on some days there will be lots of thoughts). But the body, including the brain, is in a deep state of rest, really the most efficient downtime.

The associated brain wave pattern is a type of alpha wave. (You have heard of alpha biofeedback for relaxation.) This spreads to most of the brain, creating that very quiet, restful feeling. Considerable medical research has found it very good for your health, especially for keeping the heart, which it seems could be most damaged by chronic overarousal, in good health. TM is probably the ideal type of meditation for HSPs—although, if you are enjoying another method, good! Alas, TM may be the most expensive to learn, because, ironically, it requires very skilled teaching over several days to help you learn not to make an effort! The advantages are that it is widely available in a standardized format, and substantial financial assistance is available.

Rewriting Medical History

Now might be a good time to do some reframing of your medical care experiences in light of your trait.

Think of one to three significant experiences of illness and medical care, especially hospitalizations or childhood experiences. Then follow the three familiar steps. First, think about how you have always understood those experiences, probably with the help of the attitudes of the medical profession—that you are "too sensitive," a difficult patient, afraid of pain, neurotic, and so forth. Then consider these experiences in the light of what you now know about your trait. Finally, consider if there is anything that needs to be done because of this new knowledge, such as looking for a new doctor or giving this book or the movie or the Web address to her or him.

Also, if this has been a difficult aspect of your life, look at "Practice Dealing in a New Way with Medical Professionals."

PRACTICE DEALING IN A NEW WAY WITH MEDICAL PROFESSIONALS

1. *Think of a medical situation that for you is overarousing, socially uncomfortable, or otherwise problematic.* Maybe it is your response to being undressed except for a hospital gown, to certain kinds of examinations, or to having blood drawn, teeth drilled, or getting a diagnosis or report that is delayed or unclear.

2. *Think about this situation in the light of your trait*, including your trait's potential positive role. For example, you will notice sooner if there is a problem and be more conscientious about following instructions. But above all, think about what you need (and have a right to have) to make the situation less arousing. Remember, everyone should be working to see that your body is not flooded with cortisol, since the medical outcome will be better too if you are calm.

3. *Imagine how you will get what you need.* It may be something you can do for yourself. But it probably involves at least a little bit of communicating about your sensitivity to a medical professional. So write out a script for yourself. Be sure it conveys self-respect and will generate respect from others without being rude or arrogant. Have someone whose opinion you trust look at your script. Someone involved in health care would be ideal. Then role play the conversation with them. Have them tell you afterwards how they felt as you spoke.

4. *Think about how you can apply what you have practiced to the next time you receive medical care.* At that time you may want to return to these points and practice more in order to turn the imagined into reality.

A Caution About Medical Labels for Your Trait

As you know, doctors are rapidly become aware of just how much our mental attitudes affect the immune system and illness. They are also aware that some people more than others seem to have thoughts and feelings that could contribute to illness. But because they are focused on illness, they often fail to consider whether there could be some positive aspects to a personality type which may seem to go with some illness. I say "seem" because, even if among those who have, for example, fibromyalgia, chronic fatigue syndrome, autoimmune disorders, or Type 1 diabetes there are a larger expected numbers of HSPs, it is very difficult to know the percentage who have these disorders in the larger population of HSPs. Indeed, given the differential susceptibility discussed in the Author's Note, there may be fewer HSPs with these diseases, as compared to the rest of the population, among those HSPs who had good childhoods or grew up in low-stress environments. The problem is that it is almost impossible to take a representative sample of all HSPs to see the rate of illness when given their childhoods, but it is easy to look at the percentage of HSPs being treated in a clinic for a disorder.

Especially beware of those describing HSPs as typically having a certain disorder when they offer (for a fee) treatment for it. You should ask: What is the research behind that treatment? If someone says HSPs have certain tendencies to illnesses that could be prevented with the right supplements or whatever, again be careful. How do they know that? And how do they stand to gain by telling HSPs this?

Above all, as long as HSPs experience cultural prejudices, that may be what is really doing the damage. Indeed, health professionals and those offering health advice can unwittingly perpetuate the prejudice by proclaiming with all of their professional authority that a certain kind of personality or trait is unhealthy, negative, or especially prone to disease. Remember, some HSPs, including you, may be especially likely NOT to get these same disorders.

None of this is meant to be harshly critical of doctors. But you need to be aware of it, as what I have described is obviously the case with our trait. For example, in 1989 a book called *Sick and Tired of Being Sick and Tired* was published, authored by an eminent internist from John Hopkins, Neil Solomon, and a psychologist, Marc Lipton. Its topic was the "Profound Sensitivity Syndrome," which they felt was present in many people.

Millions, in fact, have an exaggerated outpouring [of the bio-chemicals released by stress reactions and are] profoundly sensitive [to them]. They are poorly insulated against them and cannot alert the brain to stop the flow. Thus, the body is flooded with abnormal amounts and reacts with a variety of physical symptoms that cannot be traced to any other source (p. 25). . . . The key to healing . . . is in the mind's ability to perceive a problem accurately and control the flow (p. 27)

Note the phrases "exaggerated outpouring," "poorly insulated," "cannot alert the brain," and the need to "perceive a problem ac-curately." Although the book might be dated, it is the type of lan-guage most doctors heard in medical school. I truly appreciate this early effort made by Solomon and Lipton to help people with this trait. But you can read the prejudice everywhere. Their stan-dard of what is normal was not appropriate for people with this inherited trait. They did show some sense of the positive aspects of the trait, acknowledging that persons with this "syndrome" are more creative and sensitive to others. But they did not under-stand the underlying, neutral physical difference. Their sugges-tions were good, but there is an underlying condescension. We are seen as needing more rational self-control. Yet HSPs are often, if anything, overcontrolled. And it rarely helps to tell a person al-ready aroused to "get yourself under control."

Again, I do not mean to pick on Solomon and Lipton. Their book is simply an example of something to watch for as the books on health come closer to understanding us, but continue for a time to make the same old mistakes.

When Your Trait Is Thought to Be a Mental Health Problem

Several times I have suggested that you talk to your health profes-sionals about your trait. However, if you do, it is possible that you will be offered a "psychoactive" medication as a permanent solu-tion—probably an antidepressant or antianxiety medication. In-deed, many of you have probably already tried these medications. They can be very helpful if you are in a crisis or need a temporary means to control your overarousal or its effects such as not sleeping or eating well. The deeper question is whether you should take something more or less permanently to "cure" your trait. Some doctors may think you should. For example, when I first told my own family doctor about this book he was quite excited. "This problem is really undertreated by medicine," he said. "It's shameful. But thank God it's easily cured, just like diabetes." And out comes his prescription pad.

I know he only meant to be helpful, and that was twenty-five years ago. But I told him, with some sarcasm I fear, that I would try to hang on a little longer without his help.

Medications in a Crisis

There is an important distinction between using psychoactive medications in a crisis and using them to make a long-term personality change. Sometimes medication seems to be the only way out of a vicious circle of overarousal and lack of adequate functioning by day, losing sleep over it, then functioning even worse the next day. In these situations you may find a doctor like my family doctor, almost too eager to prescribe. Or you may find the other extreme, one who feels that painful states of mind should always be suffered through, especially if the cause is "external," like bereavement or anxiety about a performance. The best solution is for you to have decided ahead of time what you would do in a crisis. Become educated on the pros and cons. If you wait until you are in a crisis, you and others too may feel you are hardly in a state to be making big decisions, and there is bound to be pressure for you to do whatever the handiest doctor tells you.

Look for a psychiatrist whose philosophy on such medications suits yours. (Finding a good psychiatrist is not always easy, but family doctors are not experienced enough with these medications.) Be sure the psychiatrist understands about high sensitivity. If he or she is not interested or claims to know all about it but obviously does not, find another. If you are interested in alternative treatments, the practitioner should be informed about these, too, and be able to tell you what might work and what might not work.

About Antidepressants

As I said in the Author's Note, I am not going to go deeply into medications, except to say that HSPs have often taken antidepressants because we do develop depression easily. I know these medications have prevented suicides, relieved or ended depression, and hence, also improved the lives of people close to those who've taken them. That said, it remains the case that many find them very difficult to get off of. Some research indicates that the most commonly prescribed antidepressants are only a little better than placebos, making patients feel good to the same degree as if they had been given a sugar pill. What about the side effects? In a study of 1,500 people, from 38 countries, who had taken antidepressants, John Read and James Williams report that most had had significant negative side effects, including weight gain and loss of interest in sex. Both of these are enough to make you depressed even if you were not before. Others complained of drowsiness, emotional "blunting," and even suicidality.

There are arguments on both sides, all worth understanding, and I know they will change with time. Hence, I do not want to say more here and have it be out of date soon. Thankfully, the information is now all on the Internet somewhere (but stick to reading about scientific research, such as you can find on Google Scholar—skip the horror stories, on either side).

One thing has not changed: that antidepressants should be accompanied by psychotherapy for best results, and that in the long run psychotherapy appears to be as effective as the combined treatment.

Instant Arousal-Stopping Medications

There are countless psychoactive drugs that can stop high arousal quickly and for a few hours at least. (As you understand now, arousal does not have to be anxiety, so do not accept the label of "anxiety prone." Arousal can just be overstimulation.)

Many people swear by these medications for getting to sleep or dealing with a performance or other stressful period. However, while the effects are short-lived, the need for them may not be if one is not careful. You can become physically dependent on them quickly, in the sense that without them, you are more stressed than ever. When a new antianxiety medication appears, it is usually claimed to be less addictive than its predecessors. But it seems likely that all drugs that rapidly move us into our optimal level of arousal, from either underarousal or overarousal, are likely to be addictive to some degree. Alcohol and opiates move us out of overarousal, caffeine and amphetamines out of underarousal. All are addictive. Indeed, anything that works fast to solve a problem is going to be taken again and again and again unless the side effects outweigh the benefits. I have no idea how many HSPs self-medicate and risk, or are already dealing with, addiction. Even if a higher number of HSPs were addicted to alcohol, pain pills, and so on, than 20 percent or so of the population, it would be almost impossible to study because we don't know how all HSPs behave, especially those with good childhoods.

The point is, however, that addiction can sneak up on you, and addictive substances have the nasty effect of requiring more and more to get the same effect, until you are taking it to avoid withdrawal symptoms more than for its good effect (think of caffeine and tobacco). Further, the body's natural arousal balancing act is going to be suppressed.

Of course if you are constantly overaroused, then that balancing act is already fouled up. The break provided by taking antianxiety medications now and then may be just what you needed.

There are other ways, however, to change your bodily chemistry—a walk; some deep breathing; a massage; a snack; being held by someone you love; journaling; or dancing. The list goes on and on.

"Natural" herbal calming agents have been used since we lived in caves. Chamomile tea is a good example, so are valerian, lavender, passion flower, hops, and oat teas, or a blend. You will find individuality here as everywhere—some will work on you better than others. Used before bed, the right one will create a sleepy period that often does the trick. If you are short on calcium or magnesium, more of these minerals may calm you too.

The point is, your doctor may not mention these methods. He or she is visited often by drug company salespersons. Nobody comes around urging doctors to prescribe a walk or a cup of chamomile tea.

In Conclusion: You and the Frontiers of Medicine

Medicine is rapidly shifting toward individualized or "precision" care (not true when I wrote this chapter originally). This will have to include the trait of high sensitivity. The integration of temperament and medicine already includes research on how personality may predict future illness, which helps with prevention. Personality, the summation of innate temperament and personal history starting from before birth, is not the same as innate traits, such as high sensitivity, alone.

Interestingly, in the study of personality and prevention, neuroticism has been a confusing trait, sometimes seen as predicting better and sometimes worse outcomes. Perhaps this is because it is moderately related to high sensitivity, and some worry (an aspect of neuroticism) may help with prevention. Another trait, openness, has a low but definite association with high sensitivity and also predicts better health.

My point is that every time you explain to a medical professional about your trait, you are individualizing your medical care, which is very good for your health—and for your health care providers, since individualized medicine does improve outcomes, which is their goal. You are also advancing the attention medicine will give to this trait. It is going to be a major factor in personalized "precision" medicine soon, I am sure. Further, I know you will help medical professionals keep in mind the benefits of the trait, not just how it makes some of us, perhaps with poorer childhoods, more vulnerable to one or another illness.

A complete view of the trait is not only helpful to you, but to all of us. In other words, every time you go to the doctor's you are a pioneer and a spokesperson. I hope this book, including the new Author's Note, will help you feel prepared to speak up for yourself and for all of us.

• **Working With What You Have Learned** •

What You Would Change If a Safe Pill Would Change It

Take out a piece of paper and draw a line down the middle from top to bottom. On the left make a list of everything about yourself even vaguely related to this trait that you would gladly eliminate if there was a safe pill you could take to do it. This is your chance to be totally annoyed by the disadvantages of being an HSP. It is also your chance to dream of the perfect personality-changing pill. (This exercise is not about use of medications when you are in crisis, depressed, or suicidal.)

Now, for each item you wrote on the left, put on the right side what might be lost from your life if that negative aspect were eliminated by this wonderful pill. (One thing your pill, like all pills, cannot do is maintain a paradox.) Some examples not related to the trait: "Stubbornness" goes on the left, but without it you might lose "persistence," which goes on the right.

If you want, attach a 1, 2, or 3 to each trait—on the left according to how much you would like to be rid of it (3 being most), on the right according to how much you want to keep it. A much higher total on the left suggests that it is still difficult for you to accept who you are. Think about what might explain this, something past or present. Then imagine this part of yourself that does not like your sensitivity. Have a conversation with it. Find out what the specific problem is, and let the HSP in you practice advocating for itself.

10

Soul and Spirit
Where True Treasure Lies

There is something about HSPs that is more soulful and spiritual. By soul I mean that which is more subtle than the physical body but still embodied, like dreams and imagination; spirit transcends yet contains all that is soul, body, and world.

What role should soul and spirit play in your life? Several possibilities take a bow in these last pages, including a psychological view that we are destined to develop the wholeness so needed in human consciousness. After all, we have a deep talent for being aware of what others miss or deny, and it is ignorance which does the damage, again and again.

However, this chapter also has its share of other, less psychological voices, both angelic and divine.

Four Telltale Signs

Thinking back, I see it was almost a historical moment: the first gathering of HSPs, on the campus of the University of California at Santa Cruz, on March 12, 1992. I had announced a lecture on the results of my interviews and first surveys, inviting those who had participated plus interested students and therapists, most of whom turned out to be HSPs, too.

What I noticed first was the silence in the room before I began. I had not thought about what to anticipate, but polite quiet would have made sense. This was even a little more than mere quiet, however. There was a palpable silence, as in a deep forest. An ordinary public room had been changed by the presence of these people.

When I was ready to speak, I noticed the courteous alertness. Of course, the topic mattered to them. But I felt them with me in a manner that I now associate with all audiences of HSPs. We tend to be people very interested in ideas, taking each concept and pondering all its possibilities. We are also supportive. We certainly try not to ruin something for others by whispering, yawning, or entering a room or leaving at inappropriate times.

My third observation comes from my courses for HSPs. I like to take several breaks, including one together in silence, to rest, meditate, pray, or think, as each chooses. I know from experience that a certain percentage of the average audience will be confused, even distressed, by such an opportunity. With HSPs I have never noticed even a hesitation.

Fourth, about half of those I interviewed talked most about their soul/spirit life, as if that defined them. With the others, when I would ask about inner life, philosophy, relationship to religion, or spiritual practices, suddenly these voices had new energy, as though I had finally gotten to the point.

Feelings about "organized religion" were very strong. There were a few who were very committed, the rest were dissatisfied, even disdainful. But unorganized religion thrived; about half followed some daily practice that took them inward to touch the spiritual dimension.

Below is some of what they had to say. Reduced to glimpses, it became almost a poem.

Has meditated for years, but "lets the experiences go."

Prays daily: "You get what you pray for."

"I practice myself; I try to live a life true to animal and human nature."

Meditates daily. Has no "faith" except a faith that all will be okay.

Knows there is a spirit, a greater power, a guiding force.

"If I had been a man, I would have been a Jesuit."

"Everything alive is important; there's something greater, I know."

"We are how we treat other people. Religion? It would be a comfort if I could believe."

"Taoism, the force at work in the universe: Let go of struggle." .

Started talking to God when five, sitting in the trees; is guided by a voice during crises, is visited by angels.

Twice-daily deep relaxation.

"We're here to protect the planet."

Meditates twice daily; has had "oceanic experiences, a few days of lasting euphoria; but spiritual life is incremental, requiring understanding, too."

"I was an atheist until Alanon."

"I think about Jesus, about the saints. I have tidal waves of spiritual feelings."

Meditates, has visions, her dreams fill her with "radiant energy; many days are filled with overwhelming joy and grace."

At four years of age heard a voice promise her she would always be protected

Says life is good, in all, but it is not for comfort. It is for learning about God. It builds character.

"I am attracted and repelled by the religion of my childhood but always touched by the transcendent, the mysteries, which I do not know what to do with."

Many religious experiences. His purest came when his child was born.

Bypassed her religion, went directly to God (through meditation)—and to the needy.

Practices with a group a spiritual method from Indonesia, dancing and singing to achieve a "natural state of existence which is deeply blissful."

Prays each morning for a half hour, reflecting on the past day and the one to come—"the Lord gives insight, corrects, shows the path."

"I believe that when we are born again in Christ we are given abilities to develop so we can live our lives in the glory of God."

"True religious experiences manifest in daily life as faith in all events being for the good."

"I am a Buddhist-Hindu-pantheist: Everything happens as it is supposed to; have fun at all costs; walk with beauty above, below, and behind."

"I often feel one with the universe."

What We Are Good At—What's It Good For?

I have mentioned four repeated experiences I have had with HSPs: spontaneous deep silence creating a hallowed kind of collective presence, considerate behavior, soul/spirit directness, and insight about all of this. These four are strong evidence to me that we, the royal-advisor class, are the "priest" class, supplying some kind of ineffable nourishment to our society. I cannot presume to label it. But I can offer some observations.

Creating Sacred Space

I like the way that anthropologists speak of ritual leadership and ritual space. Ritual leaders create for others those experiences which can only take place within a ritual, sacred, or transitional space, set aside from the mundane world. Experiences in this sort of space are transformative and give meaning. Without them life becomes drab and empty. The ritual leader marks off and protects the space, prepares others to enter it, guides them while there, and helps them return to society with the right meaning from the experience. Traditionally, these were often initiation experiences marking life's great transitions—into adulthood, marriage, parenthood, elderhood, and death. Others were meant to heal, to bring a vision or revelation that gave direction, or to move one into closer harmony with the divine.

Today sacred spaces are quickly made mundane. They require great privacy and care if they are to survive. They are as likely to be created in the offices of certain psychotherapists as in churches, as likely to occur in a gathering of men or women dissatisfied with their religion as in a community practicing its traditions, as likely to be signaled by a slight change in topic or tone in a conversation as by the donning of shamanic costume and the outlining of a ceremonial circle. The boundaries of sacred space today are always shifting, symbolic, and rarely visible.

While bad experiences have caused some HSPs to reject anything striving to seem sacred, the majority feel most at home in such a space. Some almost spontaneously generate it around themselves. Thus, they frequently take on the vocation of creating it for others, making HSPs the priest class in the sense of creating and tending sacred space in these aggressively secular-warrior times.

Prophesying

Another way to look at HSPs as "priests" comes from psychologist Marie-Louise Von Franz, who worked closely with Carl Jung. She writes about what Jungians call the introverted intuitive type, the majority of HSPs. (To those who know you are not both or even one of these types, I apologize for excluding you for a moment.)

> The introverted intuitive type has the same capacity as the extraverted intuitive for smelling out the future. . . . But his intuition is turned within, and therefore he is primarily the type of the religious prophet, of the seer. On a primitive level, he is the shaman who knows what the gods and the ghosts and the ancestral spirits are planning, and who conveys their messages to the tribe. . . . He knows about the slow processes which go on in the collective unconscious.

Today many of us are artists and poets rather than prophets and seers, producing a kind of art that von Franz says "is generally only understood by later generations, as a representation of what was going on in the collective unconscious at that time." Still, traditionally, prophets shape religion, not art, and we all can see that something very strange is happening to religion today.

Ask yourself if the sun rises in the east. Then see how you feel about your "wrong" answer. Because, of course, you *are* wrong. The sun does not rise. The earth turns. So much for personal experience. We cannot trust it, or so it seems. We can only trust science.

Science has triumphed as the Best Way to Know Anything. But science is simply not designed to answer the big spiritual, philosophical, and moral questions. So we almost behave as if they must not be important. But they are. They are always being answered, implicitly, by a society's values and behaviors—whom it respects, whom it loves, whom it fears, whom it leaves to languish unhoused and unfed. When these questions are addressed explicitly, it is usually by HSPs.

But today even HSPs are not sure how they can experience or believe in anything that cannot be seen, especially given all the things once believed in that science proved untrue. We hardly believe our senses, much less our intuition, when the very fact of the sun's rising is our foolish human mistake. Look at all the dogma that the priests or priest class once insisted upon. So much of it is "now proven wrong," or worse, found to have been only self-serving.

Not all of the blows to faith have come from science directly. There is also communication and travel. If I believe in heaven and a few billion people on the other side of the planet believe in reincarnation, how can we both be right? And if one part of my religion is wrong, is the rest of it? And doesn't the study of comparative religion show that it is all just an attempt to find answers for natural phenomena? Plus a need for comfort in the face of death? So why not live without these superstitions and emotional crutches? Besides, if there is a God, how do you explain all the troubles in the world? And while you are at it, explain why so many of those troubles have been caused by religion? And so the skeptical voices speak.

There are many responses to the retreat of religion. Some of us totally agree with the skeptics. Some hang on to some kind of abstract force, or goodness. Some hold firmer than ever to their traditions, becoming fundamentalists. Others reject dogma as a source of great trouble in the world, yet enjoy the rituals and certain tenets of their religious tradition. Finally, there is a new breed of religious beings seeking direct experience, not the lessons of authorities. At the same time, they know that for some reason others have different experiences, so they do not try to proclaim their experience as Truth. They may be the first humans to have to live with a direct spiritual knowledge that is recognized as fundamentally uncertain.

There are HSPs in every category. But from my interviews and courses, I believe that the majority are in the last group. Like explorers or scientists, each probes the unknown area, then comes back to report.

Except many of us are hesitant to report. The entire business of religion, conversion, cults, gurus, and New Age beliefs can be so messy. We have all felt embarrassed for our fellow humans who carry pamphlets and have a fanatic's glint in their eyes. We're afraid of being seen that way, too. HSPs have been marginalized enough as it is in a culture that favors the physical over the soul and the spirit.

Yet the times need us. An imbalance between the royal-advisor and warrior-king aspects of society is always dangerous, but especially when science negates intuition and the "big questions" are being settled without thoughtfulness but according to what is convenient at the moment.

Your contributions are needed in this area more than any other.

Writing the Precepts of Your Religion

Whether your religion is organized or unorganized, it has some precepts. I suggest that you write them down, right now if possible. What do you accept, believe, or know from your experience? As a member of the royal-advisor class, it's good to be able to put this into your own words. Then, if you sense that someone would benefit from hearing them, you can articulate them. If you don't want to commit yourself or be dogmatic, make your uncertainty and unwillingness to preach your very first precept. Having beliefs doesn't mean they're unchanging, certain, or to be imposed on others.

How We Inspire Others in the Search for Meaning

If you're uncomfortable with the role of prophet, I don't blame you. However, in an "existential crisis" you still may find yourself elevated to a soapbox or even a pulpit. It happened to Victor Frankl, a Jewish psychiatrist who was imprisoned in a Nazi concentration camp.

In *Man's Search for Meaning* Frankl (an obvious HSP) describes how he often found himself called upon to inspire his fellow prisoners, how he intuitively understood what they needed and how badly they needed it. He also observed that, under those awful circumstances, prisoners who could gain from others some kind of meaning in their lives survived better psychologically, and therefore physically as well:

> Sensitive people who were used to a rich intellectual life may have suffered much pain (they were often of a delicate constitution), but the damage to their inner lives was less. They were able to retreat from their terrible surroundings to a life of inner riches and spiritual freedom. Only in this way can one explain the apparent paradox that some prisoners of a less hardy make-up often seemed to survive camp life better than did those of a more robust nature.

For Frankl, meaning is not always religious. In the camps, he sometimes found his reason to live was helping others. At other times, it was the book he was writing on scraps of paper or his deep love for his wife.

Etty Hillesum is another example of an HSP who found meaning and shared it with others during those same difficult times. In her journals, written in Amsterdam in 1941 and 1942, one can hear her striving to understand and transform her experience, historically and spiritually—and always inwardly. Slowly, a gentle, quiet, personal victory of the spirit grows out of her fear and doubt. One can also hear in her anecdotes how much people began to find her a deep comfort. Her last words, written on a scrap of paper and thrown from a cattle car headed for Auschwitz, are perhaps my favorite quote from her: "We left the camps singing."

Etty Hillesum leaned heavily on the psychology of Jung and the poetry of Rilke (both HSPs). About Rilke, she wrote:

> It is strange to think that ... [Rilke] would perhaps have been broken by the circumstances in which we now live. Is that not further testimony that life is finely balanced? Evidence that, in peaceful times and under favorable circumstances, sensitive artists may search for the purest and most fitting expression of their deepest thoughts so that, during more turbulent and debilitating times, others can turn to them for support and a ready response to their bewildered questions? A response they are unable to formulate for themselves since all their energies are taken up in looking after the bare necessities. Sadly, in difficult times we tend to shrug off the spiritual heritage of artists from an "easier" age, with "what use is that sort of thing to us now?"
>
> It is an understandable but shortsighted reaction. And utterly impoverishing.

Whatever the times, suffering eventually touches every life. How we live with it, and help others to, is one of the great creative and ethical opportunities for HSPs.

We HSPs do a great disservice to ourselves and others when we think of ourselves as weak compared to the warrior. Our strength is different, but frequently it is more powerful. Often it is the only kind that can begin to handle suffering and evil. It certainly requires equal courage and increases with its own type of training. Nor is it always about enduring, accepting, and finding meaning in suffering. Sometimes actions involving great skill and strategy are called for.

One freezing winter night during a blackout, a barracks filled with despairing inmates begged Frankl to speak to them in the darkness. Several were known to be planning suicide. (Besides the demoralization caused by suicide, everyone in a barracks was punished when one occurred.) Frankl called on all his psychological skills to find the right words and spoke them into the darkness. When the lights came back on, men surrounded him to thank him, tears in their eyes. An HSP had won his own kind of battle.

We Lead in the Search for Wholeness

In chapters 6 and 7 I described the individuation process in terms of getting to know one's inner voices. In this way you find your own meaning in life, your own vocation. As Marsha Sinetar wrote in *Ordinary People As Monks and Mystics*, "The point of full personhood . . . is this: that whoever finds out what is, for him, good and holds fast to it becomes whole." I would only add that what one holds fast to is not a fixed goal but a process. What needs to be heard may change from day to day, year to year. Similarly, Frankl always refused to comment on *the* single meaning of life.

> For the meaning of life differs from man to man, from day to day and from hour to hour. . . . To put the question in general terms would be comparable to the question posed to a chess champion, "Tell me, Master, what is the best move in the world?" There simply is no such thing as the best or even a good move apart from a particular situation in a game. . . . One should not search for an abstract meaning of life.

The pursuit of wholeness is really a kind of circling closer and closer through different meanings, different voices. One never arrives, yet gets a better and better idea of that which is at the center. But if we really circle, there is little chance for arrogance because we are passing through every sort of experience of ourselves. This is the pursuit of *wholeness*, not perfection, and wholeness must by definition include the imperfect. In chapter 7 I described these imperfections as one's shadow, that which contains all that we have repressed, rejected, denied, and disliked about ourselves. Conscientious HSPs are as full of unpleasant traits and unethical impulses as anyone else. When we choose not to obey them, as we should, they do not go away entirely. Some of them just go underground.

In getting to know our shadow, the idea is that it is better to acknowledge our unpleasant or unethical aspects and keep an eye on them rather than to throw them out the front door "for good," only to have them slip in the back when we're not looking. Usually the people who are the most dangerous and in danger, morally speaking, are those who are certain they would never do anything wrong, who are totally self-righteous and have no idea that they have a shadow or what it is like.

Besides the greater chance of behaving morally that comes with knowing about your shadow, its energies bring vitality and depth to a personality when integrated in a conscious way. In chapter 6 I spoke of "liberated," nonconforming, highly creative HSPs. Learning a little about one's shadow (you never know a lot or enough) is the best and perhaps only way to be free of the straitjacket of oversocialization that HSPs often don in childhood. The conscientious, eager-to-please HSP in you meets and gains the contributions of a powerful, scheming, self-aggrandizing, confidently impulsive HSP. As a team in which each respects and checks the other's inclinations, they—you—are something fine to have in the world.

This is all part of what I mean by pursuing wholeness, and HSPs can lead in this kind of important human work. Wholeness has a particular demand on HSPs because we are born at the extreme end of a dimension—the dimension of sensitivity. Furthermore, in our culture we are not just a minority but one that is considered to be far from the ideal. It might seem that we need to go to the other end, from feeling weak, flawed, and victimized to feeling strong and superior. And this book has encouraged that a little, up to now. I considered it to be a necessary compensation. But for many HSPs the real challenge is to achieve the middle ground. No more "too shy" or "too sensitive" or too anything. Just okay, ordinary, normal.

Wholeness is also a central issue for HSPs in relation to the spiritual and psychological life because so often we are already good at the spiritual and psychological. In fact, if we persist in these to the exclusion of everything else, we are being one-sided. It is very hard for us to see that the most spiritual thing might be to be less spiritual, the most insightful psychological stance might be to dwell less on our psychological insights. A call to wholeness rather than perfection might be the only way to get the message.

Beyond those two general statements, the direction toward wholeness is a very individual matter, even for HSPs. If we've stayed in, we'll be tempted out or finally forced out. If we've been out, we'll have to go in. If we've armored ourselves, we'll finally have to admit to our vulnerability. But if we've been timid, we'll start to feel all wrong inside until we're more assertive.

In respect to Jungian attitudes of introversion and extraversion, most HSPs need to be more extraverted in order to become more whole. I have heard the story that Martin Buber, who wrote so eloquently about the "I-Thou" relationship, said his life was changed one day when a young man came to him for help. Buber felt he was too busy meditating and generally being holy to appreciate the young man's visit. Soon after, his visitor died in battle. Buber's devotion to the "I-Thou" attitude began when he heard that news and saw the one-sidedness of his introverted spiritual solitude.

The Pursuit of Wholeness Through the Four Functions

Again, no one achieves wholeness. Embodied human life has limits—we cannot be fully both shadow and light, male and female, conscious and unconscious. I think people have tastes of wholeness. Many traditions describe an experience of pure consciousness, beyond thought and its polarities. It comes to us deep in meditation, and an awareness saturated with it can become the foundation of our lives.

As soon as we act in this imperfect world, however, using our imperfect bodies, we are simultaneously a perfect being and an imperfect one. As imperfect beings, we are always living only one-half of any polarity. For a while we are introverted, then must become extraverted to balance it. For a while we are strong; then we are weak and must rest. The world forces us to be one limited way at any particular time. "You can't be both a cowboy and a fireman." Our limited body adds to the limits. All we can do is constantly try to get back in balance.

Often the second half of life must balance the first half. It is as though we have worn out or become utterly bored with one way of being and have to try its opposite. The shy person sets out to become a stand-up comic. The person devoted to serving others gets burned out and wonders how he or she ever became so "codependent."

In general, anything that has been our particular specialty has to be balanced by its opposite, what we are bad at or afraid of trying. One polarity Jungians talk about is the two ways of taking in information, through sensation (just the facts) or intuition (the subtle meanings of the facts). Another polarity is the two ways of deciding about the information we take in, through thinking (based on logic or what appears to be universally true) or feeling (based on personal experience and what appears to be good for ourselves and others we care about).

We each have our specialty from among these four "functions"—sensing, intuiting, thinking, and feeling. For HSPs it is often intuition. (Thinking and feeling are both common among HSPs.) However, if you are introverted—as are 70 percent of HSPs—you use your specialty mainly in your inner life.

While there are tests designed to tell you which is your specialty, Jung thought we could learn more from careful observation of which function we are worst at. This is the function that regularly humiliates us. Do you feel like a rank amateur when you want to think logically? Or when you have to decide how you personally feel about something? Or when you need to intuit what is going on at a subtle level? Or when you must stick to the facts and details without elaborating, getting creative, or going off into imaginary realms?

No one becomes equally skilled at using all four functions. But according to Marie-Louise von Franz, who wrote a long paper on the development of the "inferior function," working to strengthen this weak and bumbling part of ourselves is an especially valuable path toward wholeness. It puts us in touch with what is buried in the unconscious and therefore makes us more in tune with all of it. Like the youngest, most foolish brother in the fairy tales, this function is the one that comes home with the gold.

If you are an intuitive type (more likely for HSPs), your inferior function would be sensing—sticking to the facts, dealing with the details. Limits in the sensing function show themselves in individualized ways. For example, I consider myself quite artistic, but in an intuitive way. Words are easier for me, although I tend to have too many ideas and to say too much. I find it very hard to be artistic in a more concrete, limited way—to decorate a room or office, to figure out what to wear. I enjoy dressing nicely but usually make do with what others have bought for me. Because the real problem in both cases is that I cannot stand to shop. There are so many *things* to overstimulate and confuse me. Plus I must come to a final decision. All of these—the sensory stimulation, the practical issues, and the decisions—are usually very difficult for an introverted intuitive.

On the other hand, some intuitives are great shoppers. They can see the possibilities in something others overlook and how it will look in a particular setting. It is difficult to make generalizations about what intuitives are good at. It is better to think about style. Math, cooking, map reading, running a business—each can be done intuitively or "by the book."

Von Franz notes that intuitives are more often completely taken over by sensual experiences—music, food, alcohol or drugs, and sex. They lose all common sense about them. But they're also very intuitive about them, seeing beyond the surface to the meaning.

Indeed, the problem when trying to get in touch with the inferior function, sensing in this case, is that the dominant function often steps in, anyway. Von Franz gives the example of an intuitive taking up work with clay (a good choice for developing sensing because it is so concrete) but then becoming caught up in how good it would be if clay work were taught in all the schools and how the whole world would be changed if everyone shaped something in clay each day and how right there in the clay one can see the whole universe, in microcosm, the meaning of life!

Eventually, we may have to work with our inferior function mainly in imagination or as a very private sort of play. But according to Jung and von Franz, it is really an ethical imperative to take the time for it. Much of the irrational collective behavior we see involves people projecting their inferior function onto others or being vulnerable to appeals to their inferior function, which the manipulative media and leaders can exploit. When Hitler was promoting German hatred of the Jews, he appealed to the inferior function of the particular group to which he spoke. When he spoke to intuitives, those with inferior sensing, he described the Jews as financial tycoons and evil manipulators of markets. Intuitives are often impractical and bad at making money (including intuitive Jews). Intuitives can easily feel inferior and ashamed about their poor business sense, which makes it a short step to feeling victimized by anyone better at it. How nice to blame someone else for one's own lack.

To feeling types with inferior thinking, Hitler portrayed the Jews as unfeeling intellectuals. To thinking types with inferior feeling, he said the Jews were selfishly pursuing Jewish interests without any universal, rational ethics. And to sensing types with inferior intuition, the Jews were hinted to possess secret, magical, intuitive knowledge and powers.

When we can spot our inferior function's inferior reactions—its "inferiority complex"—we can put a stop to this sort of blaming. Thus, it is part of our moral duty to get to know exactly how we are not whole. Again, HSPs can excel at this kind of inner work.

Dreams, Active Imagination, and Inner Voices

Achieving wholeness in the Jungian sense is also facilitated by dreams and "active imagination" with those dreams, both of which help us to become conversant with our inner voices and rejected parts. For myself, dreams have been more than mere information from the unconscious. Some have literally rescued me in times of deep difficulty. Still others have given information that I, my ego, simply could not have possessed. Others have predicted or coincided with events in an uncanny way. I would have to be a very stubborn, skeptical person not to know (for myself—for no one else) that something is there guiding me.

The Naskapi are Native Americans scattered across Labrador in small families. Thus, they did not develop collective rituals. Instead, they believed in a Great Friend who enters each person at birth to provide helpful dreams. The more virtuous the person (and virtue includes a respect for dreams), the more help the person will receive from this Friend. Sometimes when I am asked my religion, I think I should say, "Naskapi."

Angels and Miracles, Spirit Guides and Synchronicities

So far I have discussed HSPs' spirituality in terms of their special leadership in the human search for ritual space, religious understanding, existential meaning, and wholeness. Some of you are wondering when I will talk about your own most significant spiritual experiences—of visions, voices, or miracles, and of intimate personal relationships with God, angels, saints, or spirit guides.

HSPs have these experiences in abundance. We seem especially receptive to them. Receptivity seems to increase at certain times in one's life, too—for example, when in depth psychotherapy. Jung called these experiences synchronicities, made possible by an "acausal connecting principle." His point was that besides the connections we know about—object A exerting force on object B—something else not (yet) measurable connects things, too. Thus, they can influence each other from a distance. Or they're close, but in other, nonphysical ways.

When objects or situations or people are connected by virtue of belonging together, that implies an unseen organization—some intelligence, plan, or perhaps an occasional compassionate, divine intervention. When my clients report one of these events, I try gently to point out that something very significant has occurred (although I leave it to the person to decide the meaning). I also urge writing down all such experiences, so that their sheer number begins to carry some weight. Otherwise, they are buried by the mundane, derided by the inner skeptic, left orphaned by the lack of "logical explanations."

Again, these are essential moments, which HSPs are especially suited to enjoy and champion. In the mourning and healing process, which can be a large aspect of the aware life, they point to that which is beyond personal suffering or to a meaning within it, one which at times we despair of finding.

Deborah's Visitors

A series of synchronicities began for Deborah with a snowstorm, rare in the Santa Cruz Mountains. In our interview she recalled that at the time she was "depressed, dead, stuck in a

> ## TAKING UP THE TASK OF TENDING
> ## THE SOUL/SPIRIT REALM
>
> I invite you to keep a spiritual journal for just one month, a testimony of all of your thoughts and experiences having to do with the nonmaterial realm. Every day write down your insights, moods, dreams, prayers, and all the little miracles and "strange coincidences." Your efforts need not be elaborate or eloquent. They simply make you a witness of the sacred—part of a long tradition of journal-keepers, including Victor Frankl, Etty Hillesum, Rilke, Buber, Jung, von Franz, and so many other fellow HSPs.

bad marriage." Because of the snow, for the first time in their marriage her husband did not make it home that night. Instead, a stranger came to her door asking for shelter. For some reason she did not hesitate to let him in, and they sat before her fire, talking about esoteric matters until late. She had written down for me what happened next:

> I felt a very high-pitched ringing in my ears and a great emptiness in my head, and I knew that he was doing something to me but felt no fear. After an unknown amount of time (probably only seconds? minutes?), everything came rushing back into my head and the ringing stopped.

She said nothing to the stranger about it, and later a neighbor came and invited the man to spend the night at his house. The stranger apparently left in the night—there was no sign of him at dawn.

> But after that snowstorm cleared and the road opened I left my marriage and began the long and entirely different road to where I am now. The horrid depression lifted that night and all my old energy and good spirits returned. So I've always thought he must have been an angel.

Two years later, she was visited by a more peculiar creature.

One night the cat *shrieked* and leapt off my legs and out the door, so I opened my eyes in alarm, instantly awake. There at the bottom of my bed was a "creature" about four feet tall, hairless, not naked but in a sort of skin-suit, with minimalist features: slits for eyes, holes for nose, no ears, and around him was a strange light that seemed made up of colors I didn't recognize. I was not the least bit afraid. He "thought-transmitted" to me, "Don't be afraid. I'm only here to observe you." And I "said" back to him, "Well, I don't think I can handle this, so I'm going back to sleep!" Which, amazingly, I did.

In the morning Deborah still felt affected and did not discuss the experience with anyone. But after that her life took a deeply spiritual turn, and "a whole series of mysterious and wonderful events started happening that only tapered off after several years."

Part of this more spiritual phase led to an involvement with a charismatic but unstable spiritual teacher—one of those I described in chapter 8 as having evolved unevenly, so that he fairly glowed "upstairs" but was dark on the "lower floors," where the practical and spiritual must cooperate in real-life, ethical decisions. Sensing his power clearly, his weakness and her danger only vaguely, she prayed for guidance: "Please, if there really are guardian angels and I've got one, will you please let me know you're around?"

Deborah then went to her job, at a bookstore. As she walked to the front of the store, she saw a book on the floor that had fallen off one of the tables. Picking it up, she had an impulse to open it. What she saw was a poem entitled "The Guardian Angel," which began with "Yes, you do have a guardian angel, he . . ."

Still, she stayed with the entrancing spiritual leader a while longer, even when he asked his followers to give him all of their possessions. After that she often felt she wanted to leave but had no strength or will to start all over again financially. But the guardian angel seemed to remember her. One day she was alone for a moment and moaned to herself, "I don't even have a clock radio anymore!" The next day, while the group was on an outing using the car that had once been hers, she was watching a beetle climb a dirt hill. She thought sadly how that beetle was freer than she was. But then, the more she watched it, the more she realized that she could be that free. So she followed that beetle up the hill. Then she left it behind and went out to *her* car, to which she happened to have the keys because she had been asked to drive that day.

As she got into the car, to "drive off to freedom," she glanced in the back and saw a "beetle-black" clock radio just like the one she had given over to the group. Once she had arrived at a friend's house, she saw that it was her own old clock radio, with the familiar scratches. She had no idea how it had gotten into the car. It seemed that it, like the rest of the day, was the work of her guardian angel.

It is easy to think one would never become involved in a situation like Deborah's; but it happens often, especially to those with strong spiritual motivations. We seek answers, certainty. And some people possess that kind of certainty, radiate it, and believe it is their mission to share it. They have charisma, an undeniable air around them. The problem is that *all* humans are fallible, more so when others believe they're not.

Deborah was tempted one more time to return to this man. A friend warned that she was "crazy" to do it. So Deborah prayed for clarification. "If I'm thinking crazily now, let me know." Then she turned on the television.

> There came on the screen silently—no audio at all— what was obviously a scene from an old-style, 1950's sort of movie of an "insane asylum," full of obviously wacko patients! I laughed out loud. Then I lay down and asked for help and fell asleep. When I awoke, I "saw" or felt myself ringed by a ring of roses, each of which was protecting a different part of me, and I felt the recently departed presence of Christ. It was the most quiet happiness. . . .

By the time I interviewed Deborah, her spiritual experiences were occurring more and more in her dreams—perhaps an indication that her visitors had found a way to reach her without having to be projected onto outer persons. It is my experience with dreams that the more we work with them, the less we are likely to fall into bizarre situations, in life or in dreams.

When Your Spiritual Life Is Like Tidal Waves

I have spoken sometimes of the soul/spirit life as a comfort, and I think it is. But it can be intensely overarousing too, at least until we learn to keep our feet on the ground, so to speak. That's hard when tidal waves are sweeping over us. And HSPs are often in the path of the biggest, perhaps because some of us are very hard to get through to. Remember Jonah? I end this chapter and this book with a story of just such a Jonah-like HSP.

At the time of the following incident, Harper was a chronically overaroused, highly intellectual HSP. (Thinking was his dominant function.) He had undergone four years of Jungian psychotherapy and really knew how to talk the talk: "Yes, God is very real—because everything psychological is real. God is our comforting psychological projection of the 'parent imago.' " Harper had all the answers, even with just the right amount of uncertainty. By day.

By night, he often woke up in deep depressions, ready to kill himself. There was no more uncertainty. In the daylight he would dismiss such nights as "nothing but the product of a negative mother complex" due to a very painful childhood and therefore "no real threat." But then another of "those nights" would come, bringing such despair that death was the only solution his intuition and logic could produce. Something in him would try to delay carrying out his solution, just until daylight, when the worst of the despair always left him.

One night he woke in such despair, however, that he was sure he would not make it until dawn. As he lay there, he had the very spontaneous thought that the one way he could go on living would be if he could be certain God really existed and cared about him. Not as his projection. As someone real. Which of course was impossible. Impossible to believe because it was impossible to know for sure.

What he wanted was some "divine sign." The thought came as spontaneously as a drowning person's shout. He knew it was stupid. But right on its heels, he told me, came the utterly spontaneous image of an automobile accident, a minor one with a few people standing around afterward uninjured. This was the sign, and it would happen the next day.

He was immediately disgusted with himself for having the corny desire for a sign from God and a characteristically negative idea for what it should be. As an HSP, Harper dreaded hassles like accidents that overaroused his body and ruined his schedule. Then, being half-asleep and lost in his dark ruminations, he forgot about it.

The next day, the car ahead of him on a freeway on-ramp braked suddenly, and he did, too. The car behind was following too close and hit him from behind. It was an accident over which he could not possibly have had any control.

"There was this intense flood of feeling right away. It wasn't the accident. I had remembered the night before." He was filled with fear and awe, as if he were "looking right into the face of God."

The accident was minor, there were no injuries, he would just have to replace his tailpipe and muffler. He and the other driver and passengers stood around, recovering and exchanging insurance information, just as in the image the night before. Skeptical as he was, he did not believe that even the most unconscious of unconscious wishes could have caused all of this. Here was something in an entirely new category of experiences. A new world.

But did he want a new world? Being an HSP, he was not sure.

For a week he was more depressed than ever. In the daytime, however, not at night. At night he slept well. Then he realized he had been subconsciously thinking he would now have to do something for God in return. Maybe give up his career and stand on street corners professing his faith. He saw that for him God had always been someone who expected you to humiliate yourself for God's sake, to pay a huge price for any comfort received, to change your whole life, right now. In fact, exactly what Harper always had been expecting of himself. Now he reasoned that coercion and guilt did not seem to be the intention of whoever or whatever had done this. Coming as it had in response to the dark night of his despair, the whole incident was supposed to be a comfort. So he slowly began to see it as that. A comfort.

But then Harper realized that to be consistent with his new

experience, he would have to stop being so despairing and skeptical. That could be quite difficult for him. So there was a kind of task that came with the experience, after all.

At this point, thoroughly confused, he tried to discuss the incident with a few others, one of whom was as moved as he. But the two friends he respected most told him it was just a co-incidence.

"That just incensed me. For *God's* sake. I mean, God did me a favor, and am I supposed to go back and say, 'That was nice, but this time I want a sign that couldn't possibly be a coinci-dence'?"

Harper was convinced that to view the accident as a coin-cidence was deeply wrong. So he decided he would just have to grow into the experience even if it took a lifetime. He would have to make himself remember it. Ponder it. Treasure it as much as he could. And be amazed that he, who had received so little comfort all his life, had suddenly received so much more in the way of a definite sign of love than most of the saints.

"What a thing to happen to a guy like me," he concluded, laughing at himself for once. Then he remembered my research interest. "What a divine mess for a *sensitive* guy like me."

Our Worth and Partnership

The warrior-kings frequently tell us that it is a sign of weakness to have faith in the reality of the soul/spirit realms. They fear in themselves anything that would weaken their kind of physi-cal courage and power and so can only see it as that in others. But we have a different kind of power, talent, and courage. Call-ing our talent for the soul/spirit life something weak or only born from fear or from a need to be comforted is about the same as saying fish swim because they are too weak to walk, have some pitiful need to be in the water, and are just plain old afraid to fly.

Or maybe we should just turn the tables: The warrior-kings are afraid of the soul/spirit life, too weak for it, and can't sur-vive without the comfort of their own view of reality.

But there's no need to sling insults as long as we know our own worth. The day always comes when the warrior-kings are glad we have enough inner life to share it with them, just as there are days when we are glad for their specialty. Here's to our partnership.

Now, may your sensitivity be a blessing to you and others. May you enjoy as much peace and pleasure as is possible in this world. And may more and more of the other worlds open to you as the days of your life pass.

• Working With What You Have Learned •

Befriending, or at Least Making Peace With, Your Inferior Function

---

Choose something to do that calls on your inferior function—preferably something you have not tried before and that does not seem too difficult. If you are a feeling type, you might read a book on philosophy or take a course in theoretical math or physics that is appropriate to your background. If you are a thinking type, you might go to an art museum and force yourself for once to ignore a work's title and artist—just have a personal reaction to every painting. If you are a sensing type, you might try to use the appearance of people you observe on the street to imagine their inner experience, histories, and futures. If you are an intuitive type, you might plan a vacation by gathering detailed information about where you will go and deciding in advance on everything you will take and do. Or if that would be easy for you, buy a new piece of complicated electronic equipment—a computer or VCR—and use the instructions to set it up and explore *all* of its operations. Do not call in anyone else to help you figure it out.

As you gradually prepare yourself to do your activity, observe your feelings, your resistances, the images that arise. No matter how dumb and humiliated you feel by "these simple things you just can't do," take your task very seriously. According to von Franz, this is the equivalent of a monastic discipline, but individualized for you. You are sacrificing the dominant function and retreating into this other, harder way.

Be especially watchful of the urge to let your dominant function take over. For the intuitive type, once you decide on your vacation destination, stick with it. Protect your fragile but concrete decision from being undermined by your imagining all the other trips you could take. And with that electronic equipment, watch how strong your urge is to skip the instructions and start doing the "obvious" with the buttons and wires. That is all intuition working. But you are going to go slowly and understand each detail before moving on to the next.

Tips for Health-Care Professionals Working With Highly Sensitive People

- HSPs augment stimulation; that is, they pick up on subtleties. But they also experience more autonomic arousal in what others would find only moderately arousing situations. Thus, in a medical context they may appear more anxious or even "neurotic."
- Rushing or becoming impatient will only exacerbate their physiological arousal, and of course added stress does not help them communicate with you or heal. HSPs are usually very conscientious and will cooperate if they can.
- Ask HSPs what they need from you to stay calm—silence; a distraction, such as conversation; being told what's happening step by step; or some medication.
- Make use of the HSP's greater intuition and physical awareness—your patient could have important information for you if you listen.
- When more aroused, no one listens or communicates well. Encourage HSPs to bring a companion to help with these tasks, to prepare for a visit by bringing notes about questions and symptoms and to write down instructions and read them back to you during the visit, and to call you if they remember questions or points later. (Few of them will abuse this, and the "second chance" will remove some pressure when you meet.)
- Don't be surprised or annoyed by the HSP having a lower pain threshold, a better response from "subclinical" dosages of medications, or more side effects. These are all part of their physiological, not psychological, differences.
- This trait doesn't necessarily require medication. HSPs with a troubled childhood do suffer from more anxiety and depression. This is not true of HSPs who have worked that through or who had a good childhood.

Tips for Teachers Working With Highly Sensitive Students

- Teaching HSPs requires different strategies than teaching other students. HSPs augment stimulation. This means they pick up on the subtle in a learning situation but are easily overaroused physiologically.
- HSPs are generally conscientious and try their best. Many of them are gifted. But no one performs well when overaroused, and HSPs are overaroused more easily than others. The harder they try when being observed or otherwise under pressure, the more they are likely to fail, which can be very demoralizing for them.
- High levels of stimulation (e.g., a noisy classroom) will distress and exhaust HSPs sooner than others. While some will withdraw, a significant number of boys especially will become hyperactive.
- Don't overprotect the sensitive student, but when insisting that the student try what is difficult, see that the experience is successful.
- Do make allowances for the trait while the student is gaining social stamina. If a presentation is to be made, arrange for a "dress rehearsal" or the use of notes or reading aloud—whatever lowers the arousal and permits a successful experience.
- Do not assume that a student who is just watching is shy or afraid. It may be quite the wrong explanation, yet the label may stick.
- Be aware of your culture's bias against shyness, quietness, introversion, and the like. Watch for it in yourself and in other students.
- Teach respect for different temperaments as you would for other differences.

- Watch for and encourage the creativity and intuition that is typical of HSPs. To build their tolerance for group life and social status with their peers, try drama activities or dramatic readings of works that have moved them. Or read their work out loud to the class. But be careful not to embarrass them.

Tips for Employers of Highly Sensitive People

- Typically, HSPs are highly conscientious, loyal, vigilant about quality, good with details, intuitive visionaries, often gifted, thoughtful of the needs of clients or customers, and good influences on the social climate of the workplace. In short, they are *ideal* employees. Every organization needs some.

- HSPs augment stimulation. This means they're aware of subtleties but also easily overstimulated. Thus, they work better with less extraneous stimulation. They should have quiet and calm.

- HSPs do not perform as well when being observed for the purpose of evaluation. Find other ways to learn about how they are doing.

- HSPs often socialize less on breaks or after hours, for they need that time to process their experiences privately. This can make them less visible or well networked in the organization. You need to take this into account when evaluating their performance.

- HSPs tend to dislike aggressive self-promotion, hoping to be noticed for their honest hard work. Do not allow this to cause you to overlook a valuable employee.

- HSPs may be the first to be bothered by an unhealthy situation in the workplace, which could make them seem like a source of trouble. But others will be affected in time, so their sensitivity can help you avoid problems later.

To be informed of new developments regarding highly sensitive people, go to www.hsperson.com and sign up for the HSP newsletter, Comfort Zone.

Notes

Author's Note, 2020

p. xiv *published a good scientific summary of the theory and research in 2012:* Aron, Elaine N., Arthur Aron, and Jadzia Jagiellowicz. "Sensory processing sensitivity: A review in the light of the evolution of biological responsivity." *Personality and Social Psychology Review* 16, no. 3 (2012): 262–282.

p. xiv *another that I was involved in was published in 2019:* Greven, Corina U., Francesca Lionetti, Charlotte Booth, Elaine Aron, Elaine Fox, Haline E. Schendan, Michael Pluess et al. "Sensory Processing Sensitivity in the context of Environmental Sensitivity: A critical review and development of research agenda." *Neuroscience & Biobehavioral Reviews* (2019).

p. xiv *published studies my husband and I:* Aron, Elaine N., and Arthur Aron. "Sensory-processing sensitivity and its relation to introversion and emotionality." *Journal of personality and social psychology* 73, no. 2 (1997): 345.

p. xv *30 percent of HSPs are extraverts:* Aron and Aron, 1997, 345.

p. xv *one for children and adolescents:* Pluess, Michael, Elham Assary, Francesca Lionetti, Kathryn J. Lester, Eva Krapohl, Elaine N. Aron, and Arthur Aron. "Environmental sensitivity in children: Development of the Highly Sensitive Child Scale and identification of sensitivity groups." *Developmental psychology* 54, no. 1 (2018): 51.

p. xv *identifying high sensitivity in children too young to talk* Lionetti, Francesca., Elaine Aron, Arthur, Aron, Daniel Klein, and Michael Pluess. "Observer-rated environmental sensitivity moderates children's response to parenting quality in early childhood." *Developmental Psychology.* In press.

p. xv *had not been further validated or published until 2018:* Boterberg, Sofie, and Petra Warreyn. "Making sense of it all: The impact of sensory processing sensitivity on daily functioning of children." *Personality and Individual Differences* 92 (2016): 80–86.

p. xv *study looked at twenty-nine uses of it in research:* Smith, Heather L., Julie Sriken, and Bradley T. Erford. "Clinical and Research Utility of the Highly Sensitive Person Scale." *Journal of Mental Health Counseling* 41, no. 3 (2019).

p. xvi *overarching basic trait measured by the overall scale:* Lionetti, Francesca, Arthur Aron, Elaine N. Aron, G. Leonard Burns, Jadzia Jagiellowicz, and Michael Pluess. "Dandelions, tulips and orchids: evidence for the existence of low-sensitive, medium-sensitive and high-sensitive individuals." Translational psychiatry 8, no. 1 (2018): 24.

p. xvi *no more than one third of the "variance" on the HSP Scale:* Şengül-İnal, Gülbin, and Nebi Sümer. "Exploring the multidimensional structure of sensory processing sensitivity in turkish samples." *Current Psychology* (2017): 1–13.

p. xvi *Another series of studies, published in 2005:* Aron, Elaine N., Arthur Aron, and Kristin M. Davies. "Adult shyness: The interaction of temperamental sensitivity and an adverse childhood environment." *Personality and Social Psychology Bulletin* 31, no. 2 (2005): 181–197.

p. xvi *Another study the same year by Miriam Liss and others:* Liss, Miriam, Laura Timmel, Kelin Baxley, and Patrick Killingsworth. "Sensory processing sensitivity and its relation to parental bonding, anxiety, and depression." *Personality and individual differences* 39, no. 8 (2005): 1429–1439.

p. xvi *studied by Jay Belsky and Michael Pluess:* Belsky, Jay, and Michael Pluess. "Beyond diathesis stress: differential susceptibility to environmental influences." *Psychological bulletin* 135, no. 6 (2009): 885.

p. xvi *those high in what Michael Pluess calls environmental sensitivity:* Pluess, Michael. "Individual differences in environmental sensitivity." *Child Development Perspectives* 9, no. 3 (2015): 138–143.

p. xvii *had benefited from it one year later:* Pluess, Michael, and Ilona Boniwell. "Sensory-processing sensitivity predicts treatment response to a school-based depression prevention program: Evidence of vantage sensitivity." *Personality and Individual Differences* 82 (2015): 40–45.

p. xvii *only the highly sensitive boys benefited:* Nocentini, Annalaura, Ersilia Menesini, and Michael Pluess. "The Personality trait of environmental sensitivity predicts children's positive response to school-based antibullying intervention." *Clinical Psychological Science* 6, no. 6 (2018): 848–859.

p. xviii *One of the most fascinating studies:* Karam, Elie G., John A. Fayyad, Claudia Farhat, Michael Pluess, Youmna C. Haddad, Caroline C. Tabet, Lynn Farah, and Ronald C. Kessler. "Role of childhood adversities and environmental sensitivity in the development of post-traumatic stress disorder in war-exposed Syrian refugee children and adolescents." *The British Journal of Psychiatry* 214, no. 6 (2019): 354–360.

p. xviii *computer simulations about how the trait evolved:* Wolf, Max, G.

Sander Van Doorn, and Franz J. Weissing. "Evolutionary emergence of responsive and unresponsive personalities." *Proceedings of the National Academy of Sciences* 105, no. 41 (2008): 15825–15830.

p. xviii *A study of kindergarten-age children's reactions to positive and negative changes:* Slagt, Meike, Judith Semon Dubas, Marcel AG van Aken, Bruce J. Ellis, and Maja Deković. "Sensory processing sensitivity as a marker of differential susceptibility to parenting." *Developmental psychology* 54, no. 3 (2018): 543.

p. xix *having a good childhood was not associated:* Booth, Charlotte, Helen Standage, and Elaine Fox. "Sensory-processing sensitivity moderates the association between childhood experiences and adult life satisfaction." *Personality and individual differences* 87 (2015): 24–29.

p. xix *a new concept created by Michael Pluess and Jay Belsky:* Pluess, Michael, and Jay Belsky. "Vantage sensitivity: genetic susceptibility to effects of positive experiences." *Genetics of psychological well-being* (2015): 193–210.

p. xix *struggling more with negative emotions, more physical symptoms when stressed, stress at work, Type I diabetes, and anxiety:* Brindle, Kimberley, Richard Moulding, Kaitlyn Bakker, and Maja Nedeljkovic. "Is the relationship between sensory–processing sensitivity and negative affect mediated by emotional regulation?." *Australian Journal of Psychology* 67, no. 4 (2015): 214–221.
Benham, Grant. "The highly sensitive person: Stress and physical symptom reports." *Personality and individual differences* 40, no. 7 (2006): 1433–1440.
Evers, Arne, Jochem Rasche, and Marc J. Schabracq. "High sensory-processing sensitivity at work." *International Journal of Stress Management* 15, no. 2 (2008): 189.
Redfearn, Robert Alan. "Sensory Processing Sensitivity: Is Being Highly Sensitive Associated with Stress and Burnout in Nursing?" PhD diss., 2019.
Goldberg, Alon, Zaheera Ebraheem, Cynthia Freiberg, Rachel Ferarro, Sharon Chai, and Orna Dally Gottfried. "Sweet and sensitive: Sensory processing sensitivity and type 1 diabetes." *Journal of pediatric nursing* 38 (2018): e35–e38.
Hofmann, Stefan G., and Stella Bitran. "Sensory-processing sensitivity in social anxiety disorder: relationship to harm avoidance and diagnostic subtypes." *Journal of anxiety disorders* 21, no. 7 (2007): 944–954.

p. xx *research done in Denmark by Cecilie Licht and others:* Licht, Cecilie L., Erik L. Mortensen, and Gitte M. Knudsen. "Association between sensory processing sensitivity and the 5-HTTLPR

Short/Short genotype." *Biological Psychiatry* 69 (2011): 152S–153S.

p. xx   *also bestows advantages:* Homberg, Judith R., and Klaus-Peter Lesch. "Looking on the bright side of serotonin transporter gene variation." *Biological psychiatry* 69, no. 6 (2011): 513–519.

p. xx   *Chunhui Chen and his associates:* Chen, Chunhui, Chuansheng Chen, Robert Moyzis, Hal Stern, Qinghua He, He Li, Jin Li, Bi Zhu, and Qi Dong. "Contributions of dopamine-related genes and environmental factors to highly sensitive personality: a multi-step neuronal system-level approach." *PloS one* 6, no. 7 (2011): e21636.

p. xx   *away from what are called single candidate gene studies :* Border, Richard, Emma C. Johnson, Luke M. Evans, Andrew Smolen, Noah Berley, Patrick F. Sullivan, and Matthew C. Keller. "No support for historical candidate gene or candidate gene-by-interaction hypotheses for major depression across multiple large samples." *American Journal of Psychiatry* 176, no. 5 (2019): 376–387.

p. xx   *Robert Keers and Michael Pluess:* Keers, Robert, and Michael Pluess. "Childhood quality influences genetic sensitivity to environmental influences across adulthood: A life-course Gene× Environment interaction study." *Development and psychopathology* 29, no. 5 (2017): 1921–1933.

p. xx   *Finally, Marinus van Ijzendoom and Marian Bakemans-Kranenburg conducted a "meta-analysis":* van Ijzendoorn, Marinus H., and Marian J. Bakermans-Kranenburg. "Genetic differential susceptibility on trial: Meta-analytic support from randomized controlled experiments." *Development and Psychopathology* 27, no. 1 (2015): 151–162.

p. xxi *it's over one hundred:* Wolf, Max, G. Sander Van Doorn, and Franz J. Weissing. "Evolutionary emergence of responsive and unresponsive personalities." *Proceedings of the National Academy of Sciences* 105, no. 41 (2008): 15825–15830.

p. xxii *Max Wolf and his colleagues:* Wolf et al., 2008,15825.

p. xxiv *Franziska Borries did a particular statistical analysis:* Borries, F. "Do the "Highly Sensitive" exist? A Taxonometric Investigation of the Personality Construct Sensory Processing Sensitivity." PhD diss., PhD Thesis (unpublished doctoral dissertation), Univ. Bielefeld, 2012.

p. xxiv *Another study did not find two groups:* Kroenung, R. L. "The Latent Structure of Sensitivity—a Taxometric Analysis of Sensory-Processing Sensitivity." M.A. diss., MA Thesis (unpublished dissertation), Univ. Bielfeld, Bielfeld, Germany, 2015.

p. xxiv *three groups that are somewhat distinct:* Pluess, Michael, Elham Assary, Francesca Lionetti, Kathryn J. Lester, Eva Krapohl, Elaine N. Aron, and Arthur Aron. "Environmental sensitivity in children:

Development of the Highly Sensitive Child Scale and identification of sensitivity groups." *Developmental psychology* 54, no. 1 (2018): 51.

Lionetti, Francesca, Arthur Aron, Elaine N. Aron, G. Leonard Burns, Jadzia Jagiellowica, and Michael Pluess. "Dandelions, tulips and orchards: evidence for the existence of low-sensitive, medium-sensitive and high-sensitive individuals." *Translational psychiatry* 8, no. 1 (2018): 24.

p. xxiv *"Psychotherapy and the Highly Sensitive Person"* in 2011: Aron, Elaine N. *Psychotherapy and the highly sensitive person: Improving outcomes for that minority of people who are the majority of clients.* Routledge, 2011.

p. xxv *Research by Jadzia Jagiellowicz:* Jagiellowicz, Jadzia, Xiaomeng Xu, Arthur Aron, Elaine Aron, Guikang Cao, Tingyong Feng, and Xuchu Weng. "The trait of sensory processing sensitivity and neural responses to changes in visual scenes." *Social cognitive and affective neuroscience* 6, no. 1 (2010): 38–47.

p. xxv *In another study, by ourselves and others:* Aron, Arthur, Sarah Ketay, Trey Hedden, Elaine N. Aron, Hazel Rose Markus, and John DE Gabrieli. "Temperament trait of sensory processing sensitivity moderates cultural differences in neural response." *Social cognitive and affective neuroscience* 5, no. 2–3 (2010): 219–226.

p. xxv *research by Bianca Acevedo and her associates:* Acevedo, Bianca P., Elaine N. Aron, Arthur Aron, Matthew–Donald Sangster, Nancy Collins, and Lucy L. Brown. "The highly sensitive brain: an fMRI study of sensory processing sensitivity and response to others' emotions." *Brain and behavior* 4, no. 4 (2014): 580–594.

p. xxvi *Some have called it the seat of consciousness:* Craig, Arthur D., and A. D. Craig. "How do you feel—now? The anterior insula and human awareness." *Nature reviews neuroscience* 10, no. 1 (2009).

p. xxvi *A study by Friederike Gerstenberg:* Gerstenberg, Friederike XR. "Sensory-processing sensitivity predicts performance on a visual search task followed by an increase in perceived stress." *Personality and Individual Differences* 53, no. 4 (2012): 496–500.

p. xxvi *more affected by the level of chaos in their homes:* Evans, Gary W., and Theodore D. Wachs. "Chaos and its influence on children's development." Washington, DC: American Psychological Association (2010).

p. xxvii *differently in HSPs and those with autism spectrum disorders:* Acevedo, Bianca, Elaine Aron, Sarah Pospos, and Dana Jessen. "The functional highly sensitive brain: a review of the brain circuits underlying sensory processing sensitivity and seemingly related disorders." *Philosophical Transactions of the Royal Society B: Biological Sciences* 373, no. 1744 (2018): 20170161.

p.xxviii *Data from surveys and experiments:* Already cited: Aron and Aron, 1997, and Aron et al 2005.

p.xxviii *a series of studies done by Jadzia Jagiellowiczs:* Jagiellowicz, Jadzia, Arthur Aron, and Elaine N. Aron. "Relationship between the temperament trait of sensory processing sensitivity and emotional reactivity." *Social Behavior and Personality: an international journal* 44, no. 2 (2016): 185–199. Also, Jagiellowicz, Jadzia, Arthur Aron, and Elaine N. Aron. "Relationship between the temperament trait of sensory processing sensitivity and emotional reactivity." *Social Behavior and Personality: an international journal* 44, no. 2 (2016): 185–199.

p.xxviii *this reaction to positive pictures was not only:* Jagiellowicz, Jadzia, Xiaomeng Xu, Arthur Aron, Elaine Aron, Guikang Cao, Tingyong Feng, and Xuchu Weng. "The trait of sensory processing sensitivity and neural responses to changes in visual scenes." *Social cognitive and affective neuroscience* 6, no. 1 (2010): 38–47.

p.xxviii *In her studies of the brain done with Bianca Acevedo:* Acevedo, Bianca P., Jadzia Jagiellowicz, Elaine Aron, Robert Marhenke, and Arthur Aron. "Sensory Processing Sensitivity and Childhood Quality's Effects on Neural Responses To Emotional Stimuli." *Clinical Neuropsychiatry* 6 (2017).

p.xxviii *In the study by Bianca Acevedo and her associates that I mentioned earlier:* See Acevedo, Bianca P. et al., 2014, above.

p.xxviii *The brain's "mirror neurons":* For a more complete understanding of mirror neurons, see Iacoboni, Marco. *Mirroring people: The new science of how we connect with others.* Farrar, Straus and Giroux, 2009.

p.xxix *Roy Baumeister and his colleagues:* Baumeister, Roy F., Kathleen D. Vohs, C. Nathan DeWall, and Liqing Zhang. "How emotion shapes behavior: Feedback, anticipation, and reflection, rather than direct causation." *Personality and social psychology review* 11, no. 2 (2007): 167–203.

p.xxix *HSPs are far more affected by test scores:* Aron, Elaine N., Arthur Aron, and Kristin M. Davies. "Adult shyness: The interaction of temperamental sensitivity and an adverse childhood environment." *Personality and Social Psychology Bulletin* 31, no. 2 (2005): 181–197.

p.xxxi *more creative:* Bridges, David, and Haline E. Schendan. "Sensitive individuals are more creative." *Personality and Individual Differences* 142 (2019): 186–195.

p.xxxi *driven by emotions:* De Dreu, Carsten KW, Matthijs Baas, and Bernard A. Nijstad. "Hedonic tone and activation level in the mood-creativity link: toward a dual pathway to creativity model." *Journal of personality and social psychology* 94, no. 5 (2008): 739.

p.xxxi *negative emotions:* Akinola, Modupe, and Wendy Berry Mendes. "The dark side of creativity: Biological vulnerability and negative emotions lead to greater artistic creativity." Personality and Social Psychology Bulletin 34, no. 12 (2008): 1677–1686.

p.xxxi *feelings of awe:* Greven, Corina U., Francesca Lionetti, Charlotte Booth, Elaine Aron, Elaine Fox, Haline E. Schendan, Michael Pluess et al. "Sensory Processing Sensitivity in the context of Environmental Sensitivity: A critical review and development of research agenda." *Neuroscience & Biobehavioral Reviews*(2019).

p.xxxi *skills labeled together as part of the trait of mindfulness:* Bakker, Kaitlyn, and Richard Moulding. "Sensory-processing sensitivity, dispositional mindfulness and negative psychological symptoms." Personality and Individual Differences 53, no. 3 (2012): 341–346.

p.xxxi *emotional regulation and HSPs:* Brindle, Kimberley, Richard Moulding, Kaitlyn Bakker, and Maja Nedeljkovic. "Is the relationship between sensory-processing sensitivity and negative affect mediated by emotional regulation?" *Australian Journal of Psychology* 67, no. 4 (2015): 214–221..

p.xxxi *many HSPs have Seasonal Affective Disorder:* Hjordt, Liv V., and Dea S. Stenbæk. "Sensory processing sensitivity and its association with seasonal affective disorder." *Psychiatry research* 272 (2019): 359–364.

p.xxxii *would indeed be more bored:* Aron, Elaine N., Arthur Aron, Jadzia Jagiellowicz, and Jennifer Tomlinson. "Sensory processing sensitivity is associated with boredom in close relationships." Paper presented at the International Association for Relationship Research Conference, Herzliya, Israel, July 2010.

p.xxxii *have more meaningful conversations:* Mehl, Matthias R., Simine Vazire, Shannon E. Holleran, and C. Shelby Clark. "Eavesdropping on happiness: Well-being is related to having less small talk and more substantive conversations." *Psychological science* 21, no. 4 (2010): 539–541.

p.xxxiii *how HSPs experience being parents:* Aron, Elaine N., Arthur Aron, Natalie Nardone, and Shelly Zhou. "Sensory Processing Sensitivity and the Subjective Experience of Parenting: An Exploratory Study." *Family Relations* (2019).

p.xxxiv *"The Highly Sensitive Parent":* Aron, Elaine. The Highly Sensitive Parent. Citadel, 2020.

p.xxxiv *a study of the self-reported parenting styles of HSPs:* Branjerdporn, Grace, Pamela Meredith, Jenny Strong, and Mandy Green. "Sensory sensitivity and its relationship with adult attachment and parenting styles." PloS one 14, no. 1 (2019): e0209555.

p.xxxiv *An interview study:* Turner, Karen A., Ellen S. Cohn, and Jane Koomar. "Mothering when mothers and children both have sensory processing challenges." *British Journal of Occupational Therapy* 75, no. 10 (2012): 449–455. Taylor?

p.xxxiv *Finally, in a study of those raising children with Autism Spectrum Disorders:* Su, Xueyun, Ru Ying Cai, and Mirko Uljarević. "Predictors of mental health in chinese parents of children with autism Spectrum disorder (ASD)." *Journal of autism and developmental disorders* 48, no. 4 (2018): 1159–1168.

p.xxxv *A study done by Bhavini Shrivastava:* Shrivastava, Bhavini. "Predictors of work performance for employees with sensory processing sensitivity." Required research paper for M.Sc in Organizational Psychology, City University, London, 2011.

p.xxxv *Maike Andresen and her collaborators:* Andresen, Maike, Paul Goldmann, and Anna Volodina. "Do overwhelmed expatriates intend to leave? The effects of sensory processing sensitivity, stress, and social capital on expatriates' turnover intention." *European Management Review* 15, no. 3 (2018): 315–328.

p.xxxv *HSPs have also been found to have a strong entrepreneurial intention:* Harms, Rainer, Isabella Hatak, and Manling Chang. "Sensory processing sensitivity and entrepreneurial intention: The strength of a weak trait." *Journal of Business Venturing Insights* 12 (2019): e00132.

p.xxxv *reasons HSPs make exceptional leaders:* https://linkedin.com/pulse/20140903182945-1552470-3-reasons-hsps-make-better-leaders.

Chapter 1

p. 6 *under the same stimulation:* e.g., J. Strelau, "The Concepts of Arousal and Arousability As Used in Temperament Studies," in *Temperament: Individual Differences*, ed. J. Bates and T. Wachs (Washington, D.C.: American Psychological Association, 1994), 117–41.

p. 7 *observable differences:* R. Plomin, *Development, Genetics and Psychology* (Hillsdale, N.J.: Erlbaum, 1986).

p. 7 *unobserved by others:* e.g., G. Edmund, D. Schalling and A. Rissler, "Interaction Effects of Extraversion and Neuroticism on Direct Thresholds," *Biological Psychology* 9 (1979).

p. 7 *careful processing of information:* R. Stelmack, "Biological Bases of Extraversion: Psychophysiological Evidence," *Journal of Personality* 58 (1990): 293–311.

p. 10 *on the average . . . :* When unreferenced, the point comes from my own findings. When referencing studies on introversion or shyness, I assume most subjects were HSPs.

p. 10 *avoiding making errors:* H. Koelega, "Extraversion and Vigilance Performance: Thirty Years of Inconsistencies," *Psychological Bulletin* 112 (1992): 239–58.

p. 10 *conscientious:* G. Kochanska, "Toward a Synthesis of Parental Socialization and Child Temperament in Early Development of Conscience," *Child Development* 64 (1993): 325–47.

p. 10 *without distractions):* L. Daoussis and S. McKelvie, "Musical Preferences and Effects of Music on a Reading Comprehension Test for Extraverts and Introverts," *Perceptual and Motor Skills* 62 (1986): 283–89.

p. 10 *minor differences:* G. Mangan and R. Sturrock, "Lability and Recall," *Personality and Individual Differences* 9 (1988): 519–23.

p. 10 *"semantic memory."* E. Howarth and H. Eysenck, "Extraversion Arousal and Paired Associate Recall," *Journal of Experimental Research in Personality* 3 (1968): 114–16.

p. 11 *about our own thinking:* L. Davis and P. Johnson "An Assessment of Conscious Content As Related to Introversion-Extraversion," *Imagination, Cognition and Personality* 3 (1983–84): 149–68.

p. 11 *without being aware we have learned:* P. Deo and A. Singh, "Some Personality Correlates of Learning Without Awareness," *Behaviorometric 3* (1973): 11–21.

p. 11 *learn languages better:* M. Ohrman and R Oxford, "Adult Language Learning Styles and Strategies in an Intensive Training Setting," *Modern Language Journal* 74 (1990): 311–27.

p. 11 *fine motor movements:* R. Pivik, R. Stelmack, and F. Bylsma, "Personality and Individual Differences in Spinal Motoneuronal Excitability," *Psychophysiology* 25 (1988): 16–23.

p. 11 *good at holding still:* Ibid.

p. 11 *"morning people":* W. Revelle, M. Humphreys, L. Simon, and K. Gillian, "The Interactive Effect of Personality, Time of Day, and Caffeine: A Test of the Arousal Model," *Journal of Experimental Psychology General* 109 (1980): 1–31.

p. 11 *affected by . . . caffeine:* B. Smith, R. Wilson, and R. Davidson, "Electrodermal Activity and Extraversion: Caffeine, Preparatory Signal and Stimulus Intensity Effects," *Personality and Individual Differences* 5 (1984): 59–65.

p. 11 *more "right brained":* S. Calkins and N. Fox, "Individual Differences in the Biological Aspects of Temperament," in *Temperament*, ed. Bates and Wachs, 199–217.

p. 11 *things in the air:* e.g., D. Arcus, "Biological Mechanisms and Personality: Evidence from Shy Children," *Advances: The Journal of Mind–Body Health* 10 (1994): 40–50.

p. 11 *not "chronically aroused":* Stelmack, "Biological Bases," 293–311.

p. 12 *less capable of happiness:* e.g., R. Larsen and Timothy Ketelaar, "Susceptibility to Positive and Negative Emotional States," *Journal of Personality and Social Psychology* 61 (1991): 132–40.

p. 13 *sensitivity is inherited:* e.g., D. Daniels and R. Plomin, "Origins of Individual Differences in Infant Shyness," *Developmental Psychology* 21 (1985): 118–21.

p. 13 *have older brothers and sisters are more likely to be HSPs:* J. Kagan, J. Reznick, and N. Snidman, "Biological Bases of Childhood Shyness," *Science* 240 (1988): 167–71.

p. 13 *born innately sensitive:* J. Higley and S. Suomi, "Temperamental Reactivity in Non-Human Primates," in *Temperament in Childhood,* ed. G. Kohnstamm, J. Bates, and M. Rothbart (New York: Wiley, 1989), 153–67.

p. 14 *reduce sensitivity:* T. Wachs and B. King, "Behavioral Research in the Brave New World of Neuroscience and Temperament" in *Temperament,* ed. Bates and Wachs, 326–27.

p. 15 *"every thread . . .":* M. Mead, *Sex and Temperament in Three Primitive Societies* (New York: Morrow, 1935), 284.

p. 15 *other traits are ignored:* G. Kohnstamm, "Temperament in Childhood: Cross-Cultural and Sex Differences," in *Temperament in Childhood,* ed. Kohnstamm *et al.,* 483.

p. 15 *and Yuerong Sun:* "Social Reputation and Peer Relationships in Chinese and Canadian Children: A Cross-Cultural Study," *Child Development* 63 (1992): 1336–43.

p. 17 *introversion with poor mental health:* B. Zumbo and S. Taylor, "The Construct Validity of the Extraversion Subscales of the Myers-Briggs Type Indicator," *Canadian Journal of Behavioral Science* 25, (1993): 590–604.

p. 17 *performed better, and they do:* M. Nagane, "Development of Psychological and Physiological Sensitivity Indices to Stress Based on State Anxiety and Heart Rate," *Perceptual and Motor Skills* 70 (1990): 611–14.

p. 17 *the non-sensitive cope:* K. Nakano, "Role of Personality Characteristics in Coping Behaviors," *Psychological Reports* 71 (1992): 687–90.

p. 18 *protection of the planet and the powerless:* See Riane Eisler, *The Chalice and the Blade,* (San Francisco: Harper and Row, 1987); Riane Eisler, *Sacred Pleasures,* (San Francisco: HarperSanFrancisco, 1995).

Chapter 2

p. 24 *greatest when infants were tired:* M. Weissbluth, "Sleep-Loss Stress and Temperamental Difficultness: Psychobiological Processes and Practical Considerations," in *Temperament in Childhood,* ed. Kohnstamm, *et al.*, 357–77.

p. 24 *the true cause of the crying:* Ibid., 370–71.

p. 26 *adapt to the caretakers . . . :* M. Main, N. Kaplan, and J. Cassidy, "Security in Infancy, Childhood, and Adulthood: A Move to the Level of Representation," in *Growing Points of Attachment Theory and Research. Monographs of the Society for Research in Child Development,* ed. I. Bretherton and E. Waters, 50 (1985): 66–104.

p. 27 *Kagan . . . much of his career:* J. Kagan, *Galen's Prophecy* (New York: Basic Books, 1994).

p. 28 *only 10 percent showed low fear:* Ibid., 170–207.

p. 28 *born that way:* S. Calkins and N. Fox, "Individual Differences in the Biological Aspects," in *Temperament,* ed. Bates and Wachs, 199–217.

p. 29 *balance of these two which creates sensitivity:* Charles A. Nelson, in *Temperament,* ed. Bates and Wachs, 47–82.

p. 31 *ignored and neglected:* G. Mettetal, "A Preliminary Report on the IUSB Parent Project" (paper, International Network on Personal Relationships, Normal, Ind., May 1991).

p. 31 *the University of Oregon:* M Rothbart, D. Derryberry, and M. Posner, "A Psychobiological Approach to the Development of Temperament," in *Temperament,* ed. Bates and Wachs, 83–116.

p. 34 *an interesting experiment:* M. Gunnar, "Psychoendocrine Studies of Temperament and Stress in Early Childhood" in *Temperament,* ed. Bates and Wachs, 175–98.

p. 34 *caretaker is your own mother:* M. Nachmias, "Maternal Personality Relations With Toddler's Attachment Classification, Use of Coping Strategies, and Adrenocortical Stress Response" (paper, 60th annual meeting of the society for Research in Child Development, New Orleans, La., March 1993).

p. 35 *the more fear, the more cortisol:* Weissbluth, "Sleep-Loss Stress," 360.

p. 35 *last into adulthood . . .: Ibid.*, 367.

p. 36 *"archetypal" dreams:* R. Cann and D C. Donderi, "Jungian Personality Typology and the Recall of Everyday and Archetypal Dreams," *Journal of Personality and Social Psychology* 50 (1988): 1021–30.

p. 36 *developed a neurosis:* C. Jung, *Freud and Psychoanalysis,* vol. 4 *The Collected Works of C. G. Jung,* ed. W. McGuire (Princeton, N.J.: Princeton University Press, 1961).

p. 36 *"a certain innate sensitiveness . . .":* Ibid., 177.

p. 37 *educators and promoters . . .":* C. G. Jung, *Psychological Types,* vol. 6. *The Collected Works,* 404–05.

p. 37 *"a prophetic foresight":* Ibid., 401.

Chapter 3

p. 40   *"A storm threatens . . .":* D. Stern, *Diary of a Baby* (New York: Basic Books, 1990) 31.

p. 41   *"All is remade . . .":* Ibid., 37.

p. 41   *"A baby's nervous system . . .":* Ibid., 18.

p. 43   *will cry more, not less:* S. Bell and M. Ainsworth, "Infant Crying and Maternal Responsiveness," *Children Development* 43 (1972): 1171–90.

p. 43   *"securely attached" children:* J. Bowlby, *Attachment and Loss,* (New York: Basic Books, 1973).

p. 45   *"Enfolded in arms . . .":* R. Josselson, *The Space Between Us: Exploring the Dimensions of Human Relationships* (San Francisco: Jossey-Bass, 1992), 35.

p. 54   *in any darkened room:* T. Adler, "Speed of Sleep's Arrival Signals Sleep Deprivation," *The American Psychological Association Monitor,* 24, (1993): 20.

p. 56   *(Cortisol in meditators' blood decreases.):* R. Jevning, A. Wilson, and J. Davidson, "Adrenocortical Activity During Meditation," *Hormones and Behavior* 10 (1978): 54–60.

p. 57   *a powerful drug for HSPs, however:* Smith, Wilson, and Davidson, "Electrodermal Activity and Extraversion," 59–60.

Chapter 4

p. 70   *creates the situation:* H. Goldsmith, D. Bradshaw, and L. Rieser-Danner, "Temperament as a Potential Developmental Influence" in *Temperament and Social Interaction in Infants and Children,* ed. J. Lerner and R. Lerner (San Francisco: Jossey-Bass, 1986) 14.

p. 71   *"Her next gust is rushing towards me, . . .":* Stern, *Diary of a Baby,* 59–60.

p. 73   *which can be quite enduring:* Main et al., "Security in Infancy."

p. 73   *stronger-than-usual feeling of being loved:* G. Mettetal, telephone conversation, 30 May 1993.

p. 75   *"unreasonable" fears and nightmares:* A. Lieberman, *The Emotional Life of the Toddler* (New York: The Free Press, 1993), 116–17.

p. 75   *as many males as females born with this trait:* e.g., Gunnar, "Psychoendocrine Studies," in *Temperament,* ed. Bates and Wachs, 191.

p. 75   *boys and girls quite differently:* J. Will, P. Self, and N. Datan, "Maternal Behavior and Perceived Sex of Infant," *American Journal* 46, (1976): 135–39.

p. 75   *"can be interpreted as a consequence of the value-system of the mother . . .":* Hinde, "Temperament as an Intervening Variable," 32.

p. 76 *get along well with their mother:* Ibid.

p. 76 *criticism, rejection, coldness:* J. Cameron, "Parental Treatment, Children's Temperament, and the Risk of Childhood Behavioral Problems," *American Journal Orthopsychiatry* 47, (1977): 568–76.

p. 76 *both parents, for better or worse:* Ibid.

p. 78 *"shy child":* Lieberman, *Emotional Life.*

p. 81 *how normal it is:* J. Asendorpf, "Abnormal Shyness in Children," *Journal of Child Psychology and Psychiatry* 34 (1993): 1069–81.

p. 82 *one researcher:* L. Silverman, "Parenting Young Gifted Children," Special Issue: *Intellectual Giftedness in Young Children, Journal of Children in Contemporary Society,* 18 (1986).

p. 83 *better guidelines for raising gifted children:* Ibid.

p. 85 *professional achievement:* A. Caspi, D. Bem, and G. Elder, "Continuities and Consequences of Interactional Styles Across the Life Course," *Journal of Personality* 57 (1989): 390–92.

p. 86 *"quiet independence . . .":* Ibid., 393.

Chapter 5

p. 92 *seventy-five percent . . . are socially outgoing:* Silverman, "Gifted Children," 82.

p. 92 *fearful, inhibited, and timid:* H. Gough and A. Thorne, "Positive, Negative, and Balanced Shyness: Self-Definitions and the Reactions of Others," in *Shyness: Perspectives on Research and Treatment,* ed. W. Jones, J. Cheek, and S. Briggs (New York: Plenum, 1986), 205–25.

p. 93 *same negative words:* Ibid.

p. 93 *Phil Zimbardo:* S. Brodt and P. Zimbardo, "Modifying Shyness-Related Social Behavior Through Symptom Misattribution," Journal of Personality and Society Psychology 41 (1981): 437–49.

p. 96 *themselves "shy":* P. Zimbardo, *Shyness: What It Is, What to Do About* (Reading, Mass.: Addison-Wesley, 1977).

p. 96 *more noticeable . . . than it really is:* M. Bruch, J. Gorsky, T. Collins, and P. Berger, "Shyness and Sociability Reexamined: A Multicomponent Analysis," *Journal of Personality and Social Psychology* 57 (1989): 904–15.

p. 96 *just not trying enough:* C. Lord and P. Zimbardo, "Actor-Observer Differences in the Perceived Stability of Shyness," *Social Cognition* 3 (1985): 250–65.

p. 98 *more affected by their social relationships:* S. Hotard, R. McFatter, R. McWhirter, M. Stegall, "Interactive Effects of Extraversion, Neuroticism, and Social Relationships on Subjective Well-Being," *Journal of Personality and Social Psychology* 57 (1989): 321–31.

p. 99 *how introverts actually do act:* A. Thorne, "The Press of Personality: A Study of Conversations Between Introverts and Extraverts," *Journal of Personality and Social Psychology* 53 (1987): 718–26.

p. 99 *breathing in and out:* C. Jung, *Psychological Types,* vol. 6, *The Collected Works,* 5–6.

p. 99 *the "objective" world:* Ibid., 373–407.

p. 100 *They are living evidence . . .":* Ibid., 404–5.

p. 100 *the brighter the child, the more likely . . . introverted:* Silverman, "Gifted Children," 82.

p. 100 *make to a Rorschach:* R. Kincel, "Creativity in Projection and the Experience Type," *British Journal of Projective Psychology and Personality Study* 28 (1983): 36.

p. 106 *Gretchen Hill . . .:* "An Unwillingness to Act: Behavioral Appropriateness, Situational Constraint, and Self-Efficacy in Shyness," *Journal of Personality* 57 (1989): 870–90.

Chapter 6

p. 118 *"follow your bliss":* J. Campbell, *Joseph Campbell: The Power of Myth with Bill Moyers,* ed. B. Flowers (New York: Doubleday, 1988), 148.

p. 123 *the key in raising children well:* A. Wiesenfeld, P. Whitman, and C. Malatasta, "Individual Differences Among Adult Women in Sensitivity to Infants," *Journal of Personality and Social Psychology* 40 (1984): 110–24.

p. 127 *emotional sensitivity, and nonconformity:* D. Lovecky, "Can You Hear the Flowers Sing? Issues for Gifted Adults," *Journal of Counseling and Development* 64 (1986): 572–75. Much of the rest of this section is based on Lovecky's discussions of gifted adults.

p. 133 *their competence level:* J. Cheek, *Conquering Shyness* (New York: Dell, 1989), 168–69.

Chapter 7

p. 140 *self-concept:* A. Aron, M. Paris, and E. Aron, "Prospective Studies of Falling in Love and Self-Concept Change," *Journal of Personality and Social Psychology* (in press).

p. 143 *secure attachment in childhood:* C. Hazan and P. Shaver, "Romantic Love Conceptualized As an Attachment Process," *Journal of Personality and Social Psychology* 52 (1987): 511–24.

p. 145 *two themes to be most common:* A. Aron, D. Dutton, and

A. Iverson, "Experiences of Falling in Love," *Journal of Social and Personal Relationships* 6 (1989): 243–57.

p. 146 *love on the suspension bridge:* D. Dutton and A. Aron, "Some Evidence for Heightened Sexual Attraction under Conditions of High Anxiety," *Journal of Personality and Social Psychology,* 30 (1974): 510–17.

p. 146 *comedy monologue:* G. White, S. Fishbein, and J. Rutstein, "Passionate Love and Misattribution of Arousal," *Journal of Personality and Social Psychology,* 41 (1981): 56–62.

p. 147 *had not had their self-esteem lowered:* E. Walster, "The Effect of Self–Esteem on Romantic Liking," *Journal of Experimental Social Psychology* 1 (1965): 184–97.

p. 147 *first year away from home:* Aron *et al.,* "Prospective Studies."

p. 148 *fastest route to closeness:* D. Taylor, R. Gould, and P. Brounstein, "Effects of Personalistic Self-Disclosure," *Personality and Social Psychology,* 7 (1981): 487–92.

p. 153 *lose touch with their "authentic self":* J. Ford, "The Temperament/Actualization Concept," *Journal of Humanistic Psychology* 35 (1995): 57–77.

p. 158 *apart from the moment:* J. Gottman, *Marital Interaction: Experimental Investigations* (New York: Academic Press, 1979).

p. 162 *something bigger: "we":* A. Aron and E. Aron, "The Self-Expansion Model of Motivation and Cognition in Close Relationships," in *The Handbook of Personal Relationships,* 2nd Edition, ed. S. Duck and W. Ickes (Chichester, UK: Wiley, 1996).

p. 162 *much less satisfying:* N. Glenn, "Quantitative Research on Marital Quality in the 1980s: A Critical Review," *Journal of Marriage and the Family* 52 (1990): 818–31.

p. 162 *slows this decline:* H. Markman, F. Floyd, S. Stanley, and R. Storaasli, "Prevention of Marital Distress: A Longitudinal Investigation," *Journal of Consulting and Clinical Psychology* 56 (1988): 210–17.

p. 162 *(not just pleasant):* C. Reissman, A. Aron, and M. Bergen, "Shared Activities and Marital Satisfaction" *Journal of Social and Personal Relationships* 10 (1993): 243–54.

p. 163 *their caretakers are sensitive:* Wiesenfeld *et al.,* "Sensitivity to Infants."

Chapter 8

p. 169 *show* no *overlap:* J. Braungart, R. Plomin, J. DeFries, and D. Fulker, "Genetic Influence on Tester-Rated Infant Temperament As Assessed by Bayley's Infant Behavior Record," *Development Psychology* 28 (1992): 40–47.

p. 176 *writing them down:* J. Pennebaker, *Opening Up: The Healing Power of Confiding in Others* (New York: Morrow, 1990).

p. 176 *curing depression:* "Update on Mood Disorders: Part II," *The Harvard Mental Health Letter* 11 (January 1995): 1.

Chapter 9

p. 193 *two research studies on this:* One of these is under review for publication; the other was presented at a conference. Jagiellowicz, J., Aron, E. N., & Aron, A. (2007). *Sensory processing sensitivity moderates health motivations and experiences.* Presented at the Society for Personality and Social Psychology, Memphis, TN. (January)

p. 193 *rarely feel pain in their lives:* Catherine A. Nivens and Karel J. Gijsbers, "Do Low Levels of Labour Pain Reflect Low Sensitivity to Noxious Stimulation?" *Social Scientific Medicine* 29 (1989): 585–588.

p. 193 *distraction and hypnosis:* Scheffler, Michael, Susan Koranyi, Winfried Meissner, Bernhard Strauss, and Jenny Rosendahl. "Efficacy of non-pharmacological interventions for procedural pain relief in adults undergoing burn wound care: a systematic review and meta-analysis of randomized controlled trials." *Burns* 44, no. 7 (2018): 1709–1720.

p. 193 *not everyone is fully hypnotizable:* Thompson, Trevor, Devin B. Terhune, Charlotte Oram, Joseph Sharangparni, Rommana Rouf, Marco Solmi, Nicola Veronese, and Brendon Stubbs. "The effectiveness of hypnosis for pain relief: A systematic review and meta-analysis of 85 controlled experimental trials." *Neuroscience & Biobehavioral Reviews* (2019).

p. 193 *for example with dental pain:* Jensen, Mark P., Peter D. Galer, Linea L. Johnson, Holly R. George, M. Elena Mendoza, and Kevin J. Gertz. "The associations between pain-related beliefs, pain intensity, and patient functioning: hypnotizability as a moderator." *The Clinical journal of pain* 32, no. 6 (2016): 506.

p. 197 *different effects on the brain:* Travis, Fred, and Jonathan Shear. "Focused attention, open monitoring and automatic self-transcending: categories to organize meditations from Vedic, Buddhist and Chinese traditions." *Consciousness and cognition* 19, no. 4 (2010): 1110–1118.

p. 197 *Each has its purpose and merits:* Sedlmeier, Peter, Juliane Eberth, Marcus Schwarz, Doreen Zimmermann, Frederik Haarig, Sonia Jaeger, and Sonja Kunze. "The psychological effects of meditation: a meta-analysis." *Psychological bulletin* 138, no. 6 (2012): 1139.

p. 198 *keeping the heart . . . in good health:* Schneider, Robert H., Jeremy Z. Fields, and John W. Salerno. "Editorial commentary on AHA scientific statement on meditation and cardiovascular risk reduction." *Journal of the American Society of Hypertension* 12, no. 12 (2018): e57–e58.

p. 201 *"Millions, in fact . . .":* Solomon, Neil, and Marc Lipton. *Sick and tired of being sick and tired.* Wynwood Pr., 1989..

p. 203 *only a little better than placebos:* Moncrieff, Joanna, and Irving Kirsch. "Empirically derived criteria cast doubt on the clinical significance of antidepressant-placebo differences." *Contemporary Clinical Trials* 43 (2015): 60–62.

p. 203 *In a study of 1,500 people:* Read, John, and James Williams. "Adverse effects of antidepressants reported by a large international cohort: emotional blunting, suicidality, and withdrawal effects." *Current drug safety* 13, no. 3 (2018): 176–186.

p. 203 *as effective as the combined treatment:* Karyotaki, E., Y. Smit, K. Holdt Henningsen, M. J. H. Huibers, J. Robays, D. De Beurs, and P. Cuijpers. "Combining pharmacotherapy and psychotherapy or monotherapy for major depression? A meta-analysis on the long-term effects." *Journal of Affective Disorders* 194 (2016): 144–152.

p. 205 *individualized or "precision" care:* Jameson, J. Larry, and Dan L. Longo. "Precision medicine—personalized, problematic, and promising." *Obstetrical & gynecological survey* 70, no. 10 (2015): 612–614.

p. 205 *how personality may predict future illness:* Chapman, Benjamin P., Brent Roberts, and Paul Duberstein. "Personality and longevity: knowns, unknowns, and implications for public health and personalized medicine." *Journal of aging research* 2011 (2011).

p. 205 *neuroticism has been a confusing trait:* Israel, Salomon, Terrie E. Moffitt, Daniel W. Belsky, Robert J. Hancox, Richie Poulton, Brent Roberts, W. Murray Thomson, and Avshalom Caspi. "Translating personality psychology to help personalize preventive medicine for young adult patients." *Journal of personality and social psychology* 106, no. 3 (2014): 484.

p. 205 *Another trait, openness:* Lionetti, Francesca, Massimiliano Pastore, Ughetta Moscardino, Annalaura Nocentini, Karen Pluess, and Michal Pluess. "Sensory Sensory Processing Sensitivity and its Association with Personality Traits and Affect: A Meta-Analysis." *Journal of Research in Personality* (2019).

Chapter 10

p. 210 *and ritual space:* R. Moore, "Space and Transformation in Human Experience," in *Anthropology and the Study of Religion,* ed. R. Moore and F. Reynolds (Chicago: Center for the Scientific Study of Religion, 1984).

p. 211 *"The introverted intuitive . . .":* M. Von Franz and J. Hillman, *Lectures on Jung's Typology* (Dallas: Spring, 1984): 33.

p. 214 *"Sensitive people . . .":* Victor Frankl, *Man's Search for Meaning* (New York: Washington Square Press, 1946/1985), 55–56.

p. 214 *In her journals . . .":* E. Hillesum, *An Interrupted Life* (New York: Simon and Schuster, 1981).

p. 215 *"It is strange . . .":* Ibid., 242–43.

p. 216 *"The point of full . . .":* M. Sinetar, *Ordinary People as Monks and Mystics* (New York: Paulist Press, 1986), 133.

p. 216 *"For the meaning of life . . .":* Frankl, *Man's Search,* 130–31.

p. 219 *thinking, and feeling:* Jung, *Psychological Types.*

p. 219 *Von Franz . . . "inferior function":* Hillman and von Franz, *Jung's Typology,* 1–72.

p. 220 *drugs, and sex:* Ibid., 33–35.

p. 220 *caught up in how good it would be:* Ibid., 13.

p. 220 *to which he spoke:* Ibid., 68.

p. 221 *in small families:* C. Jung, *Man and His Symbols* (Garden City, N.Y.: Doubleday, 1964), 161–62.

p. 222 *"acausal connecting principle":* C. Jung, "Synchronicity" *The Structure and Dynamics of the Psyche,* vol. 8, *The Collected Works.* 417–531.

Index